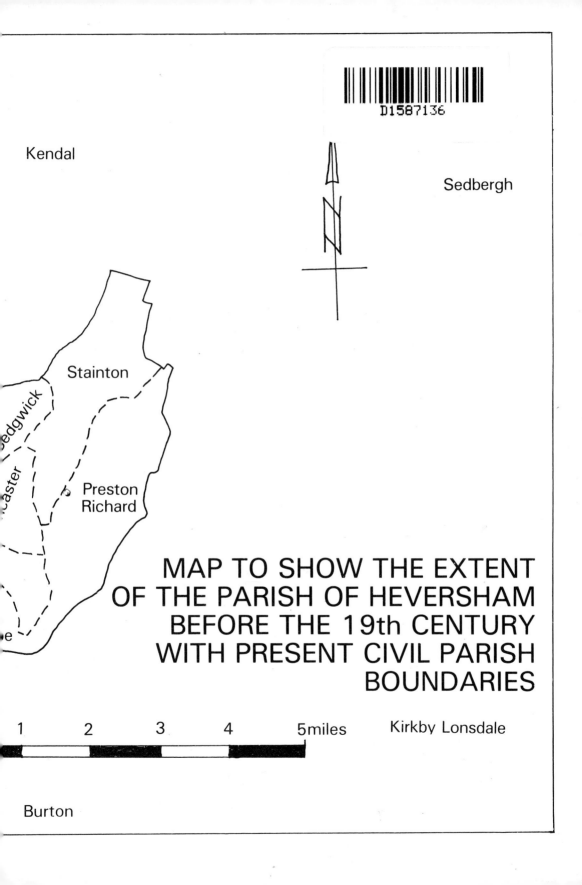

Kendal

Sedbergh

Stainton

edgwick

aster

Preston
Richard

# MAP TO SHOW THE EXTENT
# OF THE PARISH OF HEVERSHAM
# BEFORE THE 19th CENTURY
# WITH PRESENT CIVIL PARISH
# BOUNDARIES

| 1 | 2 | 3 | 4 | 5miles |

Kirkby Lonsdale

Burton

# THE CHURCH AT HEVERSHAM

By Roger K. Bingham

*The Church at Heversham with the Kent estuary behind.*

ISBN 0 950 9991 0 5

© *Roger K. Bingham 1984*

*Published 1984*
*by Roger K. Bingham*
*The Smithy, Ackenthwaite,*
*Milnthorpe*

# THE
# CHURCH
# AT
# HEVERSHAM

## A HISTORY OF WESTMORLAND'S OLDEST
## RECORDED CHURCH

Roger K. Bingham

*Roger K. Bingham*

*With my best wishes*

*Philip*

*1999.*

## DEDICATION

If this book has a theme it is simply that there are a variety of gifts and a variety of service that have been, and can be, offered to God through Christ. It is, therefore, dedicated, with hope, to those Christians of the future who will continue the 'Church at Heversham'.

# Contents

**ERRATA**

P.8      Delete lines 15 and 16.

P.84    Delete line 1.

P.128   Delete 'Priest'.

P.17    Line 8 'later' not 'latter'.

P.32    Line 47 'tolled' not told.

P.38    Line 7 Date '1661-1676' not '1616-1676'.

P.56    Photograph of the Nave not Chancel.

P.109  Line 35 1947 not 1847.

P.134  Line 16 'Fountains' not 'Fauntains'
Line 17 'Jonathon' not 'Johnathon'.

P.145  Line 15 'Geoffrey Bethell' not 'Charles'.

# FOREWORD

BY THE LORD BISHOP OF CARLISLE, THE RT.REV.DAVID HALSEY

This is an interesting and well documented history of a church and parish by one who has worshipped there for many years. Heversham is possibly the oldest recorded church in Westmorland and its history displays all the richness of parish life with its infinite variety and unceasing story of the worship and service of God which has gone on there for so many centuries. As the writer says: 'If the book has a theme, it is simply that there are a variety of gifts and a variety of service'. In 1983 the Diocese of Carlisle celebrated its 850th Anniversary, and as part of the celebrations this history of Heversham is a valued offering, as it records the lives and work of the many who have served God faithfully in Heversham in every generation.

DAVID CARLIOL

## ACKNOWLEDGEMENTS

As this book has taken me twenty years research and four to write I regret that I find it impossible to recall all those to whom I am indebted. Nevertheless the following readily spring to mind: the Vicar the Reverend J.C.Hancock M.A.; the Churchwardens W.Dawson, N.Kilshaw, M.Sisson and J.Sowerby; and the P.C.C. of 'the Church at Heversham' for their constant encouragement; the Cumbria County Archivist Mr. B.C.Jones M.A.; the Deputy County Archivist Miss S.MacPherson B.A.; her colleague Mr. Richard Hall M.A. and other staff at the Cumbria Record Office, Kendal without whose patience and advice hardly a page would have been written; the Local History Librarian at Kendal Public Library Mrs. C.Strickland; Mr. E.B.Kirtley M.A., of Lancaster University Library; the staff of the Chester Record Office; Mrs. O.R.Bagot F.S.A, for help with the early manuscript, Mr. C.M.Bagot and Mr.O.R.Bagot, Mr.J.Mashiter, Major Sandes, Brigadier C.E.Tryon-Wilson, Mrs. N.Tyson, Heversham Parish Council, the Governors of Heversham Grammar School and the Governors of Heversham C. of E. School for enabling me to consult material belonging to them. Where possible the ownership of sources is acknowledged in the chapter notes.

I am grateful to the Bishop of Carlisle for writing the Foreword, to the Reverend J.C.Hancock and Mr. B.Ormerod for taking most of the photographs; to Professor Cramp Durham University, Mrs. R.W.Hall, Mrs. L.Lister, Mrs. H.M.Phillips, Mr. A.Rumsey and Mr. M.Sisson who supplied additional illustrations; to Mr. K.Blenkharn who drew the end plate maps; to Miss. S.Crabtree and Mr. W.Unsworth who advised on publication; to Mrs. M.Bates B.A., Mrs. J.Blenkharn and Mrs. A.Johnson who typed the manuscript and to Mrs. Birch, Mrs. Dix, Miss Drew, Mr. H.East, Mrs. Frear, Mr. and Mrs. Kilshaw, Mrs. Lister, Mr. and Mrs. M.Sisson, Miss R.Sisson, Miss H.West, Mrs. J.Wilson and Miss Wright and many other friends for their valuable reminiscences.

Finally I wish to thank the Trustees of the Curwen Archives Trust for making a substantial contribution towards publication costs. Though I have expanded and, occasionally, challenged J.F.Curwen's brief article (of 1925) on the Church - previously the only study of the subject - I remain grateful for his generosity and respectful of his work.

The responsibility for all errors, omissions and faults is, of course, mine. Without the help of so many people there would have been many more.

*Roger K.Bingham*
*The Smithy, Ackenthwaite,*
*Milnthorpe, Cumbria.*
*18th October, 1983*

*Heversham photographed in mid C19 after the Church clock was donated in 1860 and before the old tower was demolished in 1869*

CHAPTER I

# The Setting and Origins

Heversham is situated at the point where the South Westmorland plain touches the Kent estuary as it meanders into Morecambe Bay. Before the nineteenth century Heversham Parish was one of the largest in Westmorland consisting of about 20,000 acres[1] spread in a rough 'U' shape centred on the lower Kent valley. In this central part are Sedgwick, Hincaster, Levens, the village of Heversham and its associated hamlet of Leasgill. Here the countryside consists mainly of undulating pasture lands grazed by sheep and friesian cattle with irregular stretches of arable cultivation especially on the drained marshes (or mosses) close to the estuary. Patches of coppiced deciduous woodland are common while there are also many taller trees like the famous oaks and beeches of Levens Park and the fine chestnuts which dominate the Churchyard at Heversham. Occasionally the predominantly green and rolling landscape is pierced by limestone crags but often, as on Heversham Head which rises 400 feet immediately to the north of the church, these are softened by more trees including darker clumps of holly and yew.

Stainton and Preston Richard (Endmoor) in the eastern arm of the old parish have a more hilly landscape with clusters of egg like drumlins in the south and, as the bedrock changes from limestone to Silurian slate, sharper featured fell land culminating in 700 foot high The Helm in the north. This area is threaded by a web of streams including Peasey, Saint Sunday's and Stainton becks which eventually join to become the river Bela. The Bela skirts the meadows along the old parishes' southern boundary at Milnthorpe before flowing through Dallam Park to reach the bay.

Contrasting with the predominantly hilly terrain are the mosses which straggling the bay run four miles north westward up the level dyke diapered Lyth Valley. Beneath the abrupt flank of Whitbarrow Scar, the lower meadows of the valley are drained by the River Gilpin. The head of the valley is terminated by the hills above Crosthwaite along which ran the northern boundary of the old parish less than two miles from the eastern shore of Windermere. Therefore, the ancient parish of Heversham linked the Pennine foothills, which start at Farleton Knott just to its south east, with the very heart of Lakeland.

Administratively the area is composed now of the civil parishes of Heversham,

7

Milnthorpe, Crosthwaite and Lyth, Hincaster, Levens, Preston Richard, Sedgwick and Stainton. The old parish had chapels at Crosthwaite and Crosscrake serving respectively the Lyth valley and Stainton. In the nineteenth century these medieval chapels were rebuilt and became independent parish churches as did also the newer foundations at Levens and Milnthorpe while Preston Richard joined Preston Patrick, formerly part of Burton but now too a separate parish.

Heversham belonged to the Archdiocese of York from before the Norman conquest until 1541 when the parish became part of the newly founded Diocese of Chester.[2] It remained part of the ancient Archdeaconry of Richmond. In 1856 it was transferred to the enlarged Diocese of Carlisle within the new Archdeaconry of Westmorland.[3] From the revival of the Rural Deaneries in the mid-nineteenth century Heversham was part of the Rural Deanery of Kirkby Lonsdale until, with the introduction of Synodical Government into the Church of England in 1974, it joined the larger Kendal Deanery. The ecclesiastical parish of Heversham as remaining in the twentieth century consists of the Civil Parishes of Heversham and Hincaster with part of Levens, including Levens Hall, Eversley House and Mabbin Hall, and the west side of Milnthorpe hill.[4] The parish church of St.Peter continues however, to be Hincaster with part of Milnthorpe including Milton Moor, the Eastern part of Ackenthwaite and the west side of Milnthorpe hill.[4] The parish church of St.Peter continues however, to be regarded as the mother church of the area formerly covered by the old parish.

For more than a millenium the typical settlement pattern of the parish was in hamlets and farmsteads. Even Milnthorpe, always the most substantial community, was composed of more or less detached groupings: these were at Ackenthwaite, on Windy Hill, near the market square and along the banks of the Bela close to the mills from which derives the Danish origin of the village's name. Milnthorpe, however, was distinguished from other places in the parish by being Westmorland's only port and by possessing a Market Charter granted in c1280 and renewed in 1334.[6] Even so Milnthorpe did not have a church of its own until 1837. As a result the main road leading north from Milnthorpe to Heversham is still

*Mount's map of Heversham, c.1826*

called Church Street and the Cross Keys Inn at the start of the street takes its name from the traditional symbol of St.Peter, the Church's Patron Saint.

According to an old estate map no distinct village of Heversham existed much before the eighteenth century. As late as 1826[7] the parish church stood virtually alone save for a few cottages, three inns: the 'Ship', 'The Bluebell' and 'The Eagle and Child', Church Farm, Heversham House and the vicarage (now 'The Blue Bell at Heversham').

As elsewhere the parish was greatly changed in the nineteenth century. The construction of the Turnpike through Heversham and Milnthorpe in 1823, and, a mile or so to the east, the Lancaster to Kendal Canal in 1819, and the main railway line in 1847 destroyed much of the ancient isolation of the area. On the other hand the distance from major centres and the lack of local coal supplies meant that steam powered industry did not develop. Indeed, with the decline of water mills the rural character of the area was if anything enhanced.

In the twentieth century the Turnpike evolved into the A6 road whose traffic pulverised and polluted many neighbouring villages especially Milnthorpe. Heversham was fortunate in being early in diverting this menace with the construction of the Princes Way by-pass in 1927. Already at that date the squat limestone rubble cottages of the old village had been joined by newer dwellings including the first of a long line of 'detached residences' and bungalows built on the higher land facing the bay. More have followed since the Second World War and the population of Heversham Civil parish has grown from 379 in 1951 to 734 in 1981.[8] Many of the newer inhabitants have been retired people and they especially have contributed to the maintenance of a relatively large congregation. There are still, however, sufficient young people in the parish to ensure the survival, for some time, of Heversham Church of England School. Heversham is perhaps best known for its Grammar School, which since its foundation in 1613, has had a continuous connection with the Church. Having been the last secondary school in Cumbria to accept reorganisation it merged in 1984 with Milnthorpe Secondary Modern School to form the Dallam School.

Today boldy set astride the main street the church is surrounded by a busy residential village. Traffic noise, buildings and also nature which has spread a tantalising screen of woods and hillocks around the estuary mask the historical significance of the setting as well as blurring the still present beauty.

Consequently, a visitor would find it rewarding if before entering the church he were to

*The Church from the south.*

take the path through the yard to the squeaky gate in the north wall. Here he could climb Vicar's Walk (so called because it led to High Leasgill, the vicarage from 1842-1948) on to Heversham Head from whose summit a glorious panorama can be surveyed. To the east are the sombre Tebay, Howgill and Bowland Fells; in the south above the bumpy green plain are bald Farleton Knott and the forested humps of Haverbrack and Arnside Knott; while over to the west the serrated line of the Cartmel range takes the eye through the blunt bulwark of Whitbarrow Scar along to the Lakeland heights far off on the northern skyline. In the foreground thrusting between the out stretched limbs of the fells is Morecambe Bay which can be the subject of an historically appropriate illusion. If viewed on an evening in late summer when the mists rise from the surrounding mosses the half mile of meadows between the estuary and the village is so contracted that the church appears to be set almost on the edge of the shore. It is then possible to imagine the seventh century Angle Haefar coming, perhaps at the end of a marauding season, to sail up this eastern extremity of the Irish Sea and establish his farmstead or 'ham' close to the site of the present church.

## The Angles

Morecambe Bay would have provided excellent access to South Lakeland for sea-borne Anglian immigrants, as it did later for the Viking invaders. Even so it is probable that most Anglian settlers came to Heversham on foot from across the Pennines. Place name evidence suggests that settlements having the '-ham' ending belong to the secondary stage of Anglian colonisation which followed the expansion to the west coast of the Kingdom of Northumbria during the reign of King Aethelfrith (A.D. 593-617). Therefore, Haefar's ham could have been founded by A.D. 650.

Haefar and his Angles did not come to a totally uninhabited region. In Romano-British times there were fairly large settlements at Watercrook and Haverbrack.[10] No doubt Celtic tribesmen had often been lured to the area of Heversham by the wild life of the mosses and by the patches of lush pasture on the lower slopes of the hills. Perhaps a summer settlement or shieling might even have been bivouacked near the spring, now known as St. Mary's Well, to be seen still on the roadside just north of the church.

Haefar was probably a pagan but the host community may have been converted to Christianity already. Although some of the Roman soldiers tramping along the military road that ran through Hincaster to Watercrook would have been Christian, Heversham was evangelised by missionaries from the Celtic Church of Ireland. They like the later Angle immigrants made their way in and out of the estuaries and bays of the north-west coast during the fifth and sixth centuries. Indeed if the legends concerning St.Patrick's foundation of Heysham Church, fifteen miles down the bay, have a factual basis then local Christianity might have a continuous history from the late Roman Period. More probably South Westmorland was penetrated by some of the missionaries who, led by St.Kentigern, had reached Northern Cumbria in c.A.D.573. It is, therefore, possible that the faith was preached at Heversham even before Augustine in 597A.D. began to spread the Roman creed in the south-east.

The presence of a Christianised host community could account for the fact that the Angle settlers were converted in the north-west comparatively early perhaps during the seventh century. Moreover, it was the Angles or their Celtic pastors who established at Heversham the only Anglian monastery known to have existed in Westmorland.[11] The monastery at Hefresham appears in the eleventh century Chronicles of the Kingdom of Northumbria,[12] making the parish one of the earliest places to be recorded in Cumbria.[12a] Thus it can be asserted that Christ has been worshipped and glorified at Heversham for 1,200 years and perhaps more.

In applying the term 'monastery' to the Anglian religious community the lofty and extensive edifices and sophisticated orders of the middle ages should not be envisaged.

10

Instead there would be a community of monks and nuns (who did try to be celibate) inhabiting a huddle of low huts made of timber, turf and field stone. Around all would go a wall or stockade designed to deter human enemies and also to keep out wild animals. Excavations at the Dog Hole on Haverbrack[13.] have shown that wolves were particularly common in the region during the Dark Ages, reminders of which are the wolf-head crest of the Wilson's of Dallam and the well known story about the killing of the 'last wolf' at Humphrey Head on the north western shore of the bay. Wild boar were also numerous and indeed the name of Heversham may be derived not from the legendary Haefar but from 'eofor'[14.] which is Old English for 'boar'. Of the crude monastic structures nothing verifiable remains though some foundation stones found in 1892 while digging a grave twenty yards north-east of the church were believed by the vicar of the day, Canon Gilbert, to be Anglian.

## The Anglian Cross

One 'most precious monument'[15] survives to provide an archaelogical link with the early Heversham Christians. This is part of the shaft of a grave cross, that for too long has been inconspicuously and ingloriously placed in the north-west corner of the porch. Though coarser in design than the famous crosses at Ruthwell and Bewcastle, it is both larger and in some respects finer than other local examples of Anglian sculpture at Kendal, Burton-in-Kendal and Lancaster and belongs, 'to the first great English school of art taught by Italian Masters in the seventh and eighth centuries'.[16] It must, therefore, have been made, at the latest, by the early ninth century.[17] So relatively numerous are examples of Anglian carving in the Lune valley region that it seems there could have been a school of sculptors at Lancaster[18] or possibly Heysham where there was a Celtic church and also suitable stone. The finished product, like the missionaries themselves, would then have sailed up the bay to Heversham.

*The four faces of the Anglian Cross. Photo courtesy Durham University.*

On the main face of the cross is a familiar Anglian design of the 'Christ' vine, bearing six bunches of grapes, entwined round two 'devil' beasts that sport bushy tails and pricked ears like those of foxes.[19] The over slim leaves, with pelta shaped terminals and rounded bunches of grapes in no way resemble the Byzantine proto-type copied by the Italian artists and indicate that the carvers were probably Angles who might never have seen a vine. Nevertheless as Collingwood stated 'the curves are squarely drawn and masterly, with plenty of spring and flow. The surfaces are quiet but by no means flat; the tendrils rise and sink perceptibly but not violently; it is a very gentle and refined art; ... it is not in the least degree weak or ineffective like what may be imitation of this style. It is a fine example of the Classic Anglian school.'[20] On the narrow faces there are similar single stemmed scrolls with side shoots springing from the bottom of the curve of the main stem. This is paralleled on Anglian sculpture at Lancaster, Heysham, Waberthwaite, Lowther and Hoddom; the carving of the leaves is similar to that on a cross from Lowther, now in the British Museum, suggesting that it was executed by the same hand.[21]

Today the cross shaft measures eleven inches by nine inches at the base and stands fifty six inches high - about half its original height. The back and side nearest the door are almost totally defaced and indicate that the stone must have been re-used for some other purpose possibly a door lintel. At what stage it was rediscovered is not known: it does not figure in any pre-nineteenth century reference to the church. In 1869 when the pebbledash rendering on the south wall was removed a further fragment of the Cross was revealed below the sill of the western window. This is a section of an arm of the cross head and is also adorned with the leaves and tendrils which were copied by J.F. Curwen when he designed the War Memorial Cross in 1919.[22]

In the south-east corner of the yard beneath the groping claws of the chestnut trees and seasonally splattered by nest debris and rook guano is a dial-less sundial. Its sandstone shaft is dated 1690 and is set in a couple of steps placed upon a slab of limestone. Curiously the steps, which are of a different hue and texture than the sundial, appear to be of the same sandstone as the cross. This led the Reverend W.S. Calverley in 1893 to suggest that they were 'part of the original cross'.[23] This was, however, mere guess-work and the steps more probably were part of a medieval churchyard cross from which monarchs were proclaimed, sinners denounced and manorial decisions broadcast.

**The End of the Monastery**

The monastery was overwhelmed by the cataclysms of the tenth century invasions by the Norse Vikings. There is a reference to this fate in the *'Historia de Sancta Cuthberte'* of c.1020 'in the time of King Eadward (c.901-925) Tilred abbot of Hefresham bought the vill named South Eden. Half of this he dedicated to St. Cuthbert in order that he might be admitted a monk of his monastery at Lindisfarne; the other moiety he granted to Norham so that he might be abbot of that place'.[24] The probable reason for Tilred's expensive removal was that he wished to escape the fury of the Norsemen and from c.905 there are no specific references to the monastery. Ironically a century earlier Northumbrian monks bearing with them the body of St. Cuthbert had fled to the Lake District after Lindisfarne had been assailed by the first waves of the Danish Viking invasion. Unlike many places in north Westmorland there are no legends concerning St. Cuthbert's body having rested at Heversham but the fact that Tilred withdrew to the north-east could have been the result of contacts made between his community and the earlier Northumbrian refugees. Probably Abbot Tilred is the bishop of the same name recorded by Symeon of Durham as having been Bishop of Lindisfarne from 915-925.[25]

As Heversham is an Anglian name in a district where Scandinavian 'thwaites', 'slacks' and 'thorpes' predominate[26] it seems probable that the Angles survived and possibly also their parish church. Certainly Anglo Nordic sculpture at Kirkby Stephen and Burton-in-Kendal indicates that the Vikings were Christianized by c.1,000A.D.[27] The lack of Anglo-Viking christian sculpture at Heversham, and also Kendal, could suggest, however, that the viking settlement of the Kent valley was more socially disruptive than elsewhere in the area. The discovery of a sword, from a Viking burial on Whitbarrow Scar, indicates that some, at least, of the invaders were pagan because the Christians followed the practice of internment without grave goods. Even so place names within the old parish suggest that the norse invaders acknowledged the Christian religion. Crosscrake[28] is derived from the Old Norse Kraka's cross or monument and Crosthwaite[29] means a piece of cleared land round a cross; Stainton is a mixed Anglo-Nordic name composed of 'ton', Angle for settlement, and 'Steinn', norse for a monumental stone which could have been a cross.

Some evidence that the area was at times peaceful during the period of the Viking invasions is provided by tenth century biography of the Scottish Prince Catroe.[30] The 'Life of Catroe' describes a pilgrimage from Fife to Rome made by the Prince in the 940's. This included a journey from Carlisle, the capital of Duncan King of the Strathclyde 'Welsh', to the court of the Norse King Eric Bloodaxe at York. Instead of taking the better known routes along Hadrian's Wall or over Stainmore the pilgrims passed through the mixed Anglian, Cumbrian and Norse population of Westmorland reaching Morecambe Bay before crossing the Pennines via the southern passes. It is possible that hospitality was provided by the surviving remnants of Heversham's monastic community, or more probably, by Anglian Christians currently being served by a secular parish church. Certainly on what was bound to have been a geographically hazardous journey the pilgrims came to no harm from the local people, indicating a measure of prosperity as well as peace.

Nevertheless the tenth and eleventh centuries were, probably the most tempestuous in the history of Heversham. For much of the period the parish remained on the border between England and the Scottish kingdom of Strathclyde and there must have been spasmodic conflict between Scot, Angle and Viking. By 1066, however, Heversham had been annexed to the Kingdom of England as it was in the possession of Tostig Earl of Northumbria, the brother of King Harold. Following the deaths of the brothers at Stamford Bridge and Hastings respectively, William the Conqueror granted Heversham to Roger de Poictou who is recorded as being lord of the manor of 'Eureshaim'[31] in the Domesday survey of 1086.

#### Notes and References to Sources   Chapter I

1. William Whelan 'History and Topography Cumberland and Westmorland' 1860. Page 829. For division of Parish in C19 see below C19 & C20 Clergy 'Canon Gilbert'.

2. Prelates and People of the Lakes Counties C.M.L. Bouch 1948 P. 188

3. *Ibid* 420

4. From information supplied by the Ecclesiastical Communion to the Rev. J.C.Hancock 1984.

5. for dedication see below Chapter II

6. 'Records of Kendal', William Farrer Ltt.D. (Cumberland and Westmorland Archaeological and Antiquarian Society Record Series Vol. V) Vol. II p.146 *obb. et. seq.* Farrer Vol. II etc.

7. CRO(K) WDAG(D)

8. Census returns

9. The Place Names of Cumberland and Westmorland W.S. Sedgfield Lit.D. 1915 *f.*154: ham from O.M. heimr = farmstead

10. Transactions of the Cumberland & Westmorland Archaeological & Antiquarian Society (C.W.A.A.S.) M.S. LXIII Mt. IV The Dog Hole, Haverbrack By Don Benson and Keith Bland p.61

11. Royal Commission on Historical Monuments H.M.S.O. 1936 F.M. Stenton P.XLIX

12. *Historia de Sancto Cuthberto*

12a. Several N.Westmorland Churches are mentioned in the stories re. translation of St.Cuthbert's body in c.9, based on c.15 accounts by

Wessington of Durham. Therefore as subject of an c.11 source Heversham has a better claim to being 'the earliest recorded Church in Westmorland'.

13. C.W.A.A.S. M.S. LXIII p61. *et.seq.*

14. Sedgfield p.154

15. W.G. Collinwood 'Lake Counties' quoted by J.L. Barnes 'All around Arnside,' Kendal, Titus Wilson, 1903. p.108

16. *Ibid*

17. C.W.A.A.S. Excursion notes July 1982 Heversham Church and Cross  Prof. K. Bailey

18. Reverend W.S. Calverley Early Sculptured Crosses Monuments in the Diocese of Carlisle C.W.A.A.S. 1899. p.202 *et. seq.*

19. Collingwood

20. *Ibid*

21. R. Bailey

22. see below 'The Churchyard'

23. Calverley p.202 *et. seq.*

24. Surtees Soc. Vol. II. p. 146, 157

25. *Ibid*

26. see Sedgfield

27. RCHM p.65, p.142

28. Sedgfield p.144

29. *Ibid*

30. 'In Search of the Dark Ages'. Michael Wood, BBC, 1981. P.148.

31. Sedgfield p.154 also Farrer Vol.I.

*A view of Heversham Church*
*Taken from 'A Tour on the Lakes of Westmorland' published by R.Ackerman*

## CHAPTER II
# The Medieval Church

The first Norman records of the church occur during the reign of William Rufus 1087-1100. Rufus having subdued the north in expeditions to York in 1091 and Carlisle in 1092 made substantial grants to his principal lieutenants one of whom was Ivo de Taillebois. Ivo's reward included the rectorial rights to the churches of Kendal, Heversham, Kirkby Lonsdale, Burton and Clapham (in Yorkshire). Between 1090 and 1097 Ivo made 'a gift in alms' of these rights to Stephen de Whitby,[1] first Abbot of the Benedictine Abbey of St.Mary at York (founded in 1088), to provide an endowment for the abbey. As rector the Abbot received about a third of the manor of Heversham, he was entitled to the income of this glebe and a portion of the tithes. In return he had to provide an adequate living for the parish priest - his deputy or vicar - out of the income of the rectory. The abbot also held the advowsom i.e. the right to present a priest to the living.

Ivo's grant was confirmed twice. Between 1120 and 1130 a deed of 'Ketel son of Elftred by the advice of Christiana his wife and William his son and at the instance of Archbishop Thurston, gave to the monks of St. Mary, the church of Clapham and one carucate of land, the church of Kirkebie Kendale, the church of Heversham, the church of Kirkebi Lonsdale, and the lands belonging to these churches ...'. By the second deed of C1212-1215 'Gilbert Fitz-Reinfred and Helwise his wife confirmed to the monks of St.Mary *inter alia* the churches of Eversheim, Bietham, Kirkeby in Kentdale with their chapels...'.[2]

For much of the medieval period the Abbot's stewards lived at Heversham Hall and, also, at Abbot Hall Kendal in order to supervise the Abbot's estates. It would seem that during the thirteenth century, at least, the Abbot did not draw his full revenue from Heversham Church lands. Thus in the Crusading Tithes[3] of Pope Nicholas IV of 1291 Heversham Church was valued at 100 marks or £66:13s:4d but the Abbot's pension was only £2. The Churches income declined as a result of devastation caused during the Scottish Wars and in the new taxation of Pope Clement V in 1318 'the true value' was set at £20 per annum.

During the fifteenth century the Abbey faced financial difficulties and in 1448 Henry VI granted a license which states that 'whereas John Abbot of the Monastery of St.Mary's York and the convent of that place are held to pay yearly to the King 200 marks for the manor of Whytgyft Co. York ... (but as) the premises are so adjacent to the water of the Ouse which ebbs and flows salt and fresh, that they cannot be preserved through floods without great costs in repairing and maintaining divers walls, weirs sluices, dykes etc. the King has granted John, now abbot, and the convent to appropriate the parish churches of Eversham-in-Kendale and Burton-in-Kendale of their patronage'. It took, however, ten years for the new financial arrangements to be implemented and it was not until 10th October 1459[6] that William Booth, Archbishop of York used the licence to appropriate the bulk of the revenue of Heversham Church to the Abbey except for 'a competent portion' for a vicar 'and an annual pension of 3s 4d to both the Archbishop of York and the Dean and Chapter of York and 5 marks to the Archdeacon of Richmond. Finally on the 6th January 1460[7] the Archbishop allocated an endowment for the vicar of '£20 a year with a manse and garden to be built and repaired the first time at the cost of the abbot.' To provide the £20 the vicar was assigned 'the annual sum of the third part of the Mill of Milnthorpe, anciently belonging to the said church, also the tithes of fishings, mills, foals, calves, pigs, brood geese, hens, ducks, bees, eggs, pigeons, lint, hemp, leeks, onions and garden fruits of the whole parish'.[8a] In return the vicar had to pay the abbot £5:6s:8d annually, to find bread, wine and wax for mass and, more expensively, 'repair the chancel'. In fact the abbot did more than meet this final stipulation for the architectural evidence suggests that the chancel was entirely rebuilt in the second half of the fifteenth century. That there were sufficient funds to carry out this work could reflect the prosperity of the area caused by the flourishing trade in raw wool and the manufacture of 'Kendal Green'. The prosperity continued and in 1535 the records of the Rural Deanery of Catterick record that the income of Henry Carbot incumbent of 'Evershame' was £39:6s:8d minus £2:13s:4d making a clear value of £36:13s:4d. This was a considerable income as the value of the rectories in the Lakes Counties immediately prior to the Reformation has been calculated at £18:15s:8d and the vicarages at £14:5s:2d.[10] Moreover, in the Diocese of Coventry and Lichfield in the possibly wealthier Midlands sixty per cent of livings were worth less than £10.

**The Dedication**

Because it belonged to St. Mary's Abbey at York the church during the Middle ages would be referred to colloquially as a 'St.Mary Church'. The same appellation would also be given to anything else connected with it. Hence the well[11] on the roadside just beyond the north-west corner of the churchyard received the name of St.Mary's well. It was perhaps inevitable that the church has been said to be dedicated to St.Mary. For example the 1844 report in the Westmorland[12] Gazette about the newly installed east window states that the centre light was the Virgin Mary 'after whom the church is dedicated'. Similarly Paley's plans for the restoration of 1868 are inscribed 'St.Mary's Heversham' while as recently as 1976 the Diocesan Directory gave the same dedication. Perhaps because of this uncertainty the early twentieth century Kelly's[14] Directories state that the dedication is unknown. In fact, from the incumbency of Canon Gilbert (1866-1921) a patronal festival[15] has been held at Peter-tide and parishioners have believed that the Church is dedicated to St.Peter. The first reference to Peter occurs in the will of Martin Redmane of Levens, proved in April 1360, in which Martin stated[16] 'I ... give and bequeath my soul to God and the Blessed Mary and All Saints and my body to be buried in the Church of St.Peter of Heversham, and my best horse by way of mortuary to the same place ...'. That the annual fair granted[17] in 1334 was to be held on the eve of St.Peter and St.Paul the Apostles could also support the contention that the Church was dedicated to Peter. Furthermore the subsidiary altar set up in the South Aisle during the

15

fourteenth century was dedicated to 'Our Lady' which presumably would not have been the case if the High Altar and the Church had the same dedication. That the confusion is long standing is shown by Machell's[18] statement in 1691 'it seems from the wall two hundred yards north-west of the church called St.Mary's well (that the church) be dedicated to the Virgin Mary, but the Rushbearing is on St.Peter's Day near Midsummer'.

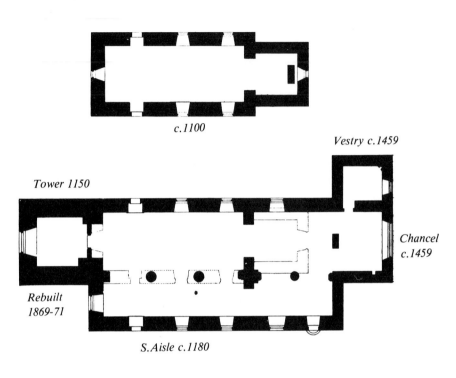

*c.1100*

*Vestry c.1459*

*Tower 1150*

*Chancel c.1459*

*Rebuilt 1869-71*

*S.Aisle c.1180*

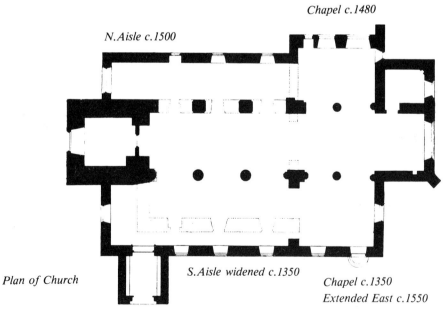

*Chapel c.1480*

*N.Aisle c.1500*

*Plan of Church*

*S.Aisle widened c.1350*

*Chapel c.1350 Extended East c.1550*

## The Building
### The South Arcade

Nothing remains of the Anglian or early Norman churches but, because of our ancestors' habit of repeatedly re-using building material, some of the stones in the present church could have come from the earlier structures on the site. The earliest surviving part is the three bay south arcade which probably marks the position of the south wall of the Anglo-Norman nave torn down when a south aisle was erected. Displaying features that are similar to the Early English style of the thirteenth century and of the Romanesque (Norman) period of the eleventh and twelfth centuries the arcade can properly be described as 'transitional'. The three pointed arches of two square orders clearly resemble the latter style but they rest on cylindrical Norman type piers. These are less massive than those at Cartmel generally dated at circa 1190 but they support an octagonal capital on the east pier and a square capital on the west that seem somewhat earlier. Moreover, the western capital has heavy water leaf or scalloped carving very similar to that at Lowther church asserted by the R.C.H.M.[19] and Pevsner[20] as being c.1165-75. On the other hand, the foliated eastern respond is clearly transitional of c.1200. However, if a central date for the arcade has to be fixed 1180 is as appropriate as any.

*Left:*
*The 'Ram'*
*Head Stop*
*Right:*
*The Western*
*capital with*
*waterleaf carving*

Curwen in 1925[21] stated that the arcade appeared to have been rebuilt probably after the fire of 1601[22] and that the capitals, piers and bases seemed to have been mixed up. This opinion can be questioned: close examination and comparison with work of similar style elsewhere suggests the capitals do, indeed, fit the piers. Moreover, the stonework of the three fifteenth century clerestory windows (each of two trefoil headed lights) is clearly original which would not have been the case if the whole had fallen during the fire. The damage obvious on the eastern pier was probably caused when the three decker pulpit and sounding board were fixed against it in c.1723.[23] The base of the pier, which was supported by scaffolding in 1868, was renewed by Paley;[24] this accounts for the disparity in its texture and composition with the pier and capital. Regarding the eastern respond it seems too small for the arch but as it is built into the pier of the Victorian chancel arch it position could date from c.1868

Curiously on the arcade's southern side is a hood mould with defaced head stops of three humans and a ram, a decorative device normally found on the nave side of an arcade. This would lend weight to a tradition that the south aisle was the original nave and the present nave (which is narrower than the aisle) was the original north aisle. However, the tower which was roughly contemporary with the arcade was at the west end of the present nave which was the normal place for a tower and not the end of an aisle.

*The Eastern Respond, South Arcade*

### The Norman Tower
In the report on the dilapidated condition of the tower in 1868 E.G.Paley stated[25] 'I think the greater portion (if not all of the walls) have been erected in the eleventh century'. He also stated that the tower was 61 feet 6 inches high and that it measured at the base 24 feet from north to south and 35 feet 6 inches from east to west. The present tower is approximately 26 feet square, the north-south extension being caused by projecting corner turrets. That the Norman tower's east-west dimension stretched three yards westward would mean that it stood virtually on the roadside wall. Thus, when during the construction of the Turnpike in 1823 the ancient track was lowered the tower's foundations would have been weakened causing the cracks in its structure that ostensibly led to its demolition. In addition Paley stated that the round uncarved tower arch to the nave was 'Norman' while 'the large west window and belfry windows were inserted at a comparatively later date'. Old[26] illustrations show that the belfry openings were of two trefoil headed lights and the west window was flat headed consisting of two long trefoil headed lights with four smaller ones above, rather like those of c.1450-1500 in the north aisle and the Dallam Chapel. The fragments of broken tracery built into the garden wall of Church Farm (the former Post Office) could have come from the west window. The belfry was corbelled and battlemented and was probably an addition like the upper stage of Beetham Church tower which it resembled.

### The Ladie Quyer
Despite reduction in funds caused by fourteenth century Scottish wars, there was some rebuilding during the period. The south aisle was widened or, alternatively, its south wall

*The battered Gargoyle*                    *The Ogee-headed piscina of c.1350*

was rebuilt. This is indicated by the three pointed windows being much wider than the lancet type opening of the Early English Period of c.1180-1200 when the arcade and the original aisle was built. On the outside these windows have medieval headstops whose features though worn can still be discerned. On the left side of the westernmost window is a small round head with prominent ears and grotesque flat nose and thick lips. It lacks a chin. The corresponding stop to the right of the window is now missing. On the left of the central window is the head of a man with a beard and moustache; to its right is a female with full coiffure and remains of what might have been a crown. On the eastern window there is a similar stop of a female head wearing a wimple; there are hands below the bust which are not clasped but clutch the body. The right-hand stop is perhaps the most interesting. It is apparently of a male whose bent arms emerge from behind the neck. The hands are applied to the mouth as if to play a musical instrument. Above this window is a battered gargoyle with large eyes and a wide, gaping mouth. The features of another gargoyle to the west can no longer be made out. During the late middle ages the aisle was known as the 'Ladie Quyer' because of the altar dedicated to the virgin. The chapel's importance, however, is indicated by the presence of a three arched sedillae below the easternmost window. This was renewed entirely in 1868 but its three ogee arches under a straight head with label probably copied medieval work. The attractive ogee headed piscina of c.1350 now in the south wall of the south-east chapel was probably originally in the Ladie Quyer.

At about the same time as the south aisle was widened an eastern extension, by a bay only, was added to form a chapel adjoining the Chancel. This chapel down to the seventeenth century belonged to the Prestons[26] of Nether Levens but earlier it may have belonged to the de Redmaynes[27] of Levens Hall who are recorded as being buried in the church during the fourteenth and fifteenth centuries. As the Ladie Altar in the Quyer seems to have been endowed by many families it would follow that the first exclusive family chapel belonged to Levens, the largest manor in the parish. Later the de Redmaynes built the north chapel.

### Chantries
The fashion set by the gentry in the fourteenth century of endowing a chantry chapel in which a priest would celebrate masses for the dead was adopted by the merchant class in the later Middle Ages. Thus in 1506 the will of Edward Brown, a jeweller of Lincoln, stated that 'I will have a preest at our Lady Altar of Hersh'm to syng there an hole yere for my fader soule, my moder soule, my brethren and systren soules and for my soule and he to have for wages £4:13s:4d. Whereas my fader and moder lyen and where I was borne'. Until the sixteenth century the dead of Crosthwaite had to be buried at Heversham although they had chapel of their own. The financial incentive of the mother church's monopoly of interment is seen in the will[28] of Myles Brigges of Crosthwaite. He, in 1517, bequeathed to Heversham

Church 'for my mortuaries after the custom of the church my best gowne. Item I give and bequeath to the said church of Seinte Peter in Eversham £100. to purchase oone Chauntrie which shall be the gifte of the heire male ...' In addition to these costly items he left to the church 'thirteen silver spones of the appostells, my great maser and paire of saltes ... to bye oone crosse with all of silver and gilted, oone baner and oone staffe' with also £13:6s:8d 'to the aforesaid chauntrie to mend it with all and the residue from the prist to be deposed to the poore the same day'.

## A Crypt?

So numerous were burials inside the church that it is not surprising that there is a tradition concerning a crypt (or large vault) beneath the nave. In 1777 Nicolson and Burn relate that a pile of bones[29] had been discovered a few years earlier under an arch beneath the south wall. A century later the Restoration Committee's notes state that[30] 'the rough cast was removed from a small portion of both the north and south outside walls in order to see the state ... and find the position of an arch known to exist in the south walls supposed to lead to a vault'. Regrettably nothing was then discovered nor, again in 1980 when during replastering work in the south aisle the pews were removed. However, on the east wall of the heating cell which occupies, in the south-west corner, the space of a large burial vault there are signs of a blocked up arch which could be either simply the line of an earlier vault or more fascinatingly could be a blocked up doorway leading to a crypt.

## Fifteenth century additions:

The chancel was rebuilt shortly after the 1459 financial agreement with the abbot of St.Mary's who probably paid for the work. It is faced in expensive sandstone ashlar whose reddy tinge suggests that it was imported from Furness, being brought no doubt up the bay on a spring tide to within a quarter of a mile of the church. The square blocks probably were shaped before their arrival but the slender tracery of the five light east window would be carved on the site. This is not only one of the largest medieval windows in Westmorland but also one of the finest examples of perpendicular architecture in the county and is not unlike the grander, and later, window at Cartmel in Furness.

That the altar stood almost immediately below the window and not further west, as for example at Kirkby Lonsdale, is shown by the position of the credence table on the narrow south wall of the sanctuary. This was originally a piscina for the shape of the removed bowl can be seen below the niche.

*East Wall*

*Above:*
*The piscina and*
*Holy Water stoop*
*Left:*
*The East Window*

The vestry is contemporary with the chancel. As it predates the Levens Chapel at first it extended north of the main building and the obviously external plinth can be seen on the east wall of the chapel. The vestry window, high up on the east wall, is of two trefoil headed lights. Its leaded lights have early, possibly seventeenth century, clear glass and there is a pane shaped to contain a stained glass shield. On the north wall is a flue, which if not contemporary with the wall is at least 300 years old as references 'to setting the vestry fire'[32.] go back to the seventeenth century.

According to Curwen the north aisle, chapels and clerestory belong to the post-reformation era c.1550, a period which saw similar extensions at Ulverston, Kendal, Grasmere and Hawkshead. This theory is not tenable because in the Levens chapel is a piscina and fragments of a Holy Water stoop while early prints show a sanctus bell cote on the east gable of the nave. All these are architectural features associated with Roman Catholic worship of before c.1540. Moreover, the styles of the three flat headed two light windows on the north wall, and also the three south clerestory windows have trefoil headed lights typical of the late fifteenth century rather than the sixteenth century. Allowing for a northern time lag in styles the date 1480-1500 for the north aisle and chapel would be reasonable.

Much of the early sixteenth century work was crude: the masonry was coarse and undressed while the north arcade was made simply by piercing the former north wall and plastering over the rough piers. These like those of similar construction at Bowness and

Grasmere lacked capitals and bases and (it was discovered in 1868) were composed entirely of rubble and mortar.

## The South East Chapel

The final addition to the church was the south-east chapel. It was probably built by Richard Buskell who acquired the rectory manor based on Heversham Hall in 1558. In his will of 1621 his descendents Jaspar Buskell stated that he wished to be buried 'according to my calling in the Quyer builded by my grandfather and uncle in or to the church adjoining commonly called the Lady Quyer'.[33] Thus a date a couple of generations earlier would put the Chapel as being c.1570-80. However, the eclectic range of styles in the chapel includes some earlier work. The three south windows are all similar to those of 1480-1500 in the north aisle. Either the builder copied an earlier style or the windows were reused, possibly from the former south wall of the chancel. The westernmost window, now blocked by the organ, is the only one in the church to contain diamond shaped panes which are set at an angle to each other giving an uneven appearance and could belong to the seventeenth century. Presumably when the other windows were reglazed in 1870 it was not worth renewing glass which would be hidden.

The tracery of the chapel's east window is Victorian yet outside it bears two defaced medieval head stops of a King and Queen. Strangely the earliest plan of the church of 1817 does not mark this or the easternmost window of c.1480-1500 which contains the Buskell arms dated 1601. However, an early print shows the chapel's east window to be similar to the chancel east window which dated from a hundred years before the chapel was built. Except for the crudely incised eastern respond the arcade is Victorian.

The church, therefore, had achieved its outward form by the mid-sixteenth century at the latest. Although the building was subsequently much repaired and altered its ground plan has not changed. The Chancel measures 39½ feet by 17¼ feet, the North (Levens) Chapel 25 feet by 16 feet, the South (Dallam) Chapel 40 feet by 19 feet, the nave, north aisle and south aisle are 45 feet long and are, respectively, 18 feet, 11 feet and 19¼ feet wide. The total area excluding the tower, vestry and porch is about 4,000 square feet. Of the 32 medieval parish churches in Westmorland, Heversham church is about the same size as Crosby Ravensworth and Kirkby Lonsdale churches and is exceeded only by Windermere (Bowness), Kendal and Kirkby Stephen churches.[34]

## Medieval Clergy

By coincidence the first reference by name of a parish priest at Heversham occurs in 1180[5] the most likely date for the completion of the south arcade which is the oldest surviving part of the building. He was called Roger and is recorded as a witness to many charters including Henry son of Norman de Redmane's grant of a Moiety of Levens, except Crosthwaite, to Ketel son of Uchtred. Either he or his namesake was still here in c.1215 for the deed[36] by which Gilbert Fitz-Reinfred and Helwise his wife confirmed to the monks of St. Mary *inter alia* the churches of Eversheim, Bietham, Kirkeby in Kendale with their chapels 'was witnessed by Roger parson of Eversheim'. His successor was probably one Thomas described as parson of Eversham when he witnessed in 1228[37] a charter of the Abbot of Furness. He was followed about 1246 by Alan de Wassand. The dispensation by which he was allowed, granted by Archbishop Richard Gray, to hold Heversham in plurality with Middleton in Yorkshire reads:[38] 'Alan de Wassand rector of the Church of Heversham has dispensation to hold the Church of Middleton in Rydal together with the said church of Heversham by reason of his probity, knowledge of letters and to enable him to support the multitude of people who resort to him'. Both he and his successor Roger de Warewike incumbent, from 1280 to 1290 are recorded as 'rector'.[39]

This implies that they were non-residents who left the cure of souls to a curate who might have been a monk from St.Mary's Abbey or from the less distant monasteries at Furness, Cartmel or Shap. Master Roger de Warewicke rector of Heversham 'was a witness to a deed in which'[40] William de Stirkeland confirmed to the prior and convent of Kermel (Cartmel) the perpetual cure and custody of the Chapel of Croscrake in the grantors territory of Staynton-in-Kendale'.

Records of the next two priests concern difficulties. In 1305 William de Hamelton[41] 'Clerk' parson of the Church of Heversham' acknowledged that he owed 800 Marks to his namesake, possibly a cousin, William de Hamelton Dean of York. In 1322[42] Simon de Baldreston parson of the Church of Heversham required the protection of the abbey. The next recorded priest is John de Wodehouse. He is important because he along with the Lord of the Manor Alexander de Wyndersore confirmed the Market Charter of Milnthorpe, granted originally in c.1280:[43] 'Grant to Alexander de Wyndersore Lord of two parts of the vill of Heversham and to the King's Clerk John de Wodehouse, parson of the church there and lord of the third part of the same vill that Alexander and his heirs and John and his successors, parsons of the said church, shall have a weekly market there on a Wednesday and a yearly fair on the eve and feast of St. Peter and St. Paul the Apostle'.

The following year John was awarded the right[44] of 'free Warren in Milnethorpe, Ascentwayt, Rouhol and Wodehouse'. Virtually the only records of parsons John de Etton King's Clerk, parson of the Church of Heversham from 1342-47,[45] of John de Neweland[46] 1343-1362 and Adam de Potthowe[47] 1362-65 are the presentation documents. John de Waltham[48] was vicar of Heversham for only a year 1365-66 but he went on to have a notable career in the church becoming Bishop of Salisbury in 1388 and on his death had the honour of being buried in Westminster Abbey. One reason for Walthams's short incumbency was a dispute about the living with Nicholas de Feriby with whom he exchanged Heversham for Steeple Langford in Wiltshire. De Waltham might never have visited Heversham but Feriby probably was resident for much of his incumbency. In the 'feet of fines' of York for 1372[49] he is described as 'parson of the Church of Eversham'. It might have been for his benefit that William de Wyndesore[50] obtained in 1377 a licence for 'religious persons to eat flesh meat at the Knight's table once a month on lawful days'. The following year Nicholas was witness of the will[51] of William de Feriby Archdeacon of Cleveland for whom he also acted as executor in 1379.[52] On 2 Nov. 1378 Nicholas received licence to be absent from Heversham possibly so that he could visit his other living of Stillington in Yorkshire. However, he continued to hold the living until his death in 1404 when he was succeeded by Thomas De Toueton or Tiverton whose ratification[53] as parson of the parish church of Eversham is dated 2nd Aug. 1404. He was a notorious pluralist. As well as being incumbent of Heversham he became Prior of St. James' Hospital Northallerton, Rector of Gosberton in Lincolnshire, Canon of St. Nicholas Pontefract and Prior of the Poor Hospital at Stillington North Yorkshire. In all he enjoyed an income of 400 Marks of which 60 Marks (£20) came from Heversham. Such worldly gain at the expense of the church did not, however, prevent Thomas from deserting his scattered flocks and in 1411 he obtained permission from the Pope to go to Rome for seven years to study.

Toueton's successor was Richard Arnall[54] or Arnold who was instituted to Heversham on 28 May 1429. From 1410 to his death in 1441 he was a sub-dean of York. He resigned the living on 17 March 1434/5 and returned to York. He was paid a pension of XL Marks by his successor at Heversham John Marschall who was presented on 4th Oct. 1455 by the Prior and Convent of St. Mary's. Having resigned the rectory of Scruton in 1434 he was allowed to hold in plurality 'the parish church of Eversham in the archdeaconery of Richmond, and Wheldrake in that Cleveland, and the Canonry and prebend of Wandestre in Wells, value altogether not exceeding £80. He was also a principal adviser and servant of Thomas Kempe, Archbishop of York 1426-1452. Kempe[55] had in fact visited Heversham, prior to Marschall's incumbency, on the 9th Sept. 1428 while en route to Furness Abbey and he might have been instrumental in obtaining the living for him. The Archbishop again visited the church on 19 Sept. 1442. Marschall was also a Canon residentiary of York where he died in 1462, and for much of his incumbency the parish was served by curates. Of these the name of only one has survived. He is Thomas Clyveland[56] who, in 1453, received a pardon of outlawry: 'Thomas Clyveland late of Eversham, alias Heversham, chaplain for not appearing to answer John Marschall, clerk, touching a debt of £40'.

When in 1459 the church was appropriated to St. Mary's Abbey the church was served by secular vicars.[57] Though they were presented by the Abbot the documentary evidence as to who the vicars were at the end of the fifteenth century is slight. In 1499 William Hudson[58] seems to have been at the chantry in the church to which in 1506/7 Edward Brown 'Jeweller of the Citie of Lincoln'[59] 'I will have a preest at our Lady Altar of Hershm to ryng there an hole yere for my fader soule, my moder soule, my brethren and sistren soules and for my soule and he to have for his wages £4:13s4d. Whereas my fader and moder lyen and where I was borne'. I.E. I will that Or Lady Altar of the same Church of Hershm have a Chalice of the value of 4 mcs'.

In 1527 Symon Senhow[60] was clerk or vicar of Heversham. He occupied the parsonage as 'fermour to the abbot and convent of Saynt Mary in York'. In 1535, at the time of the Dissolution of St.Mary's, Henry Carbot was incumbent.

### Notes and References to Sources   Chapter II

1. Farrer Vol.II p.142 (Col. Chart. Rolls 111, 115) also Vol.I appendix 1. p.377 *ex. Registro Abb. S. Marioe Eber. fol. 124*
2. Farrer Vol.II p.142 (Dodsworth M.S. CLIX F.180)
3. *Ibid* p.144
4. *Ibid* p.145
5. Transactions of Cumberland and Westmorland Archaeological and Antiquarian Society M.S.XXV Art.II Heversham Church. J.F.Curwen 1925. (C.W.A.A.S. Curwen)
6. Farrer Vol.II p.151
7. *Ibid*
8. Bouch p.25-29
8a. Valuable evidence of the Quadragesimal Tithes are contained in the Easter Books at Levens Hall. They cover the years 1581-1631 and many of the other local families e.g. Audland of Ackenthwaite, Chambers of Sedgwick, Wilson of Nether Levens and Bellingham of Levens, are recorded. The tithes continued to be collected until the Commutation of Tithes in the Heversham Enclosure Act of 1803 (See below). Also See Transactions of C.W.A.A.S., M.S.L&V 1965 - 'Notes for Excursion, by Mrs. O.R.Bagot F.S.A. Sat. 5th Sept. 1964
9. Farrer Vol.III p.222
10. Pilgrimage of Grace Ph.d. thesis M.Harrison State of Church in the Lake Counties Chap.III p.41-42 CRO(K)
11. Nicolson and Burn History of Cumberland and Westmorland (1777) Vol.I p.194
12. Westmorland Gazette (see below)
13. CRO(K) WPR/8
14. Kelly's Directories 1894, 1897, 1906, 1955, 1934, 1938
15. Local information Mrs. J.Wilson, Mrs. L.Lister
16. C.W.A.A.S. Curwen p.43
17. Farrer Vol.II p.146 Col. of Chart R.IV 312
18. Antiquary on Horseback June H.Ewbank 1963, P.55
19. R.C.H.M. 1936 p.158
20. 'Buildings of England, Cumberland and Westmorland' N.Pevsner p.273
21. C.W.A.A.S. Curwen p.43

22. see below
23. Church Wardens Account book CRO(K) WOR/8
24. *Ibid*
25. *Ibid*
26. C.W.A.A.S. Curwen p.44
27. *Ibid* p.34
28. *Ibid* and Appendix p.74
29. Nicolson and Burn Vol.I p.196
30. CRO(K)K WPR/8
31. see above; and Farrer Vol.II p.145
32. Church Wardens Accounts CRO(K) WPR/8
33. C.W.A.A.S. Curwen p.44 Appendix VII
34. see R.C.H.M.
35. Farrer Vol.II p.143
36. *Ibid* (Lancs. Pipe Rolls)
37. *Ibid* (Brit. Museum Add. Charter 17153)
38. *Ibid* Reg. Archbp. Gray (Surtees Soc) 161n
39. *Ibid*
40. *Ibid* p.144 (Copy at Sizergh)
41. *Ibid p.145*
42. *Ibid*
43. *Ibid* p.146
44. *Ibid* p.147
45. *Ibid*
46. *Ibid* (Cal. Pat. R.1342p.p.483, 515)
47. *Ibid* 1343
48. Potthowe C.W.A.A.S. Curwen p.61
49. *Ibid* p.62
50. Farrer Vol.II p.149
51. *Ibid*
52. *Ibid*
53. C.W.A.A.S. Curwen p.63 (Test Ebor Surtees Soc. Vol. 4. 1)
54. Farrer Vol.II p.150, C.W.A.A.S. Curwen p.63
55. *Ibid*
56. *Ibid*
57. *Ibid* p.151
58. *Ibid*
59. C.W.A.A.S. Curwen p.66
60. *Ibid* p.74 Appendix II
61. C.W.A.A.S. Curwen P.66

*Edwin Sandes,*
*Vicar of Heversham*
*c.1547*
*Archbishop of York,*
*1576-1588*
*(from an old*
*engraving).*

CHAPTER III

# The Sixteenth and Early Seventeenth Centuries: Reformation and Revolution

The effects of Henry VIII's breach with Rome were profound. In common with the rest of the country the changes most apparent to Heversham Christians were the substitution of English for Latin in the services, the removal of most of the statues, candles, bells and much of the ceremony associated with Roman Catholic services. The introduction of Cranmer's new liturgy in the 1549 and 1552 Books of Common Prayer was especially enduring for it shaped Anglican Worship until the liturgical changes of the 1970's.

Henry's reorganisation of Church administration led to the parish being transferred from the Archdiocese of York to the newly founded See of Chester.[1] Heversham remained part of the Diocese of Chester until incorporated in the enlarged Carlisle Diocese in 1856.

The Dissolution of the Monasteries affected the parish although it was only on the outer fringe of the area dominated administratively and economically by the great Abbeys at Shap and Furness. No longer, however, would prelates and humbler pilgrims visit Heversham on the way to these important foundations.

The Dissolution of Cartmel Priory meant that Heversham's Chapel at Crosscrake was no longer served by a Cartmel Monk. Thereafter Crosscrake seems to have been served only intermittently by curates from Heversham and by c.1691[2] the Chapel was reported, by Machell, as being almost in ruins. Though part of the building became a school regular services were not held until the Chapel was restored in c.1755.[3] This neglect of Crosscrake Chapel by the parish church combined with the distance of over three miles from it probably contributed to the growth of non-conformity in this North-East corner of the parish.

The most important consequence of the Dissolution was that the Advowson and Rectoral rights of Heversham which had been owned by St.Marys Abbey at York passed to the Crown.[4] Eventually in 1558 Queen Mary and King Philip granted the bulk of the endowment to

25

Trinity College, Cambridge except for the Corn tithes of Crosthwaite and Lythe which Edward VI had granted in c.1550 to John Southcote and Henry Cherviston. As a result the College became one of the largest landowners in the parish as is witnessed by the names of College Green Farm on Heversham Marsh and the College Meadow at Ackenthwaite.[5] As Rector and patron of the living the College ensured that most of the Vicars of Heversham down to the Reverend W.A.Cleghorn (1939-1955) were graduates of Trinity.

## The Pilgrimage of Grace

Heversham was touched by the unrest associated with the rebellion against Henry VIII known as the Pilgrimage of Grace. There are, however, few specific references to the parish in the documents recording the events of the Rebellion and its suppression. Heversham was too far from the great monasteries to have resented the loss of the abbeys which according to the leader of the Rebellion Robert Aske 'in the north partes gafe great almons to pour men and laudably served God'. [6] However, the parish would have been swept by the rumours which reportedly said that all valuables in the churches were to be appropriated by the crown, that nine out of ten churches were to be closed, that churches less than five miles apart were to be pulled down and, more believably, that fees were to be charged for baptisms.[7] However, parishioners would soon have heard and, some may have witnessed, the stirring events at Kendal where on 17th March 1537 '300 persons in the parish church of Kendal threatened to cast the curate Sir Robert Apelgarthe in the water unless he would proclaim the Pope to be head of the church'.[8] At Beetham the parson William Lancaster 'bid beads',[9] prayed for the Pope and read Rebel Communications. Subsequently Lancaster and John Stones of Beetham were hanged as rebels as were ten men of Cartmel and four of the Priory's Canons.[10] Whether Heversham folk rejoiced or regretted these executions is not known. Possibly, however, there were parishioners amongst the 500 men who met at Endmoor (within the Parish) in February 1537 towards the end of the rebellion. A reason why Heversham does not seem to have taken a large part in the rebellion could have been long standing resentment at the exactions of St.Mary's Abbey. In 1529 'the Commons' (of Heversham) had 'withheld their tithes from the farmers who had leased them from the Abbot of St.Mary's'.[11] Though there were occasional disputes over tithes and fees (especially from Crosthwaite) the parish seems to have accepted the administrative and financial settlement of the Reformation.

## Edwin Sandes

As regards the religious changes Heversham could have been in the forefront of emerging Protestantism. This is because the vicar for a period in the 1540's was probably Edwin Sandes later Archbishop of York. He was preceded by Edmund Whalley who may have been a relative of another Edmund Whalley abbot of St. Mary's from 1521-1530.[12]

From the evidence of the Letters and Papers of Henry VIII it would appear that Whalley was succeeded by Owen Sandes, A.M. 'Presentation to the vicarage of the parish church of Eversham, Westmor., which belonged to the late monastery of St. Mary York, vice Edmund Whalley, dec. Westm. Palace, 19th Feb. 33 Henry VIII'.[6] This record was repeated by Curwen in his list of Rectors and Vicars.[14] Curwen, moreover, implies that Owen Sandes stayed at Heversham until the institution of Nicholas Browne B.D. on 22nd Sept. 1570.[15] However, a commission issued to Robert Aldrich Bishop of Carlisle and others to survey chantries records 'Edwyn Sandes, Vicar of Heversham, James Hall, John Wilson, Richard Atkinson and Walter Preston Churchwardens, findeth that there is a chantry in the parish church of Heversham founded by one Miles Brigges of Crosthwaite deceased which did give £100 to purchase a Chantry'.[16] Moreover E.S.Sandys in 'The Family of Sandys' of 1930 states that Edwin Sandes was between 1546-8 'Vicar of Heversham in Westmorland and not of Caversham in Buckinghamshire which had sometimes been stated'.[18] Unfortunately there is no record of Edwin's induction at Heversham amongst the papers of the Diocese of Chester of which the Parish had recently become part. However, except for the state papers no primary source mentions Owen Sandes. Possibly Owen, which is an unusual name for that period, was a misprint or perhaps Owen Sandes did serve at Heversham c.1542 and was followed a few years later by Edwin.

26

Further support for Edwin's having been vicar is that he was a member of the locally prominent family of the Sandes of Graythwaite. He was born about 1519 at Esthwaite Hall and was probably educated at Furness Abbey. While at St. John's Cambridge he became associated with many leading Reformers, including John Bland Rector of Adesham who was burned as heretic at Canterbury in 12th July 1555. Edwin seems to have left Heversham at and end of 1548 and he became Prebendary of Peterborough in 1549 and Canon of Carlisle in 1552.

Shortly after the accession of Mary I in 1553 he was committeed to the Tower as the 'greatest heretic in England' although he protested that he had spoken 'none other than the word of God and the laws of this Realm do warrant me'. He eventually escaped, or was allowed to escape, from the Tower but not before, it is claimed, he miraculously cured the barren wife of a warder. During the latter part of Mary's reign Edwin lived in Augsburg, Zurich and Holland where he was a close colleague of the leading English Protestant exile Peter Martyr. In 1559, having refused the Bishopric of Carlisle, he became Bishop of Worcester and in 1570 Bishop of London. Finally in 1576 he became Archbishop of York which office he held until his death at Southwell Minster in 1588.

Although in such a long and distinguished career Edwin Sandes' probable incumbency at Heversham was of slight importance in his life it was possibly not without significance to the parish; for the years 1546-48 were a period which saw the introduction of important protestant reforms following the death of Henry VIII in January 1546/7 and the accession of Edward VI. These included the gradual introduction of an English liturgy which culminated in the issue of the 1549 Book of Common Prayer and the restoration of administering Communion in both kinds. Edwin Sandes was an early advocate of 'giving the cup to the laity' and indeed one of the chalices used by him for this rite has survived.[20] Therefore, it is possible to speculate that he administered the Communion cup to his congregation while at Heversham. As this did not become general until the end of Edward VI's reign it is possible therefore, that Heversham's Christians were amongst the first to partake in the restored practice.

Sandes' immediate successor at Heversham is not known. The record exists, however, that on 26th June, 1554 'William Thwaightes clerk entered his composition for first fruits' of 73s 4d being one tenth of the livings value of £56:13:4d.[21] Similar composition accounts survive for Robert Heblethwaite 7th July 1560,[22] Nicholas Browne 18th June 1571[23] and Giles Ayliffe 10th July 1573.[24] The Crosthwaite register states that 'Gyles Ailefe, clarke lait Vicar of Heversham dep'td from this world the VII day of Maye 1588'.[25] In his will proved on the 23rd May 1588 Giles requested 'Burial in the Chancell of the P'ish Church of Hev'sham' and made various bequests to his wife Jane, 'and 40 shillings to the Poor of Heaversham on this side (the Moss) 40/- to be distributed amongst them in lent next comyng'. He also gave 'to the Parishe Churche of Heversham XL towards the reparacon of the Rof (or thereof),' and, possibly anticipating Edward Wilson's Grammar School foundation of 1613 stated that 'Yf Jane my wif shall dye without ysshew of her body then I gyve and bequeath all my land being in Killington to the parishe of Heversham for ever towards the maintenance of a free scole to be kept within the P'ishe of Heversham'.[26]

Jeremiah Radcliffe was vicar from 1588-1591. He was a graduate and former fellow of Trinity College Cambridge and had been Vicar of Shudy in 1579 and Vicar of Trumpington in 1580 both in Cambridgeshire before becoming Vicar of Eaton Bray Bedfordshire between 1584-7. Having been instituted to Heversham on 17th July 1588 he only stayed until 1591 when he returned to Cambridgeshire to become Vicar of Orwell.[27] He was succeeded by Thomas Whitwell who was vicar from 1591-1604[28] during which time occurred the Fire of 1601, possibly the most disastrous event in the history of the Church at Heversham.

It was during William Thwaightes incumbency that Crosthwaite Chapel obtained parochial burial rights although it remained a dependent chapel to Heversham until the nineteenth century. This followed a petition of 1556 to Cuthbert Bishop of Chester from the inhabitants setting forth 'their great distance from the parish church, so they cannot carry their dead to be buried without a great charge and inconvenience, nor suffer their children to be baptised without great danger to the said children both of soul and body nor attend the church for divine service and sacraments without great charge and labour ... '. Heversham did not lose out financially for it was stipulated that no prejudice thereby should arise to the Mother church in tithes, oblations obventions or other ecclesiastical rights. In particular Crosthwaite had to contribute 17s for the wages of the parish clerk of Heversham and pay for every corpse above the Quire Wall at Crosthwaite 3s 4d and for every corpse buried beneath the Quire Wall 1s 8d'. In return Crosthwaite folk retained the right to elect two churchwardens and six assistants 'to make up the number of 24 sworn men' who governed the parish.[29]

In contrast the dead of Stainton, Sedgwick and Barrows Green in the Crosscrake chapelry had to be taken for burial to Heversham until the nineteenth century, as had also those from Endmoor, Deepthwaite, Milton and Milton Moor in Preston Richard. Thus Robert Atkinson of 'Thendmoore' in his will of May 1586 requested burial 'in the parishe churchyard of Heversham nigh unto my father and my owne childe'.[30]

Therefore, the sight of a shrouded corpse or of the parish coffin (from which the dead were removed prior to burial) being carried along the meadow lined lanes, or across the mosses around the estuary, of perhaps a straggle of mourners zig-zagging down the Head on the short cut from Hincaster must have been familiar for centuries. Possibly the early seventeenth century[31] Deepthwaite Bridge was built with needs of mourners as well as merchants and other travellers in mind. Certainly documentary and cartographical evidence supports the tradition that the network of footpaths which covers the parish centres on the church. Into the eighteenth century care was taken that these 'corpse routes' were kept open. Thus on the 5th April 1706 there was a presentiment 'that a common footbridge call Ings Bridge across Ings Beck in Stainton in the highway from Preston Richard to the Parish Council of Heversham is in great decay and ought to be repaired by the inhabitants of Preston Richard.[32] Similarly on 8th October 1708 James Hind of Stainton yeomen was 'indicted for obstructing a common footpath for the inhabitants of Preston Richard leading from a close called Field End in Preston Richard across a close called Bradfield there and a close called Fletcher Meadow in Stainton and from thence through several places to the parish church of Heversham'.[33]

### The Family Chapels

From the reign of Edward VI chantries were illegal. Nevertheless the founders' families continued to own the chapels and as such could sell them. In 1583 Dorothy Countess of Exeter - a decendent of Ivo de Taillebois - conveyed the north chapel to Thomas Bradley who in 1597 sold it to Sir James Bellingham of Levens Hall. Since then the north chapel has formed part of the Levens estate.[34] The descendants of Colonel James Graham (who bought Levens in 1688), the Bagot family, continues to worship in the family pew which is so elevated as to be higher even than the pulpit.

The south west chapel was conveyed by the Buskells to Edward Wilson when he bought Heversham Hall in 1630. The south east chapel belonging in the sixteenth and seventeenth centuries to the Prestons of Nether Levens was also bought by the Wilsons in 1694 from William Herbert, Viscount Montgomery, who had married Mary, heiress of Sir Thomas Preston.

The Prestons had a handsome pew in the chapel on the site of the present organ. Nicolson and Burn state that 'in the south ile of the chancel belonging to Daniel Wilson ... is the pew of Sir Thomas Preston with his arms cut in wood in the year 1602. In the middle of which pew, raised about half a yard from the floor' was a plain black marble tomb to Maria Preston.[35] This tomb along with one to Mrs. Crowle of c.1780 was removed to the south-east corner in 1870. Since 1720 when the Wilsons transferred their seat to Dallam Tower the Preston and Buskell chapels have been jointly called the 'Dallam Chapel'.

28

## The Fire of 1601

The fire is the outstanding event in the story of the church. Indeed as recently as 1911 R.Nightingale in 'The Ejected of Cumberland and Westmorland of 1662' stated that 'everything appears to date from this event'.[36] As regards architecture this is manifestly not the case[37] even though Machell, who stated in c.1691 that Heversham had 'a fair parish church burned down to the ground about a hundered years ago and now in very good repair'[38], and other commentators have asserted that the church was totally destroyed.[39] Church Records certainly appear to have been lost as the Registers (q.v) and Accounts date from c.1601. The latter are contained in a well preserved volume entitled 'A Booke of Accomptes made for the Church of Heversham ffrom the yeare of our Lord 1601' which covers all years, except 1647, 1648 and 1649, until 1828 when it was replaced by a new 'Vestry Book'. As well as financial details are included a variety of memoranda, copies of wills and agreements forming a most important historical source. In 1622 the gist (based on memory) of a financial agreement made with Crosthwaite in c.1580 was recorded. Its preamble preamble reads: 'Wheras it fortuned through the negligence of a careless workman, being a plumber, *anno christi* 1601, on Wednesday being the first day of July, the Parish Church of Heversham, in the County of Westmorland was utterly consumed with fire and all implements, ornaments, books, monuments, chests, organs, bells and all other things were perished.'[40]

Though the walls and arcades survived, the fire must have been sufficiently intense at the west end of the church for a funnel effect to have been caused in the tower so that the belfry went up in flames. Inevitably the roof, probably tinder dry in high summer, was destroyed. All the glass, save two tiny fragments in the North East Window of the Levens Chapel, and the furniture of the main body of the church were also lost.

Contrary to the sensational report of 1601 not all the monuments were lost for that of Sir William Redmayne, who died in 1482, is mentioned in 1628 as still standing in the 'Middle quyer' and that the surviving part of the inscription reads *'Redman erat certe Levens haeres, Harwode aperte Edwardo III regi meruit famulari'*.[41]

That the east end was less badly damaged is shown by the excellent preservation of the east window tracery and the survival of the vestry door which is probably fifteenth century. The only piece of furniture to have survived from before the fire is the parish chest of C.1400. Removed to the north aisle in 1977 from the vestry where it stood for five hundred years, the eight and a half feet long chest, equipped with four locks, served as a depository for records and valuables both secular and ecclesiastical until 1970. It is rightly regarded as one of the most important pieces of medieval furniture in the diocese.

*The Parish Chest*

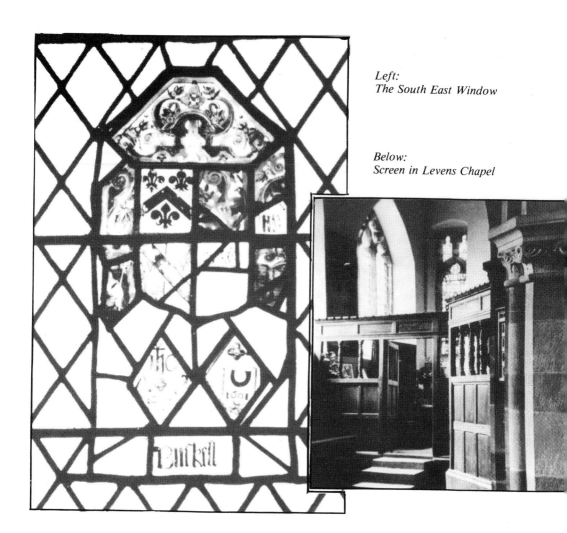

*Left:*
*The South East Window*

*Below:*
*Screen in Levens Chapel*

## Renovation

After the fire the repair work must have begun immediately as there is the Buskell coat of arms dated 1601 in the south east window of the Dallam Chapel. The Preston pew which was dated 1602 no longer survives but the same date is carved below the initials I.B.G. and the Bellingham hunting horn crest in the Levens Chapel. Apparently the repair work on the chapel was hurried for the north east corner on the outside is patched with seventeenth century brick work.

Much better work is displayed in the Levens Chapel screen. This has a panelled lower section with 14 symmetrically turned bulusters all of which are original though part of the entablature has been renewed. In two places the screen bears the initials B.I.A. and is dated 1605. There are also two rather later seventeenth century pews in the chapel. Two others were removed to Levens Hall when the Children's Corner[42] was placed in the Chapel in 1943, but were brought back in 1981 when the Lady Chapel was created. In the chancel just west of the steps leading to the Chapel is a good bench dated 1601 and carved with the initials I.A., E.W. (Edward Wilson?) and W.B. (Walter Buskell?).

The two bay arcade between the chancel and chapel shows signs of rebuilding. The pointed arches of two chamfered orders contain medieval masonry but the slim central pier and crudely incised capital and responds are probably of 1601.

*Bench dated 1601*

## The Roof

Though subsequently much repaired most of the timbers of the roof installed after the fire remain. The only complete replacement has been the chancel roof during the Victorian Restoration.[43] The north aisle roof was dismantled also at this time. However, the main timbers of its seven bay pent roof appear earlier than the tongue and groove underboarding of C.1870, and, therefore could date also from C.1601.

The Levens Chapel roof was also reset in c.1870 but its timbers are almost entirely of c.1601. It is flat pitched, of three bays and the principals, purlims and plates are chamfered. There are similar beams in the seven bay low pitched roof of the Dallam Chapel but its ridge beam is deeply scalloped on the soffit. The nave roof consists of six wide bays. Each of the

*Right: The Nave Roof*

*Below: The South Aisle Roof*

seven tie beams is over two feet thick and has a round boss in the centre. There is a large iron hook in the centre of the easternmost beam from which, originally, hung the eighteenth century chandelier. In contrast to all the other roof timbers the nave ridge beam is carved with a continuous figure of eight, or guilloche, pattern.[44] The seven bay roof of the south aisle has chamfered principals each of which has a flat central boss. The three bay low pitch roof of the porch is also constructed of seventeenth century timber. That it had to be replaced at the same time as the other roofs, although at a lower and less vulnerable level, is evidence of the extent of the fire damage.

The chancel roof, for which Trinity College was responsible was slated, the other roofs were covered with more expensive lead paid for by parishioners and Lords of the Manor. Beginning with an account of 1621 after 'all the leads of the highe roof were overblown and spoylte'[45] there are records of roof repairs every few years ever since.

Varying in colour from buff to dark brown the oak roof timbers are a fine, though often ignored, feature of the church. Being almost devoid of decoration, they reflect the austere religious observances of the Puritan period in which they are installed. At the end of the nineteenth century the church roof was much admired by the architect H.H.Austin and it may have contributed to his fondness for unstained oak seen in his designs for churches at Barbon, Field Broughton, Mansergh and Natland.[46]

Redecoration and refurnishing followed the structural repairs after the fire. In 1605 the legacy from the Reverend Thomas Whitwell, died 1604, was used to pay William Mayson £1.1s.6d for 'washing and whytinge of the chancell'.[47] The work was done thoroughly and all exposed masonry was plastered and whitewashed. Even the dressed stone door jambs of the vestry have been scored to hold plaster.

In 1606 the Clerk Thomas Parke purchased a Bible for 30 shillings and 'a Newe Sylver Cuppe' for £6.5s.11d. Contributions were received from 'Walter Preston Wyf of the End Moore towards a New Bible 6s' and from 'Thomas Brigge wyf of Staynton towards the newe cuppe 6s.8d'. On March 17th 1607 23s.9d was paid to 'William Crayston for Two Seates viz one for ye Curate & another for ye Clarke'. In 1608 twenty shillings was paid to Tom Gray for 'Writing and setting up' the ten commandments. These may have been murals in the style to be seen, for example, at St. Martin's Windermere or, possibly, were in the form of a painted 'tapestry' as the next account is 'Pd. more for the Clothe 5s.4d.' which would explain the meaning of 'setting up'.

Unfortunately the Book of Accounts does not record an estimate of the total cost or a description of the post-fire work, nor is there much information provided as to how the money was raised. Perhaps basic materials like sand, lime and timber were provided free of charge by land owners. Limestone was easily available from the Parish Quarry on the Head. However, the only references to masonry immediately after the fire are 1608, 'Mendinge and repairing of the Church Walls 8d', 1609, 'Tho. Hyne for walling of the Churchyard Walls 10d' and 'pd to Myles Hinde for Walling 10d.'

Other details of general repair work include 1608, 'Pd. for Nayles & Mending of the Queare doore 5d ... Robert Street plumbre for worke about the Church 12s', 1609, 'to Jeffray Parke for Nailes and a punchon 2s.... to William Aydland (Audland) for ironework 4d.... more for Iron Worke to Jeffray Parke 14d.... to William Kitchinge for Boardes 16d ... for 3 Jeastes (joists) 2s.... for Ernest for ye windowe frames in the Steeple 3s.4d' - and - 'for carriage of windowe frames and other seeled work from Kendall 3s.4d'.

### New Bells

It was not long before the faithful were once more told to pray. A bell was purchased in 1605. Its inscription was entered on the fly leaf of the 'Book of Accounts' as 'Me Pulsante Preces O Vos effundite Gentes Et Laudes nostros parllite Vosque Deo T.P. 1605 Johannes'.[48] ('O pour out your prayers through my ringing, you nations and praises make melody to our God. T.P. 1605 John'). That it was soon joined by other bells is shown by the accounts 1608 'pd. William Parke for 3 bell Ropes bought at Wakefield' (price omitted) and, in 1609, 'Pd. for the cariage of 2 Bell Wheeles 2s ... Pd. more in charges about 2 Bell Wheeles 4s.3d...pd. for takeing uppe the 2 Bells 10d. and the carron of the lyttle bell 9d.'[49]

### The 'Organes'

The most expensive item was the organ. Heading the accounts for 1609 is the memorandum: 'This year was a quilliet casten on this side of the Mosse towards the buying of the pare of organes ... according to the rate of Clerks wages five times (in addition) to all other assessments collected by the Churchwardens besides'. A 'quilliet', or culliet, was a rating assessment. Generally there were rates for the Poor, the Parson and the Clerk, of which the latter generally was made the basis for calculating any special rate that had to be levied. A 'pare of organes' simply meant a set as distinct from a single pitch pipe. As well as the product of the rate this first recorded 'organ fund' was augmented on '20 day of Mai 1610 Received by Walter Chamber Churchwarden at the hands of Alan Backhouse Concerning a legacy by Richard Sill of Staynton towards the organes 6s.8d.' The Book of Accounts gives the total cost of 'the organes' as £29.10s.5d. However, the actual cost appears to be £30.14s.5d, comprising 'paid for the organes £26; pd.Tho. Willan when he went to view the organes at York 25s.7d; pd. to William Parke for carriage of the Organes 24s; pd. to George Willson for his travel to York about ye organes 7s; ... for benevolences (tips) 7s; to William Parke for carriage of the organes £1.4s.0d; to Richard Benson & John Mackoroth for makeing a seat for the organes 20d' and 'to George Mashother at Bargaining of the Organes 5s.2d.' Incidentally George Mashother is the first member of the locally numerous Mashiter family to appear in the Church Records.

Mainly because of the purchase and installation of the new organ 1609 was the most expensive year in the immediate post-fire period the wardens paying out £35.1s.2d leaving a deficit of £2.16s.3d. The only indication as to how the money was raised is a memorandum of 1604 'Note also that this somme of 20s et likewise the whole of the Culliot money both of this side of the Mosse & beyond is disbursed upon the Church saving the summe of 28s.2d which is now remaining as by their true notes and perfect account made by all Churchwardens of both sides of the Mosse may appeare.' A few minor bequests are also recorded: 'Received at the hands of Thomas Brigge the 10th day of November 1604 for a Legacy which was given to Heversham Church (by) Rowland Brigge Gent his last testament the summe of 10 shilling'; also 1604 'Received of Christopher Preston of Preston Richard for a Benevolence given by him besides his Assmt. towardes the (cost) of the repairing of the Church 7s.' There is also a memorandum of 1605 which implies that a more substantial benefactor, Allan Prickett, had delayed honouring a possibly rash pledge until forced to do so at an official meeting: 'Mem. that Allan Prickett of Staynton did make his accompt before the Churchwardens and 24 this yeare last part on New Yeares even touching the summe of twenty pounds wch he did bestow and give upon Bnvolence towardes the Reedifying and repairing this Church of Eversham and paid and fully answered so much as remayned in his handes.'

To what extent the cost of repairs were supported by the larger land owners is not known. The squires of Sizergh and Levens respectively were present, however, when on 'Low Sunday being the 15th day of April 1610 the Right Worshipful Sir John Strickland and Sir James Bellingham knights according to a certain agreement set down between the inhabitants of Crosthwaite and Lyth on the one part, and churchwardens of Heversham parish on the other part did survey and view the parish church of Heversham which was newly repaired and reedified. And upon their sight and view they found the same church to be very sufficient and in good estate as the same was before the ruinous decay to their knowledge.'[50]

### Seventeenth Century Fabric

Improvement of the church's fabric continued until the iconoclastic and puritan Forties and Fifties. Although most worshippers stood or knelt on the rush-strewn floor there are several references to seating. A dispute began in 1619 concerning the pew of Edward Wilson, of Nether Levens,[52] Judge Hutton (of Cowmire Hall) and William Garnett which went on until 1622 when the Bishop of Chester's Court ruled that these gentlemen should sit 'next unto the partition betwixt the chancell and the body of the church on the south side of the chancell (screen) door, extending so far as the great pillar is, and to the Forme where William Parke's wife kneeleth ...'.[51] Nothing survives of this pew, of the chancel screen nor of the benches referred to in accounts of 1625 and 1632 'for worke about the formes'.[52]

The first references to a pulpit and of flagging the church floors occur in 1633 when the Churchwarden William Parke recorded in the Book of Accounts:

'for Pulpitt stayres . . . . . . . . . . . . . . . . . . . . . . . . . . . . . . . .6s.08

for shifting the pulpitt . . . . . . . . . . . . . . . . . . . . . . . . . . . . .0s.10

for iron worke to the pulpitt . . . . . . . . . . . . . . . . . . . . . . . .3s.00

about flagging of the church payd to a free mason . . . . . .12s.06

in part flagging church . . . . . . . . . . . . . . . . . . . . . . . . . . . . . .11s.05

in charges on a free mason . . . . . . . . . . . . . . . . . . . . . . . . . .2s.06

for Lyme & carriage from Millthorp . . . . . . . . . . . . . . . . . .2s.08    [53]

Other maintenance charges in 1633 included above average expenditure on the belfry 'new Bellropes 4s.06, Bellwheels 1s.04 and 'three Bellwheels' '2s.06 for mending Bellropes', 'for a Bondmaking and charges at the hanging of the wheels 1s.08' and 'in charges upon him that Brought them 0s.04'.[54]

There appears to have been a Church clock by this time as in 1631 one shilling was paid 'for coulours for the Diall' and 2s 'for setting up ye Diall'. The first specific reference comes in 1638 when Edward Saule was paid 13s 'for guidinge ye clocke'. In 1639 his salary was increased to 14s which remained stable for several decades.[55]

### Furniture

Apart from the carved bench in the Levens Chapel ( mentioned above) there are several other pieces of seventeenth century furniture in the church including a bench in the Dallam Chapel marked 1626 Thomas Lockey'. This is a reminder of the bequest made by Lockey 'a Loundoun Merchant Taylor, for the honour of Almightie God, the louv he boore for this his native countrie, and for the furtherance of the true religions did truly bestowe in this parish church of Hevershame, a Bible, the Booke of Martirs, Peter Mastiers Common Places, a booke of homelies and a parchment booke to be register booke for the same parishe for ever'.[56] Along with the bench went a low sloping faced desk in which the books (all of which have disappeared) were kept. It is made of the same dark oak as the bench and sinced 1976 has been kept at the Grammar School. The church also possesses a pair of seventeenth century coffin stools, and a stretch of altar rail of c.1660 now by the Preston tombs in the south-east chapel.

In 1980 the panelled eighteenth century chest in the vestry was discovered to have been built round a seventeenth century table whose turned legs are in each corner.[57] At five feet long the table is similar to seventeenth century Holy Tables and it is, therefore, probably that this was originally in the sanctuary. The panelling round it could date from 1763 when the present altar was purchased.[58]

### The Dorothy Bellingham Monument

This is the most important monument in the church and after the Clifford effigies at Appleby and the Walter Strickland tomb at Kendal is one of the finest peices of seventeenth century funeral sculpture in the county. It is set between the arches on the north face of the Levens Chapel arcade and this obscure position might be the reason why Pevsner, did not mention it in the 'Buildings of Cumberland and Westmorland'.[59]

The mural monument displays the miniature effigy of the deceased Dorothy Bellingham nee Boynton who died in 1626. She is clad in a flowing white gown, an elaborate ruff round her neck and a wimple on her head. She lies resting on her left elbow, placed on a red cushion with her hand on her brow. In her right hand is a book which touches a red swaddling clothed infant. On either side of the niche for the effigy is a black skull. Above are two pilasters crowned with spires bearing the hunting horn crest of the Bellingham's on the left

34

*The Dorothy Bellingham Monument*

and, on the right, the crescents of the Boynton's. Between is a large coat of arms of both families decorated with what seems to be either an acorn or a pineapple. If the latter, it must date from 1765 when the monument was repaired by Dorothy's co-lateral descendant Sir Griffiths Boynton whose name appears in the bottom right-hand corner. The winged cherub below the final couplet of the epitaph could also be an addition. Undoubtedly seventeenth century are the melancholy symbols of mortality decorating the pilasters. These include a skull and cross bones with Bible and spade on the left and an hour glass, book and pick on the right. All the symbols are linked by an almost playful ribbon motive.

### The Epitaph

The monument's chief interest is in its epitaph which is both explicit and poignant:

'M.S. Here lyeth the body of Lady Dorothie Bellingham Daughter to Sr. Francis Boynton of Barneston in the County of Yorke knight and wife to Sr. Henry Bellingham of Helsington in the County of Westmorland Knight and Baronett, shee dyed the 23 of January 1626 Aetate sua 39.

> 'Thrice six yeares told brought up by parents deare,
> Duely by them instructed in God's feare
> Twice seven yeares more I liv'd to one betroth
> Whose meanes yea life were comon to us both
> Seaven Children in that space I brought

35

By nature perfect and of hopefull growgth
His parents unto mee, deare as myne owne,
Theire loves were such as to ye worlde's well known,
But ere that one yeare more her course had runne,
God in his mercie unto me have showne
That all theis earthly comforts are but toyes
Being compared with those celestiall joyes
Which through the blood of Christ are kept in store,
For those in whom his word has ruld before.
To labour borne I bore, & by that forme
I bore to earth, to earth I straight was borne.'[60]

## Burials in Ecclesia

Dorothy Bellingham, probably, was buried in a vault beneath the raised floor of Levens Chapel, a practice which was followed by many humbler families elsewhere in the church. Indeed between 1609-1641 no less than 117 internments are registered as 'in ecclesia'.

Occasionally an indication was made as to the graves' position. Thus in 1609 Margaret wife of Robert Cragge was buried 'at ye chancel doore', Henry Chamber 'in the north allye' and John Hynd 'at the littell church doore'. In 1611, April 13 Christopher son of Willaim Holme was buried 'in the Bellhouse' and on May 25 Mrs Alice Mallaret (nee Buskell?) 'in her father's Queare'.[61]

The fees charged are recorded in a memorandum in the Churchwardens accounts for 1606: 'It is ordered by the Churchwardens and 24 that from hencefoorth all Burialls Above the foonte where the newe foonte now standeth shall paye the somme of 3s.4d. And beneath the foonte as hath been heartofore 20d.' Therefore, as 'Above the foonte' probably means to the east and 'beneath' to the west this memorandum indicates that the font stood in the centre of the church, perhaps by the Chancel arch, a position favoured by the sixteenth century Reformers but not adopted everywhere until the rule of the Puritans in the 1650's.[62]

During the 1630's the west end was a popular resting place. Between 1631-1633 ten corpses were interred '*supora fontem*' - beneath the font. Even after 1633 (when the church floors began to be flagged the practice hardly declined for there were 107 internal burials between 1634 and 1685. There is then a break in the records until 1691. During the eighteenth and early nineteenth centuries about another fifty corpses were given preferential burial beneath flag and pew rather than the cold sod outside.[63] All the tombstones set in the floor were removed during the Victorian Restoration except for two half hidden by the baptistry bench in the north-west corner of the church. The inscription on one reads: 'Here lieth ye Body of Agnes Crosfield, da of Anthony Crosfield of Common Myre who departed this life ye 9th Day of Oct. ...'[64] On the other the inscription cannot be made out.

## Troubled Times

Having escaped all but the milder breezes of the Reformation storms in the sixteenth century Heversham was swept, in the seventeenth century, into the maelstom of religious and political conflict. Moreover in the earlier decades the church was poorly served by its vicar Thomas Calvert who held the living from 1604-1638. He resided at Heysham where he was also rector and left Heversham in the charge of curates. An indication of poor relations between vicar and congregation is an account of 1612 'paid for charges concerning the suit at Appleby against Mr. Calvert 10s.10d'.[66] Further trouble is suggested by an entry of 1621 'pd. for an excommunication 3s.6d.' and 'pd. for public cryinge of the same 4d.'[67] This according to Curwen was done from 'the crying stone in the Churchyard opposite the (old) Blue Bell'.[68] Whether this severe penalty was imposed for heresy or immorality is not known.

References in the register are sparse and sometimes confusing regarding the curates who, served Heversham during Calvert's long absentee incumbency. The first record to the start of a curacy is 'Anno 1610 July Thomas Wyllan Clarke on the 15th day'. On the flyleaf of the register is inscribed '1621 James Wakefield's Curateshippe'. The register also records the

36

birth to Wakefield of three daughters, Isabella 1621, Alice 1623 and Agnes 1625.[69]

Wakefield was followed, it seems, by Richard Hudson whose name appears on the front page of the register for March 1627. Also recorded are the baptism of his children Maudlene in 1629, Robert in 1631 and Thomas in 1633 while the burial register gives '1631 November, Robert Sonne of Richard Hudson Clarke, and Minister of this church sepulted 27th Die'. The termination of his curacy is recorded against 'Julye 17, 1635 here ends St. Hudson's Curateshippe'. He appears, however, to have continued to live in the parish for the baptism of more of his children are registered: Jane in 1635, and twins Sarah and Dorothea in 1637. Jane died in 1636 and Sarah in 1639. Their father is registered simply as Clarke without the qualification of minister.[70]

There is no record as to how the church was served between Hudson's resignation in 1635 and the arrival of his successor Thomas Bigge in 1638.

### The Grammar School

It was while Thomas Calvert was vicar that Edward Wilson founded Heversham Grammar School, in 1613, 'in order to increase, maintaine and continue religion, good learning and discipline in the parish.'[71] From the start there was a strong connection between the Church and the school whose foundation documents stipulate that the Vicar and Churchwardens should share with other feoffees (trustees) in selecting a master. Details of the schools finances appear in 'The Book of Accounts' including: 'Received by the hands of Nicholas Benson & Roger Cragg from Thomas Saul deceased the sum of forty shillings to be employed for the use of the school September 13, 1615' and '1616 Mem ordered to the use of the School house, by the Churchwardens £7 of course Lime the year last past'. Twenty years later the building work seems not to have been completed: 'Memorandum That upon the afforesayd Day of Reckoning being the 30th Day of March: Anno Domini 1635. It was agreed upon: by the Churchwardens and Sydesmen ffor the Present yeare: as well beyond the Mosse as on this Syde that a Cessment and an halfe should be made and collected Through evrye Hamlett: according to the Cessment for the Poore ffor the finishing of the ffree Schoole. It was also agreed upon the same day that a Double Cuilliet should be collected for the sole and propper use of the Churche'.[72] Though for a long period fees were charged and periodically the 'catchment area' has varied it seems clear from this document that the founders' intentions were that the school should be free and should serve the entire parish, i.e. Crosthwaite, Stainton, Levens and Milnthorpe, and not just that fragment of the Old Parish of Heversham, that later became the Civil Parish.

### The Poor

In addition to supervising education the Church, despite troubled times, continued to fulfil its social functions. The Churchwardens acted as Overseers of the Poor and the 24 Swornmen were responsible for administering relief and levying the poor rate or 'cess', details of which were recorded annually in The Book of Accounts. Moreover, 6s.8d was paid three times a year to 'Maimed Souldiers' and there were occasional payments towards the welfare of prisoners in Kendal and Appleby Gaols. In the 1630's small sums were given to protestant refugees from the Roman Catholic Rebellion in Ireland.

Bequests to the poor were occasionally recorded e.g. 1606 'A Legacy given by Thomas Richardson to the poore of this Ende of the Mosse 40s'. Opposite the 1621 accounts two larger bequests were entered in the 'Book of Accounts':

'A true copy of a legacy in this last will and Testament of Thomas Jackson of Siggswicke Item it is my will and minde and that I dow give unto that said Church ye summe of Ten pounds for to remain for ever and the interest wherof to be distributed yearely by the Churchwardens for the tyme being in manner following that is six shillings thereof to the poore in Siggswicke to be divided by the Churchwardens and ffour and Twenty of that Hamlet and the residue of the interest to be divided amongst the poore of this parishe at Disgresstion of the Churchwardens for the tyme being that is to say to the poore of this Parishe on this side of the Mosse.'

'A true copy of a legacy ... last will and Testament of Mr. Thomas Lockey. I give and bequeath to the poore of the Hamlet of Milnthorpe in the Parishe of Heavsham within the County of Westmorland wherein I was borne the summe of fforty pounds to be imployed together with the 20 pounds formely given for the relief (?) of the said poore inhabitants at the disgression of the Churchwardens thereof and this summe accordingly To be paid Within an Yeare after my decease and I will that an acquittance under their hands & seals of the said Churchwardens be a sufficient discharge to my Executors for the same.'[73]

### Thomas Bigge Vicar 1638-1645, 1616-1676

Thomas Bigge was presented by Thomas Comber on 15th November 1638 and his bond bears the date 21 Dec. 1638. For the next twenty-five years he bore the brunt of the storm stirred up by the Civil War. He saw the parish invaded by the Scots in 1639 and 1650 and by the Parliamentary Army in 1644.

That the latter invasion, which followed the Royalist defeat at Marston Moor, had an immediate affect on the Royalist and Anglican Thomas Bigge is shown in sequestration certificate 'yt since June 1644 he hath beene kept from possession of ye Viccaridge'.[74] This occurred a year before the abolition of the Church of England and its replacement by Presbyterianism. That Bigge continued to live in fruitful, if impoverished, retirement within the parish is shown by the baptism register. For in addition to Katherine baptised 1641, and Thomas 1643 were registered Ann 1646, John 1648, Bridget 1654 and Mary 1658.[75] Presumably after 1645 they were subject to the Presbyterian baptism service though perhaps their father conducted a private and illegal form of the sacrament in accordance to the rite laid down in the Book of Common Prayer.

Thomas Bigge's place as vicar and Minister was taken in 1646 by Samuel Cole a man 'who could be depended upon to support Presbyterianism.[76] Both he and his brother William, who became Vicar of Kirkby Lonsdale, came from London and had fought in the Parliamentary Army and both had attained the rank of Captain. They also, according to the only record, so far discovered, of fighting within the Parish during the Civil War, 'had got into trouble through a struggle near Milnthorpe, where a Malignant was killed.'[77]

As an extreme protestant it can be assumed that while he was vicar Samuel Cole altered the church interior to accord with the newly introduced Presbyterian practices. Unlike at Beetham Church where in 1650, a mob led by the Puritan Richard Sill aided by Fairfax's soldiers smashed stained glass and damaged monuments[78] there are no records of specific destruction at Heversham. As however, there is no mention of an organ from this time until the early nineteenth century the instrument, installed in 1609, was probably destroyed and the puritan fashion of praising God with the raw power of the human voice substituted. In addition the communion table would also have been brought from its 'altar position' against the east wall of the chancel into the main body of the church.

The bells, however, continued to be rung. Even after the execution of the King, the abolition of the Monarchy and the elimination of Parliament by Cromwell's Generals two shillings were paid every 5th November to celebrate the failure of the Gunpowder Plot to destroy the King and Parliament fifty years earlier.[79]

While Samuel Cole was vicar the value of the living was increased by awards, from the Royalist estates and Crown property, which were sanctioned by Parliament. Thus in addition to the £40 stipend, enjoyed by Thomas Bigge, Samuel Cole was granted in 1646, 'by virtue of an order of both Houses of Parliament ... a ... remainder of ye fifths of ye impropriated rectory of Crosthwaite and Lythe ... sequestered from Sr.Richard Hutton Knt Dilinquent worth £14'[80] Later in the year £30 was awarded to 'Samuell Cole vicar of Heversham as aforesaid the vicaridge whereof is worth but £54 a yeare'.

This order was signed by Harbottle Grimston the Sequestered Estates Commissioner who was later the Speaker of the House of Commons. A further £50 was also obtained from the Rectory of Beetham (formerly held by the Crown) 'for the increase of ye maintente of Mr. Samuell Cole Minister of Heversham'.[81]

Thus it was, that the ejected Thomas Bigge, seeing his sucessor enjoying a higher income than he had obtained, petitioned on 2 November 1646 for the traditional pension, normally awarded to Clergy Widows, of one fifth of the annual value of the living. The petition was granted as 'Mr. Bigge and his wife yielding all due obedience to the said sequestracon' and accordingly Samuell Cole was ordered to pay Mrs Anne Bigge 'towards the maintenance of her and her children the full cleare fifth pte of all the tythes, rents, gleab lands and Easter booke of the said benefice'[82] Samuel Cole was replaced as 'publique preacher' by Richard Tatham' and on 9 May 1654 was instituted by the 'Com'rs for Approbation of publique preachers'. He was entitled to enjoy all rents, duties, profits, whatsoever by virtue of the said order (and) as attested by the registers of His Highnesse in that behalf and appointed voted at Whitehall 20th day of Novermber 1654'. 'His Highnesse' was, of course, the Lord Protector Oliver Cromwell!

Richard Tatham removed to Kirkby Lonsdale in 1657. He was replaced by John Wallace (or Wallas) M.A. He had 'preach'd for some time at Kendall' and had been Minister of Grasmere from July 28 1653.[83] According to Edward Calamy:

'He is reported to have been of so scandalous a life in several repects that his memory is not worth preserving. And yet I was not willing wholly to omit him least it should be charged upon me as partiality'.[84]

In fact Calamy was not expressing unfounded Royalist prejudice for Grasmere records show on:

'Last daie of July 1655 John Wallas with force and arms at Grassmire aforesaid in and upon Clara Barwis of Loughrigg being a virgin of ye age of 22 yeares then and there etc. an assault did make and ye said Clara to ravish did attempt.'

On 39th August 1655 he had been accused of assaulting John Hird 'and he did beate etc. agt. ye publique peace etc'.[85]

Wallace was apparently better behaved at Heversham where he stayed after the Restoration of the Monarchy (1660) until April 1663 when 'Brian Walker one of the Grand Jury doth p'sent John Wallas Clarke for not readinge the order of Common Prayer'. Along with

'other disaffected and suspicious persons he was later arrested for conspiracy in the Kaber Plot against the new royal regime and sent unto Appleby there to bee kept prisoner for three months ... in pursuance of ye late Act of Uniformity'.[87]

After their experience of three Republican and Presbyterian ministers one of whom was possibly guilty of homicide and another of attempted rape and assault the Heversham parishioners probably welcomed with considerable relief the return of their ejected Royalist and Anglican Vicar.

Thus it was that with the usurper Roundhead rotting in gaol Anglican Thomas Bigge successfully took his claims to the House of Lords demanding re-instatement to Heversham vicarage which he had occupied until

'about 16 yeares since when he was by the late usurped powers most illegally ejected and kept from the same and from the exercise of his ministerial duty there only for his Loyaltie and good affection to his Matie of blessed memory'.[88]

After recovering it he held the living peaceably until 1676 when the register records 'mr. Tho. Bigge vicar buried March the 18th'.[89]

**Notes and References to Sources   Chapter III**
1. See above Chapter I
2. Antiquary on Horseback
3. Cheshire Records Chester Castle EDV17/1/330
4. Nicolson, Burn Vol. 1. p.196
5. Farrer Vol.II p.150
6. Harrison p.50
7. Harrison p.125
8. Farrer Vol.I p.73 Letters, Papers Henry VIII XI p.180
9. Harrison p.136
10. *Ibid* p204
11. Farrer Vol.II p.152
12. C.W.A.A.S. Curwen p.66
13. *Ibid* Vol.XVII p.61

14. *Ibid*
15. *Ibid*
16. Farrer Vol.III p.222
17. The Family of Sandys Part I. G.O. Dandys 1930 CRO (K)
18. *Ibid* p.33 from C.W.A.A.S. Record Series Vol.IV. Records relating to the Barony of Kendal.
19. Family of Sandys Chapt. II p.33-91
20. *Ibid* p.62
21. Farrer Vol.III p.223
22. *Ibid*
23. *Ibid*
24. *Ibid*
25. Crosthwaite Register CRO(K)K WPR/3; Curwen p.67
26. Curwen Appendix VI p.77
27. Curwen p.67 Foster's Alumni Osconienses
28. *Ibid* and CRO(K) WPR/8 Parish Bundle
29. CRO(K)K WPR 3
30. Farrer Vol.II p.209
31. R.C.H.M.
32. Farrer Vol.III p.238
33. *Ibid*
34. C.W.A.A.S Curwen p.43
35. Nicolson and Burn Vol.I p.197
36. The Ejected of 1662 in Cumberland & Westmorland B.Nightingale. Manchester University Press 1911 p.968
37. see above
38. Antiquary on Horseback p.55
39. e.g. Nicolson and Burn p.197, C.W.A.A.S. Curwen p.43
40. A Booke of Accompts made for the Church of Heversham ffrom the yeare of our Lorde 1601 CRO(K)K WPR/8 (Book of Accounts)
41. The Redmans of Levens and Harewood W.Greenwood F.S.A.(Scot.) Titus Wilson 1905 p.97 (M.S.Dods 119 Fo.74)
42. P.C.C Minute Book
43. see below
44. R.C.H.M. p.110
45. CRO(K)K WPR/8 Book o. Accounts
46. Information from Miss Hilda Austin daughter of H.H.Austin to author c.1961
47. CRO(K)K WPR/8 Book of Accounts. *et seq.*
48. *Ibid.* Inscription on fly leaf
49. *Ibid et seq.*
50. *Ibid* and Quoted in C.W.A.A.S Curwen
51. CRO(K) WPR/8 Book of Accounts
52. Book of Accounts
53. *Ibid*
54. *Ibid*
55. *Ibid*
56. C.W.A.A.S Curwen
57. Discovered by author in presence of Reverend J.C.Hancock
58. Book of Accounts
59. Pevsner p.242-243
60. see also Nicolson and Burn Vol.I p.196 and Bellasis Westmorland Church Notes p.242-243
61. Church Registers (for details see below) CRO(K) WPR/8
62. Book of Accounts
63. Church Registers
64. Bellasis p.248
65. C.W.A.A.S. Curwen
66. Book of Accounts
67. *Ibid*
68. C.W.A.A.S Curwen
69. CRO(K) WPR/8 Register I also Nightingale p.970
70. *Ibid* and Nightingale p.970
71. R.D. Humber 'Heversham The Story of a Westmorland School and Village' page 2
72. Book of Accounts
73. *Ibid*
74. C.W.A.A.S. Curwen
75. CRO(K) WPR/8 RegisterI
76. C.W.A.A.S. Curwen
77. Nightingale p.71
78. Beetham Repository 1770 By the Rev. William Hutton Vicar of Beetham 1762-1811. Ed. C.W.A.A.S By John Rawlinson Ford. Kendal. (Titus Wilson) 1906, p.118.
79. CRO(K)K WPR/8 Book of Accounts
80. Nightingale p.973
81. *Ibid*
82. *Ibid*
83. *Ibid*
84. Edmund Calamy. An Abridgement of Mr. Baxter's History of his Life and Times with an account of the Ministers etc. who were ejected at the Restoration; quoted by Nightingale p.988
85. Nightingale p.977
86. *Ibid p.977*
87. Kendal Indictment Book quoted by Nightingale p.978
88. *Ibid p.978*
89. CRO(K) WPR/8 Register 2.

## CHAPTER IV

# The Later Seventeenth and Eighteenth Centuries

In the late seventeenth and eighteenth centuries the Church settled down into an era of tranquility. Generally, within the parish, there was a relative decline of the Quakers and Independents of the Civil War period, though there were still some active dissenters especially in the Milnthorpe area. Thus in 1672 after Charles II's Declaration of Indulgence Edward Briggs 'of the Parish of Heversham' obtained a licence for his home to be used for divine worship. A period of persecution followed the withdrawal of such licenses in 1675 and so on 13th October 1678 'Edward Wilson of Dallam Tower, sent several informers to a meeting held in the house of Edward Cragg of Ackenthwaite and upon their evidence convicted the worshippers, without bringing them before him, and fined by distress warrants thriteen of their number a total of £68.3s.8d.' Even more unfortunate was Joseph Gregg a distiller of Milnthorpe who for non payment of tythes was in May 1682 committed to Appleby Gaol where he stayed for five years. During this imprisonment his wife Jane was twice fined for attending dissenting meetings.

With the passing of the Toleration Act non Anglican Protestant worship became legal and in 1691 the Presbyterians Fund to assist the Country Ministry made a grant of £8 per annum 'towards the propogation of the Gospel at Milltrop in Westmorland'[1] This continued only until June 1693 when Mr.Thomas Jolly was the preacher. During the eighteenth century a Nonconformist Conventicle seems to have existed at Ackenthwaite but with few other dissenters or Roman Catholics the Established Church was accepted by most people.

When visited at the turn of the seventeenth century by the antiquarian Reverend Thomas Machell, vicar of Kirkby Thore, the church was in a good state of repair; Machell estimated it to be 23 yards broad by 40 yards long and went on to record that the 'vicarage house, a pretty good fabric, is about a hundred (yards) west of the church which I mention lest it should chance to be lost as (those at) Beetham and Burton are at this day'.

He also commented on the longevity of the population citing 'Agnes Storey of

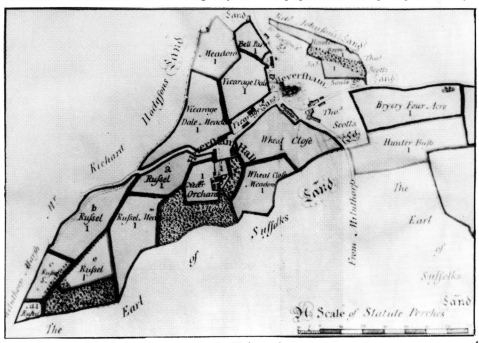

*Heversham in the Eighteenth Century*

41

Heversham buried here nine years ago. She was about a hundred years old. Edward Saal (Saul) and his wife about 20 years since lived to make up together about two hundred years. And there is one Thomas Benson at Levens Park, now living, who is about a hundred years old (and he) came to church on foot within the last three years, his house being two miles from the Church.[2]'

Compared to the stormy career of Thomas Bigge Vicar from 1638-45, and 1661-1677, little is known about his immediate successors: William Burrell M.A. 1677-1678, Thomas Milner 1678-1686, Thomas Ridley 1686-91, George Farmer M.A. 1691-1724, Mr Williams 1724-1727, Mr Murgatroyd 1727-1732 and James Smyth 1733-1757.[3] All except Burrell, Williams and Murgatroyd died in office and their deaths appear in the Registers e.g. 'Burialls 1723/4 Feb. 7. The Revrend Mr Geo. Farmer Vicar of Hevrsham Batchelor'.

In the Church Wardens Book of Accounts it is stated that 'Mr. Milner was a great Benefactor to Magdalene College Cambridge and left to it three Exhibitions of £20 per annum each for 4 years, to each of the following scholes one viz, Hevrsham, Leeds & Bradford Scholes.'

It was during the incumbency of George Farmer that it was found necessary to record, and possibly clarify the possessions and financial rights of the vicar. These included the small tithes which the vicar received in addition to the income derived from the endowment of the living valued at £66.6s.8d. They are recorded in a 'Terrier of the Rights and Dues belonging to the Church & Vicarage of Heversham' which is dated on the outside 1701: 'Imprimis our Vicarage hath two bays of building, one barn, one stable, one garden, no orchard.

2   There is no Gleabland belonging to our vicarage except two little Paddocks or yards containing by estimation one rood, and a half therabouts.

3.   We have no lands or estates tithe free within our parish.

4.   There is nothing for aformath, nor agistment For mortuaries according to the Statute. Every oblation one penny half penny. Every dwelling house one half penny. Every new calved cow two pence. Every strip corn one half penny. For calves the 1st calf one half penny 2 calves one penny 3 calves one penny half penny 4 calves two pence 5 calves nine pence 6 calves   one shilling four pence 7 calves one shilling and four pence halfpenny 8 calves one shilling five pence halfpenny and ten calves one shilling six pence.

For Roots or Herbs one penny for every one that sows any.

For hemp and flax one penny for every one that sows any. For mire Hay compositions greater or lesser summe according to quantity by meadows. Ploughs one penny. Chickens one penny. Eggs one penny. Foale one penny. Bees one swarm one penny, 2 swarms two pence, 3 swarms three pence, 4 swarms four pence, 5 swarms three shillings four pence, 6 swarms six shillings, 7 swarms six shillings five pence, 8 swarms six shillings sixpence, 9 swarms six shillings seven pence and 10 swarms six shillings eight pence. Pigs and Goose payd in kind. Composition for fruit greater or lessor summes according to quantity and Tithe for Mill greater or lessor summes For Wool every tenth fleece of Wooll and for old sheep or fold sheep one penny halfpenny, for lambs two pence five lambs, five pence, six lambs eight pence seaven lambs eight pence half penny eight lambs nine pence nine lambs nine pence halfpenny & ten lambs ten pence.

5.   All the tith corne on the East side of Sinderbarrow belongs to Trinity Coll except two tithe Barns viz Sidgswick and Stainton which belong to one Madam Strickland and no Tithes belong unto our vicar except the Tythes Hay and corne of the Ancient Desmesne Lands of Heversham Hall and no other Tythes due of our Vicar but as aforesaid.

Geo. Farmer Vic
Wm. Helme (signature damaged) ⎫
John T.P.Preston (His mark) ⎬ Church Warden[4]
Richard Cornthwait ⎪
Thomas Preston ⎭

*Wine flagons dated 1674*

Some attempt was made in the first half century after the Restoration of the Monarchy and the Church of England to relieve the aesthetic austerity imposed on the interior of the church by the Puritans. Loyalty and decoration were combined in 1665 when the 'King's Arms were set up'[5] (In 1761 there is an account: 'Spent when King's Armes was taken down & Timber 3s.'[6] Whether they were replaced by the newer arms of George III is not known although this was the contemporary practice. There are no further accounts concerning the Royal Arms, nor have any survived in the Church.) In 1674 the walls were whitened and 'adorned' and again in 1707 £3.15s was paid to Gerard Rowes for painting 'sentances'.[7]

### The Churchplate
The most important surviving link with the Restoration period are the principal items of the church's plate. In 1675 'a silver bowl and chalice'[8] were purchased for £5.15s.6d. These are probably the large Chalice and cover paten used still, for family communions. They bear a London hallmark of 1655 but are unlikely to have come to Heversham at that date as the ultra-protestant Richard Tatham was 'public-preacher' and he would have abhorred such a popish article as a silver chalice. The chalice is similar to a contemporary wine cup and thus might for its first twenty years have been used for secular purposes.

The finest items are a pair of wine flagons dated 1674 and a paten inscribed 'Yee Gifte of James Bellingham Esqe The sonne of Allan: To the service of God in the Parish Church of Heversham 1674' and were probably made for the church. According to Crawford Hodgson in 1903 there 'is a whistle at the base of the handle of the flagon a curious survival of an ancient drinking custom'.[9] Recent investigation, however, has not discovered how the whistle works or the significance of the custom. There is also a paten on stand inscribed 'For ye service of Heversham in ye County of Westmorland 1713'. The purchase of the newer paten is recorded in the acounts: 'July 19 1713. Then Taken out of the money given at the offertory the sume of £2.19s.4½d. for paying for the paten for the use of the Church as agreed upon by us

Geo. Farmer. Vic.
Christopher Bindloss
Thomas Ffletcher
Mathew Willson.'[10]

Both patens like the chalice, but not the flagons, are still used weekly.

### Eighteenth Century Accounts
From 1719 when the Council of Twenty-Four met to consider providing a seat for singers the Church Wardens' Book of Accounts provides evidence of increase and improvement of

Church wardens accounts 1745 recording expenses of one shilling when the church plate was hidden during the Jacobite invasion

furniture and fittings. In 1723 a three decker pulpit with sounding board, reading pew and clerk's desk was made by Robert Hardy and installed against the eastern pier of the south arcade at a cost of £14.10s., 'Four Tassals & Fringe for the Pulpit Quishon' cost 12s and James Scott was paid for 'making the Pulpit Quishon & Mending the Bier Cloth 2s.'[11]

Andrew Storey was paid £3.10s for a font cover in 1735; yet four years later it was decided to get a new free stone font which was to be placed once more at the west end. Since the early seventeenth century the font had stood in the main body of the church. That the restoration of a western baptistry was prompted not just by a desire to return to traditional practice but rather by consideration for the congregation is shown in the wording of the faculty issued by the Archdeaconry of Richmond on 28 June 1739 which says that a font in the chancel inconvenienced worshippers 'as persons as come with children to be baptised ... (had been) crowding into seats in the nave ... in time of divine service' .... Henceforward little children were to be suffered only if they and their attendants occupied a new christening pew that was 'to extend from the back of the great south door westwards seven feet and ... from the south wall northwards nine feet in length'.[12] The font was made by John Crakall at a cost of £2.5s; one shilling was spent 'on masons when the font was set up' and Robert Hardy was paid 12s.2d 'for work in repair where old font stood'. Anthony Cornthwaite charged £4.10s for constructing the pew and 'Joseph Johnson for a matt for Christening Pew' received 2s. A smaller 'matt' was also purchased for 4d.[13]

Detailed accounts, also survive of the replacement of the 'very irregular and much decayed seats' with box pews: in 1740 'Robert Robinson and Richard Nicholson for new seats viz. the middle pew before the pulpit measured at the top of the wainscot £18.10s' and 1s.6d' to masons for fetching three yeards of flaggs from Hutton Roof:' in 1741 'new seats in the Middle Row where the pulpit stands £17.00' and for flagging under them £12.00. A further £15.10s was spent in 1742 on 'flagging ye south side'.[14]

Two years later the twenty-four members of the council contributed £11.13s.4d towards a writing loft at the Grammar School so that 'the masters who for many years past have had the privilege and advantage of teaching their scholars in the parish church ... (causing) oftentimes great damage by mischievous scholars' could be expelled from the church. Henceforward it was hoped that the building 'may hearafter be kept clean and decent as becomes the House of God'.[15]

In 1747 lighting appears to have been improved as the accounts record

| | | |
|---|---|---|
| Pd Garard Farleton of Wiggan for the Candlestick | £5:15s:6d | |
| a box to bring it in | 1s | |
| Carriage | 2s:6d | |
| Francis Hawings for the Iron Rod for it | 2s:1d | £8:18s |
| Anthony Cornthwaite for Guilding & painting it | £0:18s:0d | |
| Spent at Robert Marshalls when it was fixed and hung up | £1:19s:7d[16] | |

The Candlestick was probably a chandelier as, later, an annual sum of generally five shilling is recorded for cleaning it. Unfortunately, it was disposed of at an unknown date, though the hook from which it hung can still be seen on the easternmost tie beam of the nave.

Caretaking costs were not great. In 1734 Henry Hudson was paid £1:10s per annum for 'sweeping and dressing the church' and Thomas Fletcher 6s for washing plate and linen. A pay rise of 2s to 8s was given to Elizabeth Harding for the same duty in 1760. This did not start a wage spiral for as late as 1828 Robert Bindloss was receiving only a guinea a year 'for cleaning the church thoroughly every week and cleaning the church walks and church yards to the satisfaction of the wardens'.[17]

On 27 March 1758 it was recorded that 'Wm. Tennant of Woodhouse was by the above said majority chosen to keep all Dogs out of the Church every Sunday for one year he to receive from the parish at the years end for so doing 7s:6d'. The whip cost 6d and was replaced for the same amount in 1768. Annual entries for 'Dog Whippers Salary' occur until 1839 when John Foxcroft was the last holder of the office.[17]

The roof gave frequent and expensive trouble. A Contract for roof repairs survives dated 4th June 1697 being an 'agreement between Edmond Birkett, Daniel Dickonson, Richard Cornthwaite Churchwardens ... with the consent of the four and twenty men of the said parish ... and Reginald Kirkbarrow of Barrowgreen (who) as often as need be shall require, amend, repaire maintaine and keep in good and sufficient repair viz. drop dry upon (sic) if fifteen days notice ... all the flatt leads gutters and water spouts belonging to the church of Heversham and the steeple and the church porch except those leads belonging to the vicar (i.e. the chancel) and the Hon. James Graham esq. (i.e. Levens Chapel) ... and that the full and just sum of two pounds of lafull mony of England and the first payment to being in and upon the first day of August next'.[18]

Eighteenth century repairs include in 1761 'paid James Wright for lead about ye weither cock £17:1s:0½d.'; the cock itself was forged by William Audland of The Smithy, Ackenthwaite at a cost of £9:17s:3d.

There are also almost annual references to whitewashing and repairs to the outside walls. In 1749, for example, John Cornthwaite got £1:5s. for 'rough casting the north side of the church'.[19]

### The Bells and Bell Ringers

The Bells and Bell Ringers figure conspicuously in the accounts. Soon after the Restoration of the Monarchy and Church of England is the memorandum 'that the Little Bell founded by Jefforie Scott of Wiggan Bellfounder was hung in the steeple of Heversham Church upon Saturday the sixt daye of September 1662'. The bell cost £15:19s:3d and was inscribed 'Dulcedine vocis cantabo tuo nominee' ('In sweetness of voice I will sing to your name'). It was joined in 1669 by a 'first' (or largest) bell that bore the inscription 'When I do cease Remain in Peace CW TC RC 1669'. It also was founded by Jefforie Scott and cost £27:5s:11d with an additional £1:12s being paid to '2 Churchwardens for going to Whiggan'. These bells were replaced by the present peal of five in 1870.

Precise duties of Bellringers were stipulated on 'March 28 Anno Domini 1687: Memorandum.

'That it was agreed upon between the 24 and Churchwardens for the parish of Haversham on the one parte and Richard Burrow, James Harrisson, John Garnot and Thomas Makorofe on the other that it is covenanted and Agreed upon between the said partys that the said Richard Burrow James Harrisson John Garnot & Thomas Makorofe ring one Bell at Seavon of the clock Every Sunday morning and Two Bells at Eight of clock and Three Bells at nine of Clock and do chyme the Great Bell soon after Every Sunday morning for one whole yoare to come in consideration whereof the said Church wardens on behalf of the said parish do promise to pay to them the sum of eight shillings by their succession and that the money given for ringing in the said parish shall be equally divided amongst them in witness whereof the said Churchwardens and the said Ringors have hereunto set their hands the day & yeare first above written.

| Signed   Churchwardens named | Ringers naimed |
|---|---|
| John Jopson | Richard Burrow |
| Edward Wilson | ‡   mark of James Harrison |
| George Mowson | John Garnot |
| Arthur Crosfield | Tho. Morkoreth  (sic)[27] |

Minor repairs are noted annually and there are occasional references to emergencies as in 1731 'spent upon the men that helped up with the middel bell when the Georgion was broke £00:1s:02d'. Otherwise there was apparently no cause to replace any of the bells installed in the seventeenth century. Indeed, judging by the wild scrawl of the vicar Dr.Lawson's memorandum, as late as Oct. 2 1821 it was with some fury that the vestry meeting rejected any suggestions that the bells were not in order! 'At a meeting held this day in the vestry in persuance of a notice given to consider of the best mode of carrying into effect the order left by the Bishop of the Diocese to have our large bell which is cracked recast it has been determined by a majority of the principal inhabitants and churchwardens being present not to carry into effect the said order but to suffer the bells to remain as they are'.[28]

Payment to bellringers marked special events. In 1660 5s was paid for 'ringing when ye king was proclaimed'. The same sum was paid on 'thanksgiving days' for five of Marlborough's victories (but not incidentally Blenheim) and for the Peace of Utrecht in 1713. At the Coronation of George I in 1714 the ringers were paid 12s but only three shillings on 11 June 1727 for 'expenses this day being the day on which the King (George II) began his happy reign'. In 1761 there occurs 'for ringers on Coronation Day (George III) 3s' and for 'the birth of the Prince of Wales (later George IV) and the taking of Havannah 4s'. Following Waterloo expenses for thanksgiving day 14 July 1815 amount to a mere 4s including '2s for a printed letter'. When Queen Charlotte died in 1818 the muffled peal cost 7s:6d and when George III died in 1820 15s.[29]

## The 45'

The peaceful, if busy, tenor of eighteenth century Heversham was punctured by the Jacobite Rebellion of 1745 in which the Parish was, for the last time, in the main path of a Scottish invasion. On 18th November 8,000 rebels entered Carlisle.[30] By 24th November, having crossed snow covered Shap, they were in Kendal. Generally the invaders did little material damage but they did confiscate food, money and plate. With the Royal army far away and the Westmorland Militia keeping a querulous eye on the Jacobite garrison at Carlisle, prudent measures were taken. Accordingly in the Book of Accounts there appears 'spent when the Churchplate was hid 1s'. On the 25th and 26th of November the rebels on their march south crossed the parish along the old high road through Endmoor. Having halted at Derby the rebel tide turned and on the foreboding date Friday 13th December the demoralized and potentially dangerous Scots straggled northwards along the same route closely followed by the forces of the Duke of Cumberland. Fortunately for Heversham the rebels made their last stand at Clifton twenty miles to the north but the alarm in the parish must have been great. Therefore, it was probably with some relief that in 1746 the Clerk was able to enter in the accounts: 'for ringing on rejoycing Days for defeating ye Rebals 5s'.[31]

## The Gallery
The largest interior change came in 1761 when 'was erected by John Maychell, Edward Johnson esquires, Richard Crompton, John Dickinson, John Preston and Joseph Backhouse gentlemen a new and handsome gallery adjoining the belfry containing 10 seats or pews sufficient to hold about 60 persons'.[20] Overhanging the western third of the nave the gallery considerably darkened the interior, cut off the north east corner and, despite a later mock Gothic wood and plaster frontal, came to be regarded as being far from 'handsome'. It was, however, necessary for the habit of encapsulating wealthy families in large box pews in the nave coincided with the rise in population. By and large it was the poor of the parish or servants who sat in the gallery except for the front seat reserved, as was seen in 1870, for certain yeomen families.[21]

## Minor Expenses
Incidental accounts such as '1765 a new bier cloth £2:12s'[22] are reminders that 'floral tributes' for the coffin were not made until Victorian times. Indeed until the mid-eighteenth century poor corpses, clad in the statutory woollen shroud, were removed from the parish coffin, after the service prior to burial.

Wet funerals were less damp, if not less depressing, for the parson after 1775 when an 'umberollo' was bought for £2:14:6d. This apparently survived until 1795 when a replacement cost only £1:10s:7½d. the last reference to a parish umbrella occurs in 1819 when Robert Walker received 3s:6d for repairing it, after which time the vicar provided his own or got wet. No Heversham vicar so far (1983) has donned a biretta. A useful convenience is recorded in 1723: 'a chamber pott for ye vestry 1s:6d'. A similar item in 1781 cost but '8d'.[23]

Another aspect of the parson and church warden's comfort provides the first evidence of what was to become the perpetual heating problem. In 1757 '5s:11d' was spent on 'Bellows fire shoval and tongs for the vestry'. Coals and carriage cost 5s:6d a half ton and Thomas Saul was paid 5s p.a. 'for setting the vestry fire'. The same fee was paid until well into the nineteenth century. Coal, however, became cheaper presumably after the opening of the Lancaster/Kendal Canal in 1819 for a ton cost but 8s in 1828.

There are almost no records of contributions to either civil or religious charities after the seventeenth century. The only regular payment was for the relief of poor prisoners in Appleby Gaol which started at £1:10s:6d in 1708, rose to £2:12s:0d in 1712 before being fixed (as it turned out for over a century) at £1:6s:2d per annum in 1718.

## Vermin
The Council of Twenty-Four had a number of non-ecclesiastical responsibilities. Amongst the most frequently recurring in the Book of Accounts is payment for the extermination of vermin. For example, in 1609 the Clerk Thomas Parke recorded 'Mr.Chamber man for a fox head 12d' and Anthony Johnson for a fox head, 4 Catts and 2 Brocks 2s:10d'. In 1682 1s:6d was paid for a fox head and 1s for a badger. By 1761 the rate was respectively 5s and 2s:6d. A stipulation was made in 1805 that 'every fox head in future be presented at the annual meeting, shall be accompanied with a ticket stating the day and place where and when the fox was roused and killed by whose dogs. The ticket to be attested by two or more respectable and credible inhabitants. N.B. No payment for a Dog Fox'. In addition to piles of festering skulls the atmosphere of the vestry meeting was further perfumed by 14 foulmarts (Pine marten) heads in 1805 for which the wardens paid 2s:6d. Evidence of a good days hunt and that the stipulation about where the fox was roused was followed appears in an account for 1809: 'for Staveley fox killed at Levens 5s'. The means by which the vestry meeting sought to prove the origins and sex of a fox by inspecting its mask and skull is not recorded![25]

**Answers to Queries**

Much evidence of the state of the parish during the incumbencies of the Rev.Henry Wilson (1757-97) and Rev. Dr.George Lawson (1797-1842) is provided in the answers to queries made prior to visitations in 1778, 1789, 1084, 1814 and 1821.[32] All the queries and answers are full and detailed compared to records of earlier visitations. In 1755 eighteen answers were written on one sheet. Curiously in this document the answer to question number nine concerning the presence of ancient seats ignores Levens Hall and several Manor Houses and states 'we have no ancient seats, halls or granges in our parish'.

The pattern of the 1778 queries and answers was followed at the later visitations although the 1824 document is more like a modern form. The most important questions concern the area and population of the parish, the presence within it of any Roman Catholics, non-conformists and disaffected persons, the state of the dependent chapelries, the form of worship, the availability of schools and the condition of the church building and fabric.

Estimates of the extent of the parish varied: for example, in 1778 it was stated to be fourteen miles long by seven broad while the 1789 dimensions were twelve to fourteen miles long by three broad. According to the ordnance survey the distance from Bowland Bridge on the extreme Western limit of the Crosthwaite Chapelry to Peasey Beck in the east is seven miles and from the Paradise Lane on the southern edge of the parish to Barrows Green in the north is five miles. The distance of the Crosscrake and Crosthwaite Chapels from the parish church was given respectively in 1789 at four and nine miles and in 1804 at three and seven miles. The 1982 distances by car are three and half miles and seven and a third miles.

There is some indication of the growth of population. The 1778 estimate was 600 people in 460 families while in 1789 600 families were recorded and 'the number of inhabitants, however, has greatly increased of late years owing to various manufacturys established here'.

The number of Roman Catholics declined during the period as did apparantly the support given to the Quakers and Presbyterians. The 1778 answers to 'Are there any papists in your parish?' was 'we have not more than six or seven Roman Catholic Families in the Parish, and these extremely poor. Their Priest resides at Kendal'. In 1789 there were six families of Roman Catholics: Day labourers and poor mechanics 'who had 'neither school nor chapel'. Dr.Lawson, in 1804, 'was aware of no papist whatever in the Parish except a poor family consisting of two people', in 1814 he said there were two Roman Catholic families and in 1824 one.

As regards the non-conformist nine families of Quakers were recorded in 1778 'who had a meeting house at Stainton' but 'no duty was done in it as there are only two families near it ... There are only a few Methodists and I do not think the number increases'. However, in 1804 there were '60 people of the Methodists in the township of Levens'. There were two presbyterians and six or eight families of Quakers remained in the Stainton area 'where there was a very numerous school taught by a Quaker'.

In 1814 the Levens Methodist Congregation had 'variable teachers..., but I believe their number declines rather than increases'. Nevertheless the Methodists were still active in Levens in 1824 and their Church still (1983) survives.

The answers to the question 'are there any persons who profess to disregard Religion'? - vary between complacency and off-hand concern for the neglected poorest section of parish society. The 1778 answer is full and significant:

'Milnthorp and Ackenthwaite form, as it were one large village, consisting of near two hundred families, the nearest at more than a miles distance from the church, and bad weather, therefore, in winter is their excuse then, for absenting themselves from public worship, but hence is contracted an habit, by which, they become more careless and indifferent about Religion in general. But in the country if a clergyman cannot draw His Parishioners together on Sunday to instruct them in their Duty to God, their neighbour, and themselves, it will be in vain to look after them in the week following, being for the most part engaged then at a distance from their own houses and in so extensive a Parish their houses so far from the Vicarage.

48

But if a chapel was built in this part and a sermon preached every Sunday afternoon by the vicar there (who can scarce get a congregation (of) them at the church) it would be a means to prevent the spread of irreligion and profaness among 'em.

Yet how this good matter is to be effected I know not, the inhabitants are themselves poor and gentlemen who have property there, too indiferent about Religion to think of erecting a Chapel at their sole expense.

Your Lordship, perhaps some time, hereafter, may be able to put us in a way to effect it - By the assistance of the present Lord BP. of Ely we got a chapel and a sallery of near fifty pound a year to the curate at Crosscrake where a chapel was not equally wanted - nay I suppose, the odds may be as seven to one in favr of Milnthorp. N.B. Milnthorp from its situation being the only seaport in the county is a very improving village, and since my coming hither (i.e. 1757) has received an increase of twenty families'.

The briefer answers in 1789 stated that regular absentees from service are 'the lowest and worst part of the parish and their number increases with that of the inhabitants'. In 1804 there were 'no instance of continued absence' other than two cases caused by infirmity while 'we have none who profess disregard of religion'. However in 1814 Dr.Lawson returned to the question of a chapel for Milnthorpe - but stated 'that my neighbour Mr.Wilson of Dallam Tower wishes to build a chapel at Milnthorp'. He supported this plan because 'I derive from thence the principal part of my audience'. He would be prepared to preach a 'sermon there in the afternoon only and prayers read in ye morning'. A further reason for building a chapel of ease was derived from the circumstances of 'Milnthorp being much resorted to during ye bathing season by Multitudes from the country around'. An opportunity for the visitors to hear a sermon would, Dr.Lawson believed, 'prevent much of the Disorders and Profaness which are often attendant on such associations'. The plans were not successful at this stage and Milnthorpe had to wait until 1837[33] for St.Thomas' Church to be built without, incidentally, the assistance of either the Diocese or the owner of Dallam Tower.

As regards the existing chapels at Crosthwaite and Crosscrake the early answers refer to the need to augment their income. Crosthwaite in 1789, was served nominally by the absentee Reverend Mr.Peek, Grammar School Master of Hawkshead who had a stipend of £32 p.a. The Vicar, Reverend Wilson, in urging augmentation did so 'not for the Benefit of the Present Curate (who is a most worthless character) but for future curates'. In 1814 Dr.Lawson stated that the Crosthwaite curate was Mr.Strickland and the Crosscrake Curate Mr.Cartmell. Mr.Rushton was an additional curate assisting the vicar while 'Mr.Wilson's Chaplain officiated at his house at Milnthorpe'. This was presumably Dallam Tower which is situated, actually, within Beetham Parish.

Some indication is given in the 1789 answers about possible disputes regarding the mother church's authority over the chapels. Referring to Crosscrake the Reverend Wilson stated 'to this chapel the vicar of Eversham has undoubted Right to put a curate. But at Crosscrake the inhabitant pretend a right of choosing their curate whom the vicar is to nominate. It is a pity that popular elections are not everywhere set aside as occasioning animosities and quarrels between neighbours, friends and relations seldom to be made up'. Despite this the vicar continued to exercise his patronage even after the chapels had become independent Parish Churches in the late nineteenth century.

There is remarkable little evidence provided about worship. As elsewhere the principal service was on Sunday Morning and consisted of Morning Prayer, The Litany, a sermon and, occasionally, Ante-Communion. The liturgical psalms were sung and there would be one or two hymns. Although there is no record of an organ between the early seventeenth century and 1800 when a 'seraphine',[34] an early form of harmonium, was placed in the north aisle it is reasonable to assume that this large and prosperous church had a musical accompaniment to the services. That there was in fact a musical tradition is indicated by several references in the Book of Accounts including: 1718, 'when the young men of Cartmel came to sing', 1773, 'when a singing master came here 1s', 1791, 'paid to Crosscrake singers 5s' and 'spent when Sunday Scholars came first at Church to sing 2s', and in 1828 when a 'gratuity' of 15s was paid to 'treble singers'. In 1822 a Pitch Pipe was purchased at the cost of 7s:6d while, in the same year, 'Candles 8lbs for singers' cost 4s:8d.[35]

Throughout the period 1771-1824 Holy Communion was celebrated only four times a year at Christmas, Easter, Trinity Sunday and Michaelmas. At Easter, however, there was generally a celebration on Good Friday as well as on Easter Day. Although the average congregation at Sunday Morning service was estimated at about 250 the number of communicants was small. The 1781 answer stated that 'as a great part of the Parish lies very distant from the church, the number of communicants depends much on the good or bad weather, sometimes 80 or more, at other times not much above half that number'. The 1814 figures were 60-90 at the 'Great Festivals' (Christmas and Easter) and 40-50 at the others. The 1824 average number of communicants was 50.

Although at that time there was not a charity or National School in the parish, attention was given to the general as well as religious education of children. Prior to all visitations information was provided about the parish's two free Grammar Schools at Crosthwaite and Heversham whose deeds were kept with the church records in the vestry chest. Throughout this period the Master of Heversham Grammar School was a Clergyman and often acted as a curate for Crosscrake.

Younger children were catechized in Lent and during the Summer after Evening Service. In 1789 Reverend Wilson said that he used 'Bunday's Catechical Lectures' but in 1804 Dr. Lawson said that he did not use 'a printed form but devised questions of his own judgement'. A Sunday School for boys was started on 1st. Jan 1786 and rather later a separate one for girls was established. The 1814 'answers' said that there were a great many schools in different parts of the parish free and voluntary on Sundays. 'The number of children taught in each may vary from 10 or 12 to 40 or 50'. Fifteen schools were recorded in 1824.

On all returns the condition of the fabric was recorded as good. Surprisingly in view of the bad condition to which they had apparently deteriorated in Victorian times the tower and vicarage were also stated to be sound. In 1778 Reverend Wilson recorded that he had had the vicarage 'new slated' at a cost of £200 of which Trinity College paid £50. Dr. Lawson in 1804, mentioned more repairs but also said that because 'he had no condition of finance' he had been unable to rebuild it.

Both clergymen lived consistently in the parish. The Reverend Wilson stated that he was absent, at most, on one Sunday a year while Dr.Lawson claimed to be away for no more than three or four Sundays per annum.

### Notes and References to Sources   Chapter IV

1. J.F.Curwen 'History of Heversham with Milnthorpe'. p.53 *et seq.*
2. Antiquary on Horseback P.55
3. List in Book of Accounts apparently written by Reverend Henry Wilson (vicar from 1757 to 1797)
4. CRO(K) WPR/8 parish bundle
5. Book of Accounts    6. *Ibid*
7. *Ibid*    8. *Ibid*
9. Transactions of C.W.A.A.S. IV M.S. 1904 Report of Proceedings: 'While Viewing the Church Plate Mr. Crawford Hodgson F.S.A. pointed out the whistle at the base of the handle of the flagon, a curious survival of an ancient drinking custom'.
10. Book of Accounts
11. *Ibid*
12. Quoted by Curwen C.W.A.A.S. XXV, Art.II page 49-50
13. Book of Accounts
14. *Ibid*    16. *Ibid*
15. *Ibid*    17. *Ibid*
18. CRO(K) WPR/8 Additional Records deposited 21 Jan. 1970.
19. Book of Accounts
20. Nicolson and Burn Vol. 1 p.197
21. See below
22. Book of Accounts    23. *Ibid*
24. *Ibid*    25. *Ibid*
26. Re. Jeffrie Scott Book of Accounts; Inscription Nicolson and Burn Vol. 1 p.19
27. Book of Accounts
28. *Ibid*
29. *Ibid*
30. 'A History of Cumberland Westmorland' by William Rollinson, Phillimore Press 1978, P.81
31. Book of Accounts
32. Answer to Queries Charts Record Office. Ref. EDA6/7/59, EDU7/1/330.
33. See 'Our Village', Roger Bingham
34. Book of Accounts
35. *Ibid*

*Watercolour Painting Mid 19th Century*

## CHAPTER V

# Early Nineteenth Century Improvements

Extensive and costly alterations and repairs took place in the early nineteenth century. According to Curwen the battlements round the church were taken down in 1813.[1] Even so there is an account of £1:12s:6d being paid for repairs to the battlements in 1822. Perhaps 'battlements' is an archaism such as 'steeple' for tower used in an 1821 account for '7s. to Robert Bindloss for removing soil from about the church steeple'.[2]

By far the biggest expense concerned the reflagging and repewing of the church between 1814-1817. The faculties and accounts survive[3] along with the plans drawn up by the contractor John Burrow of Sandside who charged four guineas for a detailed estimate and 6s 6d 'for measuring the church'.

The work was supervised by the Clerk and curate the Reverend Joseph Fawcett of the 'Eagle and Child' whose salary was raised from £8 to £10 per annum in 1814. It was he who ordered the paving contractors John and George Atkinson of Hutton Roof to ensure that the flags were 'three inches thick and perfectly square upon the edge' and that 'tombstones were to be laid exactly as they are now'. The floor of the south aisle formerly a foot lower than the nave and north aisle was raised to make it level necessitating the porch floor to be relaid (by John Hudson for £8s 17s) so that it sloped outwards from the threshold of the door.

Burrow of Sandside, the joiner, was required to construct the pews of oak 'five eighths thick' with doors except for six in the south aisle and ten in the north. All were still arranged preaching shop style to face the pulpit which was moved from the eastern pier of the arcade to the south pier of the chancel arch (near the site of the present vicar's desk). This arrangement meant that occupants of the family pews of Daniel Wilson and the vicar in the nave had to turn their back on the altar as also did the Wilsons of Heaves whose pew, installed ten years earlier,[4] was in the north aisle. Judging from a section of dark oak panelling traditionally said to be derived from a pew, surviving as window shutters, at the Audland House in Ackenthwaite, Burrows pews were carved with a crude Gothic design.[5]

51

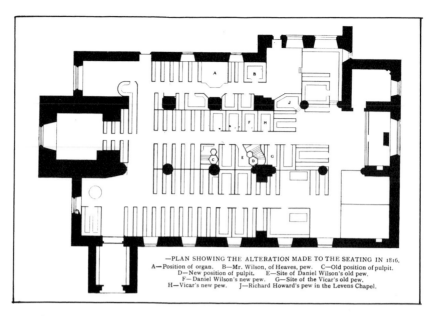

—PLAN SHOWING THE ALTERATION MADE TO THE SEATING IN 1816.
A—Position of organ.   B—Mr. Wilson, of Heaves, pew.   C—Old position of pulpit.
D—New position of pulpit.   E—Site of Daniel Wilson's old pew.
F—Daniel Wilson's new pew.   G—Site of the Vicar's old pew.
H—Vicar's new pew.   J—Richard Howard's pew in the Levens Chapel.

The gallery was also repaired with 'Good Dantzick oak well seasoned and moulded and with staircase Balusters to be 1½ inches square turned to correspond with the Communion rails.[6] A section of the bannister is now at Holly Bank, Leasgill.[7]

Though the work was carried out during a post war recession it was extremely costly: the paving bill alone came to £248:2s:4d while the pews cost £145:15s:9d. The last bill however, was nearly met by the sale by public auction of pews numbered 17, 21, 41 and 48 respectively to A.Huddleston of Milnthorpe for £49, William Atkinson of Burton for £24, William Maling of Kidside for £50, and Mr. Cragg of Milnthorpe for £21:10s.[8]

### Improvements during Archdeacon Evans' Incumbency 1842-66

No sooner had Robert Wilson Evans been inducted as vicar in 1842 than he set about persuading his parishioners to pay for extensive improvements to the church. As if to make up for the neglect of the church during the incumbency of Dr. Lawson, with whom she had quarreled for nearly forty years, Mrs. Howard of Levens Hall donated a neo-gothic front for the gallery. Rather pointedly this involved the removal of an inscription on the gallery[9] recording the re-pewing and repairs carried out under Dr. Lawson.

Other parishioners paid for the repair of the north arcade which received stone capitals and bases to the piers and an imitation stone veneer in stucco. The square north clerestory windows were replaced with windows in the perpendicular style similar to those on the south side. Possibly this work was carried out in red sandstone for the clerestory wall, rebuilt in 1869, contains pieces of the stone and, moreover, there is a fragment of a nineteenth century neo-gothic window spandrel built into the garden wall of the Old School.

The most expensive item was stained glass costing £160 raised by public subscription and inserted in the east window in 1844. It was the work of Warrington of London. At the time it was extravagantly praised as having 'wonderful richness and beauty so as quite to match the best ancient specimens'.[10] This had the result that 'the fine old chancel with its roof recalling forcibly to mind on a smaller scale that of the nave of Ely Cathedral is now filled with a mellow light which adds a deep solemnity to its architectural features'.[11] Succeeding generations have, however, felt that the 'deep solemnity' is a little too deep for the dark colours, rendered even darker in summer when the trees outside are in full leaf, can look gloomy. The composition is also unbalanced with the middle third of the window being filled with a yellow, brown and purple representation of five elaborate gothic canopies. These surmount large flattish figures of the gospel makers standing on either side of a seated Christ

52

who wears a red and white robe with a Saxon wheel head cross as halo. His right hand rests on the tightly curled head of a kneeling toddler who is clad in a purple frock, blue socks and gold slippers. His left hand holds an open book inscribed in Latin with Matthew 8 verse 2 - 'And behold there came a leper and worshipped Him saying, Lord if thou wilt, thou cans't make me clean'. Certainly the child looks leprous!

On either side are Mark and Luke, with purple haloes, carrying their gospels. They like Matthew, on the extreme left, sport long beards and balding heads. The clean-shaven John looks appropriately younger and, like Matthew, has a green halo. In his hand is a chalice from which emerges a red eagle. The angel, griffin and hart symbols of the other saints appear in the upper lights. Scrolls bearing their Latin names appear at the top and bottom of the window.

In the three larger of the upper lights are represented on the left St.Peter with his key and on the right St.Paul with a sword. In the centre holding the Christ Child is a crowned 'Virgin Mary, to whom the church is dedicated' (sic). In the apex lights are angels holding the text 'In Excelsis Deo'. This started an angelic trend because the upper lights of most of the other stained glass windows, all of which were installed after 1844, contain angels. Indeed in 1914 the wardens stipulated that coats of arms in the design of the upper lights of the window (showing St.Oswald) dedicated to Sir Josceleyn Bagot should be replaced by angels.[12]

## The reading desk and pulpit

On the death in 1849 of their father John Evans M.D. The Reverend Evans and his sister donated a new octagonal pulpit and reading desk as a memorial. The former was first set against the south pier of the chancel arch and originally had a door and a bannister for the steps. It was designed by Messrs. Sharpe and Paley and carved by Mr. Hatch of Lancaster, with linen fold panels and crocheted spires at the corners.[13] On the stone plinth was carved the words 'their sound went into all the earth and their words unto the ends of the world'. The reading desk has four linen fold panels and poppy head ends, five and a half feet high. It can seat a brace of slim clergymen.

## The Organ

Under the terms of the will of Thompson Bindloss Esq. made 24 Jan. 1858 the church received in 1855 a handsome bequest of £700.[14] Of this £300 went to purchase a new organ and £400 was invested in government bonds along with funds from Suart's Charity providing a salary for the organist.[15]

Within a few months an instrument was obtained from Messrs. Holt of Bradford. It was described as having 'nine stops and a swelling organ with seven stops, two octaves and a quarter of pedal pipes and two coupler stops with precision in excellent taste.'[16] It was placed 'in the vacant space between the windows of the north aisle and adds much to the fine structure already rich in ecclesiastical furniture and wanting but this to make all complete'.

The new organ was first played at a grandiose service held in 'brilliant weather before a large attendance' on 30th September 1855. The local choir was augmented by that of St.George's Kendal under the direction of its organist Mr. Smallwood who 'performed in precision and excellent taste'. Apparently there were two addresses, one by the Venerable E.Bickerstead, Archdeacon of Buckingham: the other by Dr. William Whewell, Master of Trinity College, 'was of peculiar interest on account of the allusions which he made to his having been in his early days a member of that church'. This would be when he boarded at the grammar School from 1809-1812 .

Contemporary approval of the improvements was summarised in the 'Westmorland Gazette': 'this church has become one of the most interesting objects of our neighbourhood and doubtless will attract the notice of many of our summer visitans and tell them that the North will not quietly yield to the south with the palm of good taste and good spirit'.[17] Notwithstanding such complacency many of the 'improvements' were swept away during the restoration only twenty years later. It was in 1870 that the organ was moved to its present site in the Dallam Chapel.

**The later history of the organ**

Despite the glowing estimates of the usefulness of the 1855 organ it was decided in 1888 'that after 34 years (sic) its old fashioned strains should be replaced with a better more modern instrument'. As on previous occasions 'friends were not lacking' and Mrs. Argles in particular contributed £500 to provide 'a chased and handsome case beautifully carved' by Miles and Morgan of Lancaster to designs by Paley and Austin.

The works were by Messrs. Wilkinson of Kendal who incorporated part of the Holt's instrument of 1855 in the new organ. The result was regarded as being infinitely superior and the organ was claimed to be the finest in the area.

When the organ was first played in July 1888 there was a great musical service attended by no less than twelve clergy. Choral Evensong was led by the choir of Lancaster Priory under the direction of the organist Mr. Haythornthwaite. Psalm 34 'O taste and see how gracious the Lord is' was sung as the anthem. The preacher was the Reverend Canon Ware, vicar of Kirkby Lonsdale. He used the text 'Let everything that hath breath praise the Lord' to emphasize how 'poor and feeble was the noblest and most gracious worship of earth as compared with those angelic songs in which they hoped some day to join.' He concluded by exhorting the members of the congregation to demonstrate their interest in the 'beauty of worship' so that 'it might lead them to pay off the remaining debt upon the organ'. To the tune of 'Onward Christian Soldiers' £23 was collected and the bill was cleared.[18]

Unfortunately the organ proved to be a perpetual drain on the church's finances. Within ten years, at Christmas 1897, Wilkinson's tuner discovered dry rot in the case. The general consternation is reflected by an emergency meeting being called on December 30th. it was resolved 'that the ground be excavated to a depth of fully sixteen inches, and that a layer of concrete be placed at the bottom and along the side. Also that concrete, brick or stone be substituted for wood in the supports and that care be taken to have through ventilation provided'.[19]

Apart from regular maintenance no further alterations were made for a quarter of a century. When in 1924 'new leathers' were fitted the organist Mr. Dobie suggested that substantial repairs should be carried out. Estimates from Messrs. Willis of London and Manchester of £92 were rejected in favour of £50 for 'repairs and cleaning' from Wilkinsons of Kendal, with a further £27 for 'various improvements to pedals and reed stops'.[20] The cost was met by the relatives of Mr. Rogers Shaw, of Greenside House 'who was so fond of music and had (before living at Greenside) played the organ at the church which he attended'. The Shaw relatives paid up only after being assured that the 'improvements would be of permanent value'.[21] Ironically successive organists have believed that the tone deteriorated after the 1925 re-fit.

Also in 1925 the Parochial Church Council suggested that the organ be 'blown by mechanical means owing to the difficulty of providing an organ blower'.[22] Hydraulic pressure was the method first considered. This would have involved laying pipes, altering the village water supply to provide the necessary 50lbs pressure and the installation of bulky apparatus in the Dallam Chapel. The cost was estimated at £150 for the apparatus excluding 'the laying of pipes to or from the church plumbing work and a wooden casing for the apparatus'.[23] Not surprisingly the P.C.C. decided against the scheme in 1928 and 'the vicar was asked to ascertain if electricity made at Kendal could be supplied at Heversham'.[24]

The organ, however, continued to be pumped by hand until 1935 when through the generosity of Frederick Astley (who had bought Greenside House from the family of Roger Shaw) electricity was installed in the church. Mr Astley also under-wrote the cost of an electric organ blower and in 1938 after 'a credit balance on the organ fund' had been paid to him allowed the outstanding debt to 'be regarded as liquidated'.[25]

Almost immediately a further £90 was required for 'pneumatic action, mechanism for the pedals'. This was met in April 1939 by an envelope subscription throughout the parish.

No organ repair was needed during the Second World War and with the coming of peace organ recitals were arranged. In 1946 the organ accompanied the Eversley Choral Union when it performed Messiah in aid of the 'Save Europe Now' appeal. Woodworm was again discovered in the case in 1952 and as a result the whole organ was dismantled and 'rebuilt' by Wilkinsons for £235. After such a large bill, maintenance was reduced to a minimum and in 1954 it was decided not to replace the tremulant stop at an estimated cost of £25, as it was 'so little used'. Five years later a bill for £10.2s.6d was off-set by the sale to Wilkinsons of a harmonium for £5.[26]

Even a few years of relatively scanty maintenance had dire consequences for in 1961 a new set of pedals was required. Fortunately Mr. O.R.Bagot of Levens Hall, in the tradition of his ancestors, came to the rescue and paid the bill of £298. No major repairs were required for another fifteen years until with an increase in musical activities following the induction of the Reverend John C.Hancock in 1976 the deficiences in tonal quality became apparent. After some debate a thorough restoration was carried out by Rushworth and Dreaper of Liverpool, the firm which had taken over Wilkinsons of Kendal. This was completed in June 1979 with the result that 'the original tonal quality' was restored and, also, the Great Mixture not completed in 1888, was finished.

Specifically the 'tracker' was thoroughly regulated making one of the greatest improvements from the player's point of view because the action had become very heavy and lacking in depth tone. The wind pressure, lowered for reasons unknown in the past, was raised. Once these two items had been dealt with, the re-voicing was started with the intention of achieving the original balance.

The cornopean on the swell was removed to the organ builder's works in Liverpool for extensive work but the rest of the re-voicing was carried out in the church. Above treble C the Great Mixture had played only at the octave but it was completed with the addition if the fifth. The entire cost of the repairs amounted to £2,900. [27]

**Notes and References to Sources   Chapter V**

1. C.W.A.A.S Curwen
2. Book of Accounts
3. CRO (K) WPR/8
4. *Ibid*
5. Family tradition related to author by Mrs. V.M.Audland (1900-1981)
6. CRO(K) WPR 8
7. Information Miss B.Sisson
8. CRO(K) WPR/8 mentioned C.W.A.A.S. Curwen
9. see below
10. Westmorland Gazette. 20 Jan. 1844
11. *Ibid*
12. Vestry Book (H)
13. CRO(K) WPR/8 also Westmorland Gazette
14. CRO(K) WPR/8 Thompson Bindloss Charity papers.
15. CRO(K) WPR/8 Edward Suart of Leasgill, Heversham, gent, will made 8 September 1849 with codicil 1 November 1850 bequest 'to augment salary of Grammar School master, pay organist and provide for poor persons in Leasgill and Milnthorpe with Heversham'.
16. Westmorland Gazette.
17. *Ibid*
18. Westmorland Gazette 14 July 1888.
19. Vestry Book.
20. Minutes of Parochial Church Council at H.
21. *Ibid*
22. *Ibid*
23. *Ibid*
24. *ibid*
25. *Ibid*
26. *Ibid*
27. Notes written by Reverend J.C.Hancock July 1979.

*The Organ*

# CHAPTER VI
# The Victorian Restoration

Between 1868-71 the church was subjected to a transformation fashionably if euphemistically described as 'restoration'. Dating from the middle years of Queen Victoria's reign, the work displayed all the enthusiasm for thoroughness typical of the High Victorians. Inspired by often misplaced antiquarian zeal, the 'restorers' threw out much that had contributed to the varied character of the building, including every piece of furniture, except the Holy Table of 1763,[1] and every scrap of woodwork installed over the previous 150 years. So, in Betjeman's words, 'the church's restoration left for comtemplation not what there used to be'.[2]

The overt objects were a commendable desire to break the shackles stuffily imposed by the eighteenth century preaching shop form of worship, while at the same time repairing the structure and lightening and brightening the interior. Motivating all, was an urge not to be outdone by other parishes, for, in the previous 13 years, no less than 110 churches within the Diocese of Carlisle had been restored or rebuilt including 26 out of the 84 in Westmorland.[3] However, to quote the 'Westmorland Gazette' of the period, Heversham 'was remarkably fortunate; situated in one of the choicest parts of the county, a large number of residences are here and there with the result that any movement for the good of the people is warmly and liberally supported'.[4] Thus within four years £6,557 was spent on the church; out of 154 churches restored in the Diocese between 1869-92 this sum was only exceeded by £20,000 at Kendal, £12,000 at Crosby Ravensworth, £9,415 at Kirkby Lonsdale, £8,000 at Ulverston, £7,185 at St.Michael's Workington, £7,100 at St.Martin's Windermere and by £6,728 at St.Mary's Windermere.[5]

At Heversham there were two main driving forces: a new broom of a vicar, the Reverend T.M.Gilbert (inducted in 1866) and the Argles family who had lived at Eversley since 1859.[6] Although the Argles were regarded as 'nouveaux' by the gentry and as 'off-comers' by the lowly their conspicuous generosity to the church could provide a firm foundation for social influence akin to that already enjoyed by the owners of Levens Hall and Dallam Tower.

*The Chancel*
*(Photo: A.Rumsey)*

On 21 February 1867 the churchwardens Messrs. Argles, Wakefield, Sharples, Holme, Tattersall, Rawlinson and Squires called a vestry meeting to consider plans drawn up by E.G.Paley of Lancaster 'for the partial restoration of the Parish Church including the removal of the gallery, the rebuilding of the north arcade, the pointing and restoration of the outside walls'.[7] On 1st March the plans were approved and a committee appointed. With the exception of G.Squires, yeoman farmer of Lower Haverflatts, the Vicar and the Reverend J.H.Sharples who was Headmaster of the Grammar School, the Committee members were all principal landowners: Lieut. General the Honourable A.Upton of Levens Hall, G.E.Wilson of Dallam Tower, Frank Atkinson Argles of Eversley, A.D.Keightley of Old Hall, Preston Patrick, W.H.Wakefield of Sedgwick House, C.W.Braithwaite of Plumtree Hall, John Harrison of Summerlands, W.Tattersall of St.Anthony's House, J.Rawlinson of Leasgill and John Holme of Owlet Ash. A subscription book was opened and initial entries included £500 from the Argles and £200 each from the Vicar and Mr.Wakefield.[8]

Contracts were tendered and work began in April 1868 when the nave was boarded off from the chancel and the organ which was insured for £250 was dismantled by Wilkinson of Kendal and stored at the vicarage. By the end of the year the gallery and pews had been removed, the south arcade shored up and scaffolding erected preparatory to removing the roof and demolishing the old plaster and rubble north arcade.

Finished in July 1869, the north arcade matched the height of the transitional arches to the south but was modelled on a more exact Early English style. The three pointed arches consisted of two chamfered orders resting on octagonal abbaccii decorated with water leaf carving supported by circular piers on square bases. A continuous label without stops decorates the upper arch while above a string course are three deeply set clerestory lancets. All the exposed masonry is of machine-cut red, brown and buff sandstone which in certain lights glistens a warm soft pink against the white plaster. The cost of the arcade was £231.

Despite many precedents of costly 'work about ye leads', 15 tons 6 cwts 3 qtrs and 141lbs of lead was obtained for the roof at 24s.6d per cwt., part of which was rebated at 17s per cwt. for the old lead, which weighed 12 tons 7 cwts and 371lbs.[9] Other financial details included £20 for a new three light flat-headed window (similar to those of two lights installed c.1500) placed above the blocked-up aisle door, four buttresses at £10 each to correct a still noticeable outward lean on the south wall and, for £30, a renewed sedillae of three ogee arches in the north aisle.

Regarding the floor, it had been proposed that 'the whole area be excavated to a depth of two feet and covered with four inches of concrete ... the aisles to be laid with tiles on hollow flooring ... and the pews to have Baltic deal floors'.[10] On the grounds of expense not all this work was completed for tiles were not laid in the nave but all except two tombstones in the north-west corner of the baptistry were removed. Unlike at Kendal where cartloads of bones were removed from the nave in 1850,[11] it is not known whether human remains were disinterred and, if so, what was done with them. Similarly there is no record of the fate of the Burrow of Sandside's pews, then scarcely fifty years old and presumably capable of being reused.

During 1870 the work was interrupted until the ownership of the chancel arch and of those arches between the aisles into the Levens and Dallam Chapels could be determined. Eventually it was decided that the parish owned the western half of the arches and Trinity College and the two estates the eastern. Thus Levens paid half of £45 for the northern arch, the College half of £52 for the chancel arch and Dallam half of £58 for the south arch. Harmonising with the north arcade, the restrained carving of two ordered arches emphasised the solidity of the structure while the fluted responds of the chancel arch provided a touch of originality with the northern responds being dark red and the southern one buff in colour. When at length on 13th November 1870 the nave and aisles were reopened for worship the total cost was accounted as £2,408.19.0d.[12]

## The Restoration of the Chancel
Even before the work on the nave was completed, the restoration committee's attention was

directed to the chancel. It was proposed to rebuild the roof of which 'the timbers were ill constructed, rough and partially decayed owing to their having been cut out of small and sappy wood', relead it and erect a cross on the gable end[13] to match that set in the place of the sanctus bell cote on the nave. Estimates for 'screens' at £70 and new seats for £84 were also submitted though not taken up after the College (despite a protracted correspondence between the vicar and the bursar had refused to foot the bill for furnishings). £160 was also saved by slating the roof and not covering it with lead as everywhere else. The total cost of the chancel repairs was £422.1s.8d. At the Rededication in 1871 the bishop revealed the munificence of the Rev. T.M.Gilbert when he stated that 'he could not say that the college itself had been very liberal and the greater part must have come out of no other pocket but the vicar's ....'.[14]

Owing to lack of finance only minor embellishments could be afforded. New altar rails were installed at a cost of £21:13s:3d by Mrs. Haslam of Woodhouse, while a ladies' committee headed by Miss Evans, surviving sister of the late Archdeacon, raised £17.7s.0d to purchase Tables of Commandments. Despite a plethora of gilt lettering and decoration these have never been easy to read owing to their position high up in the narrrow spaces on either side of the east window. At the same time the vicar and Trinity College paid for the paving of the central chancel aisle and sanctuary.[15] The chancel has red tiles set in broad polished oolite limestone surrounds. The sanctuary also has red tiles with yellow patterns of roses and birds with green and white chequered bands.

## The Reredos

In 1880 the Reverend Gilbert's mother-in-law, Mrs Edmund Harrison, presented a new alabaster reredos after permission for the removal of a wooden neo-gothic one donated by the Bindloss family 25 years previously had been negotiated.[16] Though of a material unsympathetic to the plaster and ashlar textures of its surroundings, the excellent restrained quality of the reredos carving makes it one of the most handsome as well as the most prominent features in the church. It is in three parts, the longest section behind the altar being slightly higher and emphasised by square pilasters with capitals carved with vine leaves and grapes. The frieze is crenellated and bears badges of a lily, tudor rose and fleur-de-lys. A large relief cross fills the central panel with four flower patterns fillings the corners between the arms and the frame. On either side is perpendicular arcading bearing the symbols of the evangelists: winged ram of St.Luke, Griffin of St.Mark, flaming chalice of St.Matthew and the eagle of St.John. A crown above a shield bearing I.H.S. projects over the altar cross. There is blank arcading on either side.

## The Choir Stalls

Seven years later in 1887 Mrs. Argles enabled the deal choir seats to be removed when she donated the fine oak choir stalls. These were designed by Paley and are extensively carved with over 100 oak leaf, rose, pomegranate and acorn patterns all different. The two larger benches to the west have poppy heads taking up the theme of the reading desk of thirty years earlier. The panel fronts bear perpendicular window tracery and a curvilinear type frieze. A further elaboration

*Carvings on the choir stalls.*

is two statuettes on both ends but too low to be seen easily.

## The Chapels

The restoration of the chapels was concurrent with that of the chancel. Mrs Howard spent £168[1] on the Levens Chapel, which included the cost of directing its flue into that of the vestry and making the ashlar faced chimney 'as ornamental as possible'.[18] She also repaired the family pew which is inscribed with the initials H. and M., F.G. for Mary, and Fulk Greville Howard. At £228 G.E.Wilson spent rather more on the Dallam Chapel caused by his meeting wholly the cost of rebuilding the chancel south arcade.

Except for the reused chamfered stones and incised capitals of the late fifteenth century eastern responds, all the masonry was renewed. Moreover, Mr. Wilson, reseated the chapel with pews carved with the family crest of a flaming crescent. He also agreed for a nominal rent of one shilling[11] a year to allow the organ to be installed in the south-west corner, after the alternative position against the east wall of the Levens Chapel and the south-east corner of the Buskell Chapel had been rejected for accoustic reasons. Unfortunately the organ's new position involved the blocking of the western south window and the removal of

*Left: The Wilson Crest*
*Below Left:*
*Paley's Architectural drawings*
*of the small South Door*
*Below Right: The small South Door*

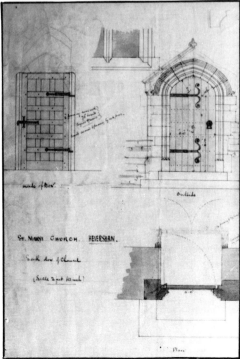

the tombstones over the Preston vault to the south-east corner so no one lies under the stones - they are under the organ.

Paley's skill in producing a deceptively simple design for the church is well seen in the renewed north doorway to the Dallam chapel installed for £35. This has a tiny sandstone porch with a fleur-de-lys on its gable and an oak door which fits the tudor style arch outside but is straight-headed within. When open the door is entirely contained within the three foot thickness of the wall and does not impede the inner flat-headed double doors.[20] Until about 1900 when they were accommodated in the south aisle, the Heversham Grammar School boys used this entrance as they sat in the block of pews at the east end of the Dallam Chapel.[21] Their hob-nailed boots no doubt made a major contribution to the curved doorstep: the only piece of Victorian masonry to show pronounced wear and tear.

Fittingly on his death, the friends and tenants of George Edward Wilson installed stained glass by Clayton and Bell[22] to his memory in the Dallam Chapel's east window. This is perhaps the best window in the church with deep, almost medieval, blue panes well set against a silvery background emphasising the more varied colours of the main figures. In the centre light is a seated and crowned Christ holding an orb, and surrounded by the text 'As ye have done it unto my brethren ye have done it unto me'. On His right is a female figure completely enveloped except for a sharp featured face, in a purple and green medieval gown and flowing wimple illustrating 'I was naked and ye clothed me'. In the northern light is a male holding an Italianate wine jug and a square yellow dish with the text 'I was hungry and ye gave me meat'. On Jesus' right is a red robed matron (she has a wedding ring) holding a bunch of keys and a text reading 'Welcome' with the words 'I was as stranger and ye took me in' wrapped round her. The southern light illustrates 'I was sick and ye visited me' with a male figure holding a bunch of herbs and a huge stone bottle. In the upper lights are the Latin labelled saints Andrew, Peter, James the less, John, Matthew, Thomas, Simon, Jude, David, Bartholomew, Mark, Luke, James Magnus and Matthias. It is surprising that room could not have been found for England's patron saint and namesake of the subject of the memorial.

### The Tower

By far the most conspicuous and controversial change concerned the rebuilding of the tower. On 22nd August 1868 Paley had reported that 'owing to vibrations it is not advisable to add to the present light peal of three bells' and he estimated that it would cost £500 for the belfry and foundations to be strenthened sufficiently for a peal of six bells, which the Misses Woods of Elm Lawn wished to donate to the church, to be installed. Although he admitted that there was 'no immediate cause for alarm', he concluded that 'no effectual remedy can be found and no permanent cure can be made to a building so cracked and disturbed on every side ... in some instances the wall has separated nearly three inches'. Only a month later on September 21st, before the committee had considered the matter officially, Mr. Argles 'offered to pay the cost of rebuilding except for the west window'.[23] The exception was because a new five light perpendicular style window with a pointed head had already been designed by Paley for the Archdeacon Evans' memorial committee which would meet its costs. In the end Argles paid everything and the Evans' memorial glass was put in the south aisle. As soon as Argles' offer was made, Paley had a plan to hand which leads to the speculation that either he had anticipated the contract or he had the designs 'in stock' drawn without reference to the church.

In February 1869 Messrs Dixon and Wilson of Kendal began the demolition of the old tower and in April it was reported that 'the travelling public have ... been amused and some-times alarmed during the last five or six weeks by the continual avalanche of stones and mortar falling from this venerable pile upon the Milnthorpe Turnpike ...' During this work it was discovered that the fears about the safety of the old tower had been justified as 'the masonry was of the rudest kind, not one through stone was found, nor was the limestone of which the mass chiefly consisted ever touched by chisel or pick but was built in with the mortar exactly in the rude state in which it lay upon the hill surface. Built upon the edge of

 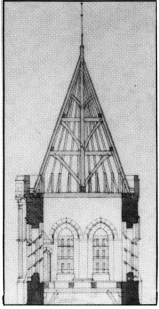 

*Left and centre: Paley's Drawings.     Right: The tower at the present time.*

the escarpment of the limestone rock part of the tower stood upon a base of adamant, part on very different stuff, nor was any effort made by the builders to supply the outward and deficient foundation by proportionately solid work but they took what they found whether earth, clay or rock'. Moreover, this inadequate foundation had been weakened further by internments and 'a complete skeleton of a female or young person was found right under the middle and in the line of the north wall of the tower. This must have been let in from outside and a cavity of at least 6 feet long cut out of the substance of the wall for the purpose.'[24]

Set well away from the steep edge of the churchyard on firm foundations reinforced by a reconstructed roadside wall the new tower was impressively solid. Unfortunately the use of machine-cut squared limestone with pale yellow sandstone dressings scarcely matched the course rubble of the nave walls newly revealed by the removal of whitewash and pebble-dash rendering.

Yet, viewed in isolation, the tower is a handsome structure in an academically correct Early English style, uniform at a glance but with asymmetrical details on closer inspection. It is partly embraced by the aisles while the outlying western half is raised on a stepped sandstone plinth.[67] Both the western corners project though only the southern one containing the stairs reaches to the unembattled sandstone parapet. This is supported by corbels carved in six differing patterns. The lower slit lights of the stair turret are flat headed but the upper one is rounded while on the upper stage the turret has sandstone corner pilasters.

### The Clock

On the north and south sides of the second stage is the round clock face set in a square panel flanked by blank arches which correspond with four arches on the west and east sides. The dial is ornamented with a flaming gilt sun on a maroon background with sun and star roundels in the corners and with a black and white border. The clock's works were those presented to the previous tower in 1860 by Mary, widow of Samuel Holker Haslam of Woodhouse.[25]

Above the clock are twin deeply set lancet belfry openings on the north, south and west sides and a larger single lancet on the east. Capping (crowning would be too grand a term) the tower is a leaded spire from which points the green copper weathercock. Though too stumpy for so massive a tower, the lines of the spire are fortunately clearer than in the original design, which showed an ugly projection on the south-west corner over the stair head.

In the south-east corner was inserted the flue to the boiler house installed in the crypt below the font. As no chimney protrudes from the parapet, smoke and fumes issue apparently from the roof giving the unfortunate impression that the tower is on fire.

Inside, the ground floor of the tower was opened to the nave by a fine pointed arch of two rolled orders resting on foliated capitals whose leaves point up on the north side and down on the south. The responds are keel-moulded on rounded bases. The west window consists of two lancets below which is the brass inscription 'To the Glory of God': the ancient tower of this church having become unsafe was taken down and rebuilt at the sole expense of Frank Atkinson Argles and Susanah his wife in the years 1869-70'.

In the window went glass described by the Westmorland Gazette of 1871 as 'being a kind of stained mosaic with illustrative figures which we understand was done at the cost of Mr. Argles'.[26] According to a surviving letter of Canon Gilbert it was the work of Burrow of Sandside. However, when the window to Thomas and Agnes Argles was inserted in 1924 it was taken out and stored on top of the inner porch where it lay completely forgotten until rediscovered during repairs carried out in 1980.

### The Bells
Into the belfry went a peal of 6 bells cast by Messrs. Warner of London for £438.2s.10d with a total weight of 57 cwts. The sixth bell records that the peal was given 'for the service of God in the Parish Church of Heversham by Margaret and Mary Woods A.D. 1870'. The texts on the others are:

> One:     'Let him that is athirst come'
>
> Two:     'Whomsoever will let him take of the water of life freely'
>
> Three:   'Jesus Christ the same yesterday today and forever'
>
> Four:    'Blessed be the God and Father of our Lord Jesus Christ'
>
> Five:    'Praise the Lord O my soul and forget not all his benefits'.[27]

The bells were further augmented in 1871 by the gift of a set of handbells by G.E. Moser.[28] So sound was the main peal that it required no attention until 1915 when £102.12s.0d was spent on repairing the bearings - Canon Gilbert writing that 'though unfortunate that the expense should have to be incurred at the present time it is a thing that in our judgement cannot be avoided'.[29] These repairs were sufficient to last for sixty years until 1978-79 when the bells were re-hung and many repairs carried out.

Even contemporary opinion on the aesthetic value of the restoration was mixed. In 1880 a Westmorland Gazette article stated that 'inside the church presents much of that element of novelty which focuses on the antiquarian; albeit the work in the interior as regards innovation has been conducted with marked skill and delicacy ... yet the truth however ... it is quite impossible to improve sacred edifices in order to qualify them for modern acceptance without entirely robbing them of their characteristic hold on the mind'.[30]

That the Argles at least were pleased with the tower is shown by their choosing a similar design for the one built for Crosthwaite Church in 1878.[31] This time they chose Joseph Bintley of Kendal as the architect. Paley was perhaps rejected on the grounds that his estimate of £1,300 for the Heversham Tower had been exceeded considerably because the total cost was £2,054.

### The Rededication Service 1871
There could have been few doubts, financial or aesthetic, to the value, importance and success of the restoration when on the 3rd June 1871 almost every parishioner, the grammar school boys, half the 'county' and a dozen clergy came to witness the rededication of the church and to hear the Bishop of Carlisle preach.

As the occasion also included the consecration of the new burial ground the bishop chose the 'unspeakable sad and solemn curse' from Jeremiah XXII, 18, 19 as his text and dwelt at length on 'there being something unspeakably solemn in the parish churchyard' despite burial being 'the sure slow foot with which death advances all'. By coincidence this proud and peaceful ceremony occurred during the week when over in France, Paris was being burnt by the Communards, its churches desecrated and clergy murdered while in England republicanism was raising its occasional and ugly head. Inevitably then, the bishop stressed the stabilizing influence of established religion: without doubt in ultra-conservative mid-Victorian Westmorland his lordship was preaching to the converted! Finally 'he exhorted his audience to complete the work on the church by clearing off this small remainder of debt (estimated at £50) which they might easily do that day'.[32] In fact the collection brought in £42.

Eventually after two hours a flurry of coaches, broughams and barouches took 43 top-hatted and be-bustled guests including ten clergy off to a luncheon at Eversley where in glorious sunshine no fewer than nine toasts were drunk at the tables set out in the grounds. Lesser folk like the Choir and the Bell Ringers were entertained more soberly at the vicarage under the Chairmanship of Rev. J.H.Blackman of Endmoor - Canon Gilbert having gone with the great ones to Eversley.

## Later additions to the fabric

The interior arrangement of the church in 1880 remained virtually unchanged for a century. Thus compared to the elaborate augmentation of the fabric by the early and mid-Victorians the catalogue of subsequent additions is relatively brief. In 1897 after two lengthy meetings with many resolutions and amendments the vestry agreed to a proposal by the Heversham Diamond Jubilee Committee 'to commemorate the Long Reign of Queen Victoria by the erection of a new inner porch and by other alterations including an external approach to the heating apparatus'.[33]

Accordingly H.H.Austin designed a new pit for steps to the outside door and the inner porch which skilfully contained a closet in the south west corner for 'trestles, two buckets and a cistern'.[34] The screen is constructed of oak linenfold panels alternately embellished with roses and blank shields with glazed and leaded upper lights, double doors to the nave and a crenellated frieze beneath which was carved the legend: 'This screen was erected to commemorate the many mercies of God to the country during the long and happy reign of Queen Victoria A.D. 1897.' Identical panelling was installed around new, rather low, baptistry seats, according to the inscription on the northern corner seat 'to the Glory of God and in loving memory of Susannah Argles of Eversley who died 11 July 1895 these seats with the bread cupboard above were placed here by her son T.A.Argles Easter 1899'[35] Ironically the donor and his wife were childless and no Argles child was christened there.

Strangely there are no records concerning the font which, however, appears to date from the restoration of c.1870 when the marble font noted being in the church in 1820 must have been thrown out. It is of freestone with a round bowl supported by four columns and a central pier round whose bases are carved the words 'Arise and be baptised and wash away thy sins'.

## The Argles Memorial

The font is now surmounted by a crocheted spire canopy installed by 'past and present parishioners' to the memory of Agnes and Thomas Atkinson Argles who died in June and September 1923. Following their death a special meeting had met to consider a 'definite memorial to two such workers' and it had been decided that 'as so much had already been given to the west end of the church by the Argles the completion of the Baptistry by the provision of a font cover and new glass for the window[36] would be suitable. Funds were insufficient for the window so its red, white and purple/blue glass of 1857 which shows the Alpha Omega, Dove for the Holy Spirit and Lamb of God remains.

The cover itself was the work of Messrs. Hatch of Lancaster, cost over £50 (more than had been collected originally) and arrived too late for the dedication by the Bishop. It is carved in the Victorian Gothic tradition with open work tracery and the text 'one faith, one baptism,

*Kneeling Angel on Font Cover*

one God and Father of all' carved round the square base. At the corners are kneeling angels, two female with crossed arms and two male with hands clasped in prayer. These fit the tops of the supporting piers showing that the canopy was designed specially for the font and not just ordered from one of the catalogues sent to the Parochial Church Council by Messrs. Hatch. The old flat font cover was stored for nearly half a century until presented to Crosscrake Church to commemorate its restoration in 1967.

**The West Window**
The major Argles Memorial was new stained glass for the Tower window which had been ordered by Thomas Argles in the brief interval between his wife's and his own death. His wishes were fulfilled by his heirs who also presented a large silver alms dish to the church.

The window was designed by Archibald Nicholson of London and is in the militaristic war memorial medieval style of the time. In the left window (to Thomas Argles) is the blue-robed St.Chad of Lichfield (with the ecclesiastical activities of which city Mr.Argles was closely associated') and Archbishop Theodore of Tarsus and King Oswy of Northumbria. Below is the enthroned figure of Thomas a Becket wearing red vestments, a kneeling acolyte at his feet and King Henry II and Canterbury Cathedral in the background.

The right light to Agnes Argles shows a green-robed St.Ursula, the patroness of young women, which refers to Agnes' interest in the Girls' Friendly Society and Casterton School. With Ursula are Eutherus, the English prince who wished to marry her, and Bishop Cyriachus, both of whom were martyred in Germany with 'her mission train of virgins'. Below is a red-robed St.Cecilia, patron of musicians, a tribute to Agnes' patronage, along with her sister Mary Wakefield, of music in Westmorland. The red robe could, also, refer to Agnes Argles' own love of red clothes and decorations: the Athenaeum (founded by Frank Atkinson Argles in 1872) and the cottages in Leasgill were all painted red.

At a great ceremony held on the 5th October 1924 the window was dedicated by the Bishop of Barrow-in-Furness. His address was redolent of the slushier Victorian eulogies for, after dwelling on the sad fact that the 'couple were denied that happy crown of marriage, children's love and laughter',[37] he went on to state that to be in contact with such generous, such noble, and such utterly modest goodness is to pass judgement on one's poorer nature. This sentiment is reflected in the window's inscription: 'They were lovely and pleasant in their lives and in their death they were not divided'.

Although the Argles' cousin, Mrs Ethel Macleod (daughter of Canon Argles of Hawbarrow) remained a member of the Parochial Church Council until her death in 1955 the passing of Thomas and Agnes Argles snapped the link with the heyday of Victorian restoration. Moreover, though Heversham continued to have some parishioners, happily including the Drews, the Argles' successors at Eversley, able to give substantial support to the church never again would benefactions be either so lavish or so conspicuous.

APPENDIX TO CHAPTER VI

# The New Pews and Christianity at Heversham

In the restoration programme the largest item of expenditure, was for the new pews which were to be 'low and open', i.e. without doors. Estimates of £750 from Johnstone of Whasset and of £480 from Clarkson of Carnforth were rejected in favour of one from Charles Blades of Kendal, who quoted the extremely neat figure of £666.6s.6d.[1] Like their predecessors of c.1820, the pews were constructed of excellent polished oak but had neo-gothic ends supported by miniature stepped buttresses and a series of panels displaying quatre-foils, trefoils, circles in triangles, arcading and curvilinear rose window type tracery. The pews under the tower had much narrower seats and panelled backs possibly from the Burrows pews of c.1820 and incorporate a gothic frieze which might have come from the gallery frontal of 1844.[2]

### Controversy
Regretably the new seating arrangements caused the church's most fierce nineteenth century controversy. Under the sceptical headline 'Christianity at Heversham', the tart comment appeared in the press that 'it appears that Heversham Christians have more love for one another's pews than they have for their own bodies and souls ...'[3] The cause of this alleged apostasy went back to 1868 when the possessors of the seats in the doomed gallery agreed to relinquish them on the understanding that new seats should be given in compensation; of these 'at least half should be in the middle aisle'. Superficially Blades' plan achieved this for, despite the loss of sixty seats in the gallery, he planned accommodation in the nave and aisles for 357 worshippers compared to the pre-restoration figure of 363.

Notwithstanding a resolution of 10th December 1868 that there should be 'no assignation of pews',[4] when the church was reopened in November 1869 places were indicated to the former gallery seat holders: Lt. Col. Gandy of Heaves, Messrs. Kieghtley, Harrison, Holme, Hardy, Cragg and G.Squire. The latter was particularly pleased when he was shown to the front seat on the north side of the nave. However, a year later the churchwardens re-allocated the seven giving the front pew on the north side to Mrs. Jemmet Browne of Heversham House and providing alternative accommodation for Mr. Squire further back on the south side. Mr. Squire however, continued to occupy his old seat at the front.

As a result the churchwarden M.Whittaker, William Ruttledge and William Handley wrote to Mr Squire on March 31st 1871 'We the undersigned formally make known to you that we did in the month of November of last year and before the thirteenth day of the said month in the exercise of our lawful authority as churchwardens of the Parish Church of Heversham and with the consent of the vicar of the said church, assign to you a certain seat in the said church which seat is situated on the south side of the nave of the said church in which seat we have directed the cushion, kneeling stool and other articles belonging to you to be placed ... at the same time we did assign to certain other persons a certain seat upon the northside of the nave of the said church which seat notwithstanding remonstrances from us, without any appeal from us to any superior authority and to the great annoyance to the persons to whom the seat was by us assigned you have hitherto persisted in occupying - Now, therefore, we hereby give you formal notice in the exercise of our lawful authority that we do not intend to permit you any longer to occupy the said seat upon the northside of the nave ... in the event of your attempting after this notice to persist in occupying it we shall use such lawful means to prevent you, from doing so and to enforce our lawful authority in this respect as shall to us appear most convenient ...'[5]

At Easter 1871 'the first signs of aggression' appeared when on arriving for morning service Mr Squire discovered that his books and cushions had been removed to No. 15, on the south side. According to the partisan 'Kendal Mercury' 'he took them out and again placed them in the seat first allocated to him but it was to no purpose for week after week they were removed and Sunday after Sunday they were put back. On Sunday last matters began to take a more serious turn. Mr Squire attended the church as usual and found the seat which is capable of holding six or eight people occupied by two ladies from Heversham House but a word from him caused one of them to rise to make room for him'. Stirring up the parochial teacup he attended Evensong as well only to find 'two functionaries (presumably Churchwardens W.Ruttledge and William Handley) stationed like sentries on each side of the entrance to the seat as to prevent his family from entering'.[6] After an excruciating staring match the Squires then chuntled out.

Next week they turned up with supporters to find 'a policeman in the yard ... in readiness should anything more serious transpire'.[7] Undeterred they swept into church where loud noises were exchanged by the occupants of the front pew, drowning the vicar's opening intonation 'When the wicked man turneth away from his wickedness' and then stormed out again, this time followed by half the congregation'. All this was grist to the mill of the 'Kendal Mercury' which in opposition to the conservative 'Gazette' took a radical line and, perhaps with a dig at the Argles, denounced 'the moneyocracy part of our population who have little or nothing else to do but raise up monuments to their temporal glory'.[8] Furthermore a correspondent pointed out that if Mr Squire owned 6,000 acres and not 60 he would have got a place in the main aisle that now appeared 'to be reserved for those who keep a carriage'. Inevitably the incumbent was censored as 'not being a manly man who would sternly put his foot upon attempts to trench upon individual and well defined rights ...'[9] In fact the poor vicar was in a tricky position: work had begun on the chancel but the college (which had been expected to bear most of the costs) had been proved to be stingy and if the Reverend Gilbert did not keep in with his carriage trade he would have to pay up himself.

Surprisingly quickly tempers calmed down for on the 26th April Mr. H.Swindlehurst of Hincaster House wrote to the 'Westmorland Gazette' stating that 'the earthquake that had upset the equanimity of the parish,[10] had subsided: Mr. Squire had regained the front pew which, becoming known as the 'faculty pew', was occupied by his family until the son Robert's death in 1946.[11]

The ousted ladies from Heversham House, Mrs. Warham Jemmett Browne and her daughter, did not occupy their new humbler places for long as Mrs. Browne died almost immediately afterwards and her family moved away.

The presence of a mere yeoman in the nave exasperated some of his social superiors one of whom, Colonel Gandy of Heaves, continued the pew quarrel for another decade. Gandy had lost six seats in the gallery and ten from a family box pew at the front of the north aisle. In return he had only been given two pews containing twelve seats in the aisle and accordingly he demanded a third pew to provide the outstanding four seats. The churchwardens refused on the grounds that a third pew would give him eighteen seats and, furthermore, according to warden John Audland, the Gandy's would not need more than two pews as they 'rarely attended and then only in the afternoon',[12] when there was plenty of room to spare. Seven letters on the issue written between 1871 and 1880 by Gandy to 'My Dear Canon Gilbert' survive along with counsel's opinion that as the family pew had been installed in 1807 by H.Wilson, the then owner of Heaves, the east end of the north aisle belonged to Heaves in the same way that the Levens and Dallam Chapels belonged to their estates. As late as 1879 the Colonel stated that the churchwardens must be 'laughing at him' and 'had he known' he would not have contributed to the restoration appeal.

Even though he continued to 'press his rights for the sake of those who came after him',[14] he seems to have been mollified before his death. In 1881 his wife donated stained glass for the west window of the north aisle to the rather belated memory of her parents, who died in 1857 and 1858. The window's predominant colours of red, blue and green are similar to the glass by Clayton and Bell in the Evans' Memorial window but the composition is, if anything, more banal and could therefore be the work of Burrow of Sandside. It shows the miracle of Jairas' daughter above the inscription 'The soul of the child came unto him again' and of Our Lord blessing the children, inevitably entitled 'Of such is the kingdom of God'.

Finally in 1885 a memorial brass plaque was placed on the north wall above the Gandy pew inscribed: 'In loving memory of Jane Gandy of Heaves Born March 14th 1818 Died March 1st 1883 and of her husband Fredric Gandy (formerly Brandreth) Lt. Colonel Scots Guards. Born September 16th 1812, Died May 25th 1883'. It also bears the family crest and the 'motto' *'Nemo me impune lacessit'* and the initials J.C.G., A.L.H.F., A.E.D.

In addition, the Gandy children presented the oak eagle lectern in memory of their parents. This was placed directly under the chancel arch until 1922 when, following the anonymous gift of the Fald stool, it was moved to the narrow space to the west of the vicar's desk so that its sabre beak and gripping talons loom over the occupants of the front pew.

**Continued 'Dispewtes'**
Seating troubles did not end with the mid-Victorian controversy. In 1880 when one Humphrey Hallows visited the church the wardens maintained a low profile for there was no one to show him his place and, as a result, he 'inadvertantly turned a parishioner out of his accustomed seat'.[15] However, with commendable charity by the standards of ten years earlier, 'the parishioner allowed him to stay for the rest of the service'.[15] Even so a plan for sidesmen collectors of 1909 shows only twelve out of 67 pews in the nave and aisles unallocated and these were either by the door behind the grammar school boys or in the north-west corner where altar, lectern and pulpit could not be seen. In more recent times in 1925 Parochial Church Council member Herbert Kilshaw complained of the 'difficulty of a non-parishioner getting a seat in Heversham Church'. The difficulty it seemed was caused by 'new houses being built in the parish and from the system of appropriating certain pews to certain houses irrespective of number of persons occupying them'. Therefore, it was resolved that 'all seats be free and unappropriated as soon as the minute bell is rung and that no one seated should be disturbed'. This was notwithstanding the fact that a notice to the effect that 'all seats are unappropriated' had been hung in the porch for half a century. Even so twenty-five years later the Parochial Church Council had to declare yet again that 'all seats were free' and as late as the 1980's occasional worshippers rising from introductory devotions might meet the quizzical gaze of the regular occupant of the pew.

## Notes and References to Sources   Chapter VI

1. Book of Accounts
2. The Churches Restoration (poem).
3. Bouch Prelate and People of the Lakes Counties Book IV. Appendix VI p.401-402. Book VIII Appendices IX, XI, p.462, 465-369.
4. Westmorland Gazette 6 October 1855.
5. Bouch Appendices IX, XI, p462, 465-469
6. History of Heversham with Milnthorpe John F.Curwen p.33 1930
7. CRO(K) WPR/8
8. *Ibid*
9. *Ibid*
10. *Ibid*
11. Kirkebie Kendal John F.Curwen Titus Wilson 1900 p.232
12. CRO (K) WPR/8
13 *Ibid*
14. Westmorland Gazette 3 June 1871.
15. CRO(K) WPR/8
16. CRO(K) WPR/8 and Vestry book (H)
17 *Ibid*
18. CRO(K) WPR/8
19. Vestry book (H)
20. CRO(K) WPR/8 Additional Docs. desposited 13 June 1975
21. CRO(K) WPR/8 list of sittings 1892.
22. Signature on glass.
23. CRO(K) WPR/8
24. Westmorland Gazette 3 April 1869.
25. see plaque in Tower; also Bellasis p.256.
26. Westmorland Gazette 3 June 1871
27. CRO(K) WPR/8
28. Vestry book (H)
29. *Ibid*
30. Westmorland Gazette 12 June 1880. N.B. the Church is called 'St.Mary's Church'.
31. Pevsner p.278.
32. Westmorland Gazette 3 June 1871.
33. Vestry book.
34. CRO(K) WPR/8
35. *Ibid*
36. P.C.C. Minute book.
37. Westmorland Gazette 12 October 1924.

## Appendix to Chapter VII

1. CRO(K) WPR/8 Restoration Committee papers.
2. see above
3. Westmorland Gazette Kendal Mercury April 1871.
4. Vestry Book.
5. Letter preserved in family papers of Mr. John Mashiter, kinsman of the Squire family.
6. Kendal Mercury 2 April 1871.
7. Westmorland Gazette 2nd April 1871, 9th April 1871.
8. Kendal Mercury 15 April 1871.
9. *Ibid*
10. Westmorland Gazette 29 April 1871.
11. Memories of many parishioners e.g. Mr. M.Sisson (godson).
12. Vestry Book (H).
13. CRO(K) WPR/8
14. *Ibid* (14)
15. Westmorland Gazette 12 June 1880.

*The tablet over the Dallam Chapel Door.*

*Right: The tomb in the south-west corner of the Dallam Chapel.*

CHAPTER VII
# Monuments and Memorials

**Monuments and Memorials**

Of the monuments and memorials not referred to elsewhere in the text the oldest, according to date of death, is the black marble tablet over the Dallam Chapel door. It is to the nephew of the founder of the Heversham Grammar School, Edward Wilson, and reads 'In memory of Thomas Wilson of Heversham Hall who departed this life 1656 aged 64 years'.[1] However the style of the lettering as well as the more modern euphemism 'departed this life' suggests that the tablet might have been installed by Thomas's descendents, the owners of Dallam, long after his death.

The two tombs in the south west corner of the Dallam Chapel which originally were placed over the vault on the site of the organ belong to Maria Preston and Dorothy Crowle. Constructed of a polished black marble emblazoned with a fine cartouche and deeply cut arms of the Preston-Molyneux families Maria's tomb is the more opulent. Its epitaph reads:

> Hic Jacet Dna Maria Preston Filia illustrismi Dni Carylii Molineux vicecomitis de Maryborough Conjux Nobilissmi Dni Thomae Preston Baronetti quoe obiit die VI Julii ano Dni MDCLXXIII.[2]

> (Here lies Lady Mary Preston daughter of the most illustrious Lord Charles Molineux Viscount of Maryborough, wife of the most noble Lord Thomas Preston Baronet who died on 6th July 1673 A.D.)

Nicolson and Burn's reference 1776 to the Crowle tomb states that 'it is to Mrs. Crowle of Froyston (sic) in the County of York great grandmother of the present Daniel Wilson esquire over whom is raised an handsome monument of freestone but without inscription.' Dorothy Crowle was in fact the widow of Squire William Crowle of Frystone and died on 23rd July 1716.[3]

There are monuments related to three former scholars of Heversham Grammar School who according to Atkinson's 'Worthies of Westmorland' 'must as long as education endures throw over the vale of Levens intellectual sunbeams of no ordinary attraction and renown.'[4] To the west of the three light window in the north aisle is a plain white tablet incised in very thin hardly discernible letters reading:

Juxta Marmor

S.C

dus

REV Thomas Watson

Annos prope quinquaginta Ludi magister

haud inutilis.Ob.Nov.22 d an.Sal.(C17)53.

AET 81[5]

Close by the marble (monument) lie buried the Reverend Thomas Watson for almost 50 years a far from useless schoolmaster. He died on 22 November 1753 aged 81.

During his 39 years as headmaster from 1698 to 1737 Watson created a reputation for the school that lasted along after the 'rod of power fell from his hands'. He encouraged boys from outside Westmorland to be educated at the school. They had to lodge in the village, his own house at Plumtree Bank being too small for boarders. Nevertheless his greatest protegees were all local. Of these his son Richard, Bishop of Llandaff from 1782 - 1816, was the most renowed or, perhaps, notorious. His obiturary in the 'Quarterly Review' must be the bluntest ever bestowed on a Hevershamian. 'We are to say that in point of self-ignorance, vanity, rancour, and disappointed ambition united with great original ability our country has produced nothing similar since Swift - and for the quiet of this church and state or rather for the sake of human nature we sincerely and devotedly wish that it may never be our lot to animadvert on a third'![6]

Watson was certainly the epitome of the 'Cankerworm' erastian eighteenth century parson for he only visited his diocese ten times and his North Wales rectory once, preferring to spend his time debating in the House of Lords, hunting, cockfighting or landscaping Calgarth Park on Windermere. He was also Professor of Divinity and Professor of Chemistry at Cambridge. No one else has ever held both chairs. None of his scientific works 'showed either originality or power or in any way extended the landmarks of science'. He also committed a notable gaffe when, on finding a lump of slag from an iron forge on the Helm near Stainton, he declared that there had been volcanoes in the Parish of Heversham. Nevertheless Richard Watson remains one of the most distinguished persons to be associated with the church.

Further down the north aisle is a monument set up to his mother by Richard Watson's contemporary and brother bishop, William Preston. It is by J.Stewart of Dublin and consists of a black marbled niche containing a freestone urn and coat of arms. A bishop's mitre is carved on the wall above. The inscription on the urn reads:

Aetatis Suae LXXII

in piam mem. Tam optimae quam delectissimae

matris annae Preston A.D. MDCCLXVII defunctae

hoc marmor ponendum curavit filius moerens guls.

Preston DD.[7]

(William Preston DD. the grieving son of the best as well as the most delightful mother Ann Preston who died in 1767 aged 72 had this marble monument erected in dutiful memory.)

According to 'The Worthies of Westmorland' Preston's intellectual powers were the least of his virtues. He was a man whose life was pious, whose mind was enlightened by genius, enlarged by travel and softened by society'. Yet his pursuit of worldly ambition followed much the same course as Watson's. From Endmoor via the Grammar School he went to Trinity, Cambridge. After ordination, eschewing the role of parish priest, he became a Fellow and concentrated instead on tutoring the sons of noblemen, one of whom, the Duke

70

*The Ann Preston monument*

*The Alan Chambre memorial
with that to Archdeacon Evans below*

of Rutland, later employed him in the diplomatic service. The Duke later made him his secretary while he was Lord Lieutenant of Ireland and as a reward he was given the Irish bishoprics of Ferns and Killala. These he certainly never visited more frequently than Richard Watson visited Llandaff! The inscription on the tablet gives details of his career:

'In memory of the Right Rev. William Preston D.D. Late Lord Bishop of Ferns, Fellow of Trinity College, Cambridge, Rector of Okeham in Surrey, Chargé des Affaires several years at the Courts of Vienna and Naples, private Secretary to the late Duke of Rutland, when Lord Lieutenant of Ireland, Bishop of Killala, and afterwards translated to the Bishoprick of Ferns in that Kingdom.He died at Dublin 19 April 1789 Aged 60.'[8]

In the south aisle is a white mural monument to the Bishop's nephew inscribed: In memory of John Preston of Leasgill, Nephew of Dr. William Preston late Bishop of Ferns who died 28 June 1816 Aged 52 years. Also of Jenny his Daughter (Wife of John Nunns of Lancaster) who died 18 August 1819, Aged 25 years.'[9]

Next to the Preston tablet in the north aisle is a large mural monument surmounted by an urn with white swags set on a black background to Reverend James Backhouse who was also one of Thomas Watson's pupils. It reads to 'Rev. James Backhouse S.T.B. Senior Fellow of Trinity College, Cambridge, And for many years Dean and one of the Principal Tutors of the said College, Chancellor of Bristol and Peterborough, Rector or Scotter, Lincolnshire. He deceased at Helsington Laythes, His Brother-in-Laws Mr Richard Bindloss's, 30 Sept. 1790 In the 74th Year of his Age. His loving and grateful Brother and Sisters Erected this Monument To His Memory.'[10]

To its left is another white block tablet to his nephew Bateman Backhouse of Milton, gentleman d. 23 Aug 1823 aged 84 and Isabella his widow daughter of Edward Johnson Esquire of Old Hall d. 28 July aged 66.

According to Bishop Watson 'If schoolmasters may properly be allowed to participated in the honours of those whom they have educated, the greatest honour of my father's life will be the education of Ephraim Chambers'.[12] Ephraim was born at Milton in the parish. After leaving the grammar school he went to London where he was first apprenticed to an instrument maker before becoming a journalist which led him to produce the Dictionary that later developed into the Encyclopaedia - making his name a household word. Nicolson and Burn state that in the church adjoining the chancel is an inscription 'In memory of Mary wife of Richard Chambers who died in the year 1764 which Richard was father of Ephraim Chambers, author of the celebrated Dictionary of Arts and Sciences.'[13] This information was also quoted by R.D.Humber in 'Heversham, the story of a Westmorland School and Village' of 1968.[14] Unfortunately no such monument has existed in living memory. There is, however, one on the south wall of the Sanctuary whose inscription reads 'Sacred to the memory of the Rev. Alan Chambre A.M. Minister of the Cross Crake Chapel who died at Heversham 20 November 1800 and was interred in this place aged 31 yrs.'[15] This has a book, often pointed out as 'Chambers' Encyclopaedia!' depicted leaning against an urn at the top of the plaque.

Opposite on the north wall is the black and white marble monument in the form of a scroll to Dr. Lawson. The inscription reads: 'This tablet is placed by his parishioner and friends in affectionate remembrance of the Reverend George Lawson M.A. formerly fellow of Trinity College Cambridge, and upwards forty-four years Vicar of Heversham, he died June 14 1842 aged 77. The blessings of him that was ready to perish came upon him; and he caused the widow's heart to sing with joy'.[16] Below is an oval plaque to 'James Smyth A.M.Vicar of Heversham who died Jan 27 1757 aged 50 and of Mary Smyth his widow who died July 14 1791 aged 71'. As there was space to spare Smyth's successor Henry Wilson d. 12 April 1797 aged 77 is commemorated on the monument along with his son 'Henry Wilson A.M. Scholar of Queen's College Oxford who died July 23 aged 20'.[17] It was Henry Wilson (Senior) who endowed several scholarships for Heversham Grammar School Boys at Oxford and Cambridge.

To the south of the vestry door is a table to Richard Birkett of Milnthorpe d. 15 January 1829 aged 90 and his wife Mary died 12th day of March 1842 aged 93. This serves as a reminder of the Julian calendar for his birth is given as 14 May 1739 O.S. - for old style. According to the Gregorian Calendar adopted in 1752 his birthday would have been the 28th of May.

Higher up to the east is a bulky Grecian style black marble tablet to one of Milnthorpe's greatest sailors and the builder of perhaps its finest house, Harmony Hall. It also tells of a probably forgotten naval disaster during the Napoleonic Wars: 'To memory of Captain Joseph Fayrer of Milnthorp who died at Cape Coast Castle on the Coast of Africa Jan. 11 1801 aged 55. Also of Bridget his Wife who died March 14 1807 aged 52. Also Edward Birbeck Fayrer, their third Son, A Midshipman of the Royal Navy who died in the Service of his Country being one of the unfortunate Crew of H.M.S. Defence lost in a storm off the entrance to the Baltic Dec. 23 1811 aged 21. This Stone is erected to the memory of his deceased Parents and Brother by R.I.Fayrer, Lieutenant of the R.N.'[18]

A tragedy which occured within the parish is recorded on a marble tablet in the south west corner, (now within the broom cupboard). It is inscribed;'Near this Place are buried the Remains of John Hudson second son of Robert Hudson Esq. of Todworth Court, Surrey, And also of Issac Hudson of Long Sleddale his schoolfellow, who were drowned bathing on the sands on the 24 of June A.D. 1792, both aged 16 years.'[14] Nearby is a tomb-like mural monument to 'Benjamin Hunter late of Kendal who died during his Mayorality on 23rd day of November 1821 aged 34 years.[20]'

On the south wall of the chancel is a monument to a member of a notable local family. It

> Near this Place are buried
> the Remains of JOHN HUDSON
> second Son of ROBERT HUDSON Esq
> of Tadworth Court Surry.
> And also of ISAAC HUDSON,
> of Long Sleddale his Schoolfellow.
> who were drowned bathing on the Sands
> the 24th of June AD 1792:
> both Aged 16 Years.

reads: 'Near this place in hope of glorious resurrection are the remains of Revd. William Fisher Audland D.D. senior fellow of Queen's College Oxford, he died at Ackenthwaite May 3rd 1861 aged 57 years'.[21] 'Mark the perfect man and behold the upright for the end of that man is peace.' Contrary to the implication of the inscription William was not buried 'in ecclesia' but lies with his parents John died 2 March 1853 aged 82 and Ellen Audland died 5 September 1861 aged 83. They lie in the south yard with his nephew William Grant Audland and his sisters Jane and Ellen.

William was ordained in 1827 and held one or two curacies but most of his life he spent at Queen's College where he was a tutor before ultimately becoming senior fellow. He was unmarried and was cared for by his sisters who were devoted to him. This is the only monument within the church to a member of the family which has the longest continuous connection with the parish. The Audlands are possible descended from the de Astenthwaites recorded in the thirteenth century. No less than thirteen John Audlands were discovered in the church records by Brigadier Gordon E. Audland when he researched the family pedigree in the 1960's. For at least ten generations, moreover, John's eldest son was christened William and William's John.[22] Until the late nineteenth century when Dr. John Audland was church-warden the family held a church office in almost every generation. Though never able to compete with the great landowning dynasties of Levens and Dallam the Audlands as small farmers and blacksmiths were typical of the fairly well to do yeomanry that traditionally were the backbone of Old England and who were the staunchest supporters of the Established Church. Fittingly in view of their unique links with the mother church (and also with its daughter of St. Thomas Milnthorpe), the heads of the family down to Brigadier G E Audland d. 1976 have continued to be buried at Heversham though their careers have taken them far afield.

Incidentally, it was at The Smithy, Ackenthwaite, purchased from the Audlands in 1978 by the present writer that this book was written.

Between the second and third windows of the south aisle is a large very black hulk of marble to Richard and Bridget Crampton d. March and July 1797 of Howlet Ash (Milnthorpe).[23] Just to the east of the main door Thomas Watson's successor as headmaster, the Reverend John Wilson who died 12 November 1798 aged 71 is eulogised 'as a Teacher he was beloved and respected, as a Clergyman he was exemplary and revered. Multis ille bonis flebilis occidit'. (He died lamented for many good works).

An inconspicuous memorial is a pink alabastor monument very high up on the north side of the tower wall in the north aisle. Below a free standing urn set in a deep niche its epitaph reads simply 'William Cragg who died 9th March 1820 aged 31'.[25]

The only old brass in the church is over the wall offertory box in the baptistry. In remarkably florid script it refers to some of the many burials in the vicinity:

'Here under lieth the Body of Mr. Wm. Jonson of Old Hall Preston Richard who Died December the 9th 1713 aged 63 also Wm. son and Heir of the above 2nd Wm. Johnson who Died Decembr 30th 1748 aged 68. Margaret wife of the former and daughter of Mr. Tho. Newton of Burton Hall Oct. 6 1685 aged 30. Also Margaret wife of the latter and daughter of Mr. Wm. Birkhett of Kidside, died 20th February 1767 aged 77.'[26]

In the north aisle are newer brasses to the Gandy's of Heaves and to Canon William Crane of Manchester and formerly rector of St.George's Hulme who 'entered into rest' 1903. The erection of this memorial caused controversy as Canon Crane 'had had no very great connection with the area'[27] and it was only installed after the vicar Canon Gilbert had given a casting vote in its favour.

**The Levens Families**
Similarly a marble tablet to Richard Bagot d. 1921 and his wife Sophia Louisa was almost prevented from being installed when a description of the deceased's foreign distinctions 'Knight of Honour of the Sovereign Order of Malta and Grand Officer and Commendatore of the Order of the Crown of Italy' was found to be different to that on the faculty. A hidden reason for the objections could have been Richard Bagot's conversion to Roman Catholicism and open hostility to Protestantism.[28] The church-wardens had already objected to a coat of arms in the upper lights of the stained glass window installed in the north east of the Levens Chapel to Richard Bagot's brother Sir Joscelyn. Instead the Bagot arms were inserted in the north window and glass bearing pictures of angels put in the north east window above the figure of St.Oswald.

No such objections occurred in 1850 when the huge white marble and freestone memorial plaques were set in the chapel's east wall to Fulk Greville Howard 1773 - 1846 and his wife Mary, the owner of Levens 1784 - 1877. The Honourable Fulk's memorial records that he was 'the second son of Clotworthy, First Baron Templetown, of Castle Upton Co. Antrim and sometime in the first Gren.Regt. of Guards' and that he 'was wise and good and let the void left by his death in the hearts of those who mourn his loss bear testimony how deeply he was beloved.'[24] Both Fulk and Mary Howard's twin tablets record that she was the owner of Elford in Staffordshire, Castle Rising in Norfolk, Ashstead in Surrey as well as Levens but Mary's states also that 'she resided frequently at each of them and has left in all ample proof of her wise and Christian benevolence but nowhere has the care she had for her own people been shown more abundantly than in this county and neighbourhood.' [30]

Beneath the north Windows of the chapel is a similar memorial to the Howard's heir at Levens General Arthur Upton 1807 - 1883 and his wife the Hon. Frederica Blake with the text 'the righteous shall be held in everlasting remembrance'.

**Newer Memorials**
Since 1921 no private monuments have been erected in the church. Tangible memorials have taken a more practical form. In 1927 a faculty for brass candlesticks and cross was obtained for the Reverend F S and Miss Milner in 'memory of many happy times of worship in this church' and the vicar having 'spoken of the symbolism of the gift there were no votes against [31] in the P.C.C. Accordingly the cross, inscribed 'In memorium Alexander Milner 1835 - 1919' and candlesticks were installed. However, sometime later these were removed, by an unknown person and hidden in the churchyard.[33] Fortunately they were recovered undamaged and the desire to see the Holy Table set only with two flower vases, as in Canon Gilbert's day, has never again been expressed.

The local historian J.F.Curwen was commemorated in 1932 by a specially woven carpet that reaches from the foot of the chancel steps to the sanctuary where the Curwen arms and crossed keys of St.Peter and initials J.F.C woven in the pattern stare up at the communicants kneeling at the rail.

In 1936 additional brass vases were presented to the church in memory of Mrs. Lloyd of Woodhouse by her daughters. Further sanctuary adornments have been a wafer box presented in memory of churchwarden Herbert Valentine Kilshaw in 1953, silver and crystal wine and water cruets donated by Mrs. Cleghorn to commemorate her husband

Reverend W.A.Cleghorn in 1955 and oak flower stands installed by the Mother's Union in 1978.

In 1946 an oak and brass engraved flower tub was purchased by the P.C.C. as a thankoffering for the work of Robert Squire, parish clerk for 40 years. A photograph of 'Robbie' was also hung in the vestry. The churchwardens' silver-headed staffs were given in 1953 in memory of Frederick Astley of Greenside, a churchwarden for over 20 years, while a silver chalice and paten of 'Icelandic' design presented by his family in 1968 commemorate another churchwarden Mr. G.L.Brownson. In 1980 the collection taken at the funeral of John Chew in 1977 was used to purchase a handsome brass and oak standard Cross. This now leads the robed and surpliced choir as it processes from the new choir vestry (installed by Norman Kilshaw in 1978) to the chancel before family communion. A brass vase was purchased by the choir in 1978 in memory of Kenneth Daly, Organist from 1976 to 1978. In 1981, after many years discussion, a side altar for mid-week communion was installed in the Levens Chapel. The oak Holy Table and Rails, made by Jim Frearson and Norman Kilshaw and designed to harmonise with the Jacobean screen, were 'dedicated to the Glory of God and in memory of Kathleen Joan Sanderson on Sunday 6th December 1981'. The creation of this 'Lady Chapel' meant that there was no longer room for a 'Children's Corner'. An octagonal oak table made for the children's corner by James Sisson in 1943 was put at the west end. On it are placed the elements presented in the Offertory at Family Communion. In the baptistry there is an oak bookcase for children's books bearing the dedication plaque: 'In memory of a dear friend Roselind Whittaker Given by The Young Wives Group and Sunday School 1979'.

**Notes and References to Sources  Chapter VII**

1. See Bellasis, Westmorland Church Notes p.275 N.B. all inscriptions have been checked by the present author (1982).
2. *Ibid 265*
3. *Ibid* Nicolson and Burn p.197.
4. George Atkinson 'Worthies of Westmorland or Notable persons born in that County since the Reformation' 1849 p.185-230.
5. *Ibid 273*
6. *Ibid p.184-229*
7. *Ibid*
8. *Ibid*
9. *Ibid*
10. *Ibid p.240*
11. *Ibid*
12. *Ibid p.191*
13. Nicolson and Burn p.194
14. 'Heversham, the Story of a Westmorland School and Village' R.D.Humber Titus Wilson 1968 p.21.
15. Bellasis p,246
16. *Ibid p.262*
17. *Ibid p.269*
18. *Ibid p.252*
19. *Ibid p.259*
20. *Ibid*
21. *Ibid p.240*
22. CRO(K) Audland Family papers.
23. Bellasis p.248
24. *Ibid p.274*
25. *Ibid p.248*
26 Not in Bellasis's transcription by present author. (1982)
27. Vestry Book.
28. Information Mrs. O.R.Bagot.
29. Bellasis p.258
30. *Ibid*
31. P.C.C. Minutes.
32. Reminiscences of parishioners; N.B. no reference in the Vestry Book or P.C.C. Minutes.

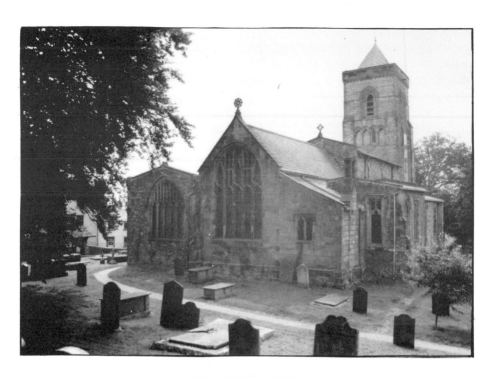

CHAPTER VIII

# The Churchyard

The Churchyard possibly has a longer history than the church for the early Christians often worshipped around the cross set under the open sky,[1] a fact which is implied in the names of the daughter communities of Crosthwaite and Crosscrake.[2] Moreover the Christian burial rite in eschewing cremation and internment with grave goods, was a challenge to heathenism, and hence the burial ground probably was treated originally with greater reverence than the first, rough, church building. When the church was built burials probably took place to its south, as the tradition that the Devil haunted the north side in order to take wandering souls off to hell, seems to have been observed by local Angles and Normans. Beetham and Burton churches, for example, have almost no yard to the north. Evidence that Heversham's yard might have extended three hundred yards to the south-east was produced in 1948 when skeletons were dug up during the building of the Bay View Council houses.[3] However, these remains could simply have been those of suicides buried outside consecrated ground or, possibly, have come from the cemetery of the Anglian villagers situated away from the monk's graves near the church.

The size of the northern yard implies a long history, and the supposition of a pre-reformation consecration has enabled Roman Catholics to be buried there in recent times.[4] Although, before the eighteenth century when gravestones became common, the same ground could be used over and over again Heversham had to have a large yard as it was the only consecrated burial ground in the parish. Crosthwaite got a burial ground in 1555 but place names inscribed on the monuments show that burials from Crosscrake, Levens and Milnthorpe regularly occurred at Heversham until the late nineteenth century.

After the consecration of Milnthorpe Churchyard in 1838 there were frequent complaints, recorded in the vestry book, about the burial at Heversham of paupers from Milnthorpe Workhouse, for which wardens received only five shillings compared to £5 'for what are conceived a double grave'.[5] The cause of the problem according to Canon Gilbert in 1916 was that Milnthorpe was 'not a separate parish because the licence under which marriages were celebrated there was revocable'. However, he believed that if the vicar of Milnthorpe 'Mr Pickering applied for an irrevocable license Milnthorpe would then become separate and the right of sepulchre would cease'[6] (for Milnthorpe corpses) in Heversham yard. Independence for Milnthorpe was achieved in 1923 when ironically there were no longer any paupers, for the Workhouse had become the 'Mental Home'.

Of the hundreds of pauper funerals conducted at Heversham only one received the attention of the press. This occurred when 'an interesting dwarf, a native of Kendal named Simpson' was buried on the 15th February 1895. 'She was 26 years of age and stood exactly 3ft. 5ins. in height and her weight was four stone four pounds. She was fairly proportioned in all parts of the body but the head was abnormally large and the spine had been indented from birth which was the probable cause of the stoppage in development. She was not able to speak, but could hear and apparently understood anything that was said to her, and she was of a happy disposition.'[7]

Although the northern yard is ancient, burials to the south were more numerous and may have caused the south yard to be raised several feet higher than the land surrounding it. An eighteenth century plan even shows graves in the main pathway leading to the south porch, some of which were disturbed in 1823 when the Turnpike road encroached on the yard. As compensation the vicar received an annual fee until 1870, which evidence he used in 1906 when he persuaded the Turnpike's successor, the District Council, to pay for repairs to the roadside wall.[8] The age of the spiky iron railings running along the terraced wall is uncertain although they appear in a watercolour dating from before the restoration of 1869-1871.[9]

## Expenses

Churchyard expenses figure in the account books in the eighteenth century. They include 1735 'Richard Hudson a quart of Ale when he walled the churchyard: £0 0s.4d', new spades in 1736 at 1s.6d and in 1786 at 2s.6d.,1739 £2 9s.10d. for new walls for which James Scott was paid '5d. for 7 bushells of stones', 1743 'Henry Hudson three days and a half laying walks 3s.6d.' and in 1765 '13s.6d. for Gravel walks and edgestones'.

In 1739 Anthony Crosthwaite was paid £2.10s for the 'Churchyard gate and painting it'.[10] He was also a mason and this account could be a reference to the eighteenth century gates with handsome ball top piers now at the west entrance. These were transferred from the south entrance in 1894 (at a cost of £4.10s. paid to Charles Hargreaves) when the lychgate was erected. The lychgate had been offered by the family of Dr. John Audland at a vestry

*Churchyard from The Head*

meeting held in November 1893. As there were 'only two persons present' it was left to a subsequent meeting to resolve that there should be 'some substantial memory of the long and faithful service rendered to the church by the late Mr. ( sic) John Audland, and to agree to its erection'.[11] Since then the lychgate's quaintly curving hipped roofs have provided a welcome umbrella from rook droppings from the overhanging chestnuts. In 1965, having been damaged in several collisions with double decker buses, the first in 1951, it was set back a couple of yards northwards. The inscription, on the west pier, hints at Anglo-Catholicism untypical of Victorian Heversham, as it states that 'John Audland M.R.C.S for nearly 13 years churchwarden of this parish died on the eve of the feast of the purification 1892'.

Over the centuries there were difficulties about boundary walls. The most detailed settlement was made on the 14th October 1831 when it was agreed that 'the fence on the north side of the churchyard adjoining the property belonging to George Wilson, Dallam Tower, esq., should be rebuilt with a good strong stone wall at the joint expense of the Parish and the said George Wilson (disputes having arisen)' ... and ...' it also resolved that the fence should be divided in the middle by a double groin: the higher division to the east to be considered in future as belonging to the parish and the low division to the west as belonging to the owner of the adjoining garden now the property of the aforesaid G. Wilson'.[12] Fifteen years later this wall was demolished when the school and schoolhouse were built.

Though labour was cheap the maintenance of the yard was fraught with difficulties in the nineteenth century. The sexton's duties and fees were stipulated with increasing detail. Thus in 1829 he was to be allowed to charge 'for a grave 3 feet deep, 2 shillings for every grave made deeper 1 shilling for every foot above three ... and he should charge one shilling each for tolling the passing bell and the funeral bell'. In 1861 it was resolved that 'no double fees in future be paid to the sexton on the burial on non-parishioners but in place thereof the sum of one guinea or half a guinea ... to be charged on a sinking (!) fund to be laid aside for additional burying ground'. On the appointment in 1879 of sexton Henry Nicholson a niggardly rule was made that: 'stones taken from graves were to be placed by the sexton without extra payment either in the churchyard or just outside as the churchwardens may direct'. A customary lawn trimming service was dispensed with in 1885 when it was resolved that 'after the sheep have left the churchyard at May day the churchwardens do instruct Henry Nicholson to keep it in order by mowing and for that purpose they be authorized to pay him an additional salary of £12.' It was doubtless to ward off sheep rather than body snatchers that railings were put round so many graves before 1885.

Nicholson's successor, John Proctor, received a salary of only £10 in 1888 and he had 'as well to look after the spouts of the church itself'. He was however helped by Henry Varley who 'attended to the grates and doors for £8 p.a.' The wardens could well afford additional wages for in 1890 the churchyard fund stood at £328.7s.7d. Not surprisingly money from the fund was used for other purposes thereafter.

There are regular records of sexton problems in the vestry books. Thus in December 1874 it was resolved that 'the conduct of Bindloss (the sexton) in allowing an improper person to dig the grave of Mr. Burrows children deserves severe censure', and for this grave crime he was dismissed in April the following year.

Notwithstanding apparently thankless taskmasters, elections for the office of sexton were invariably contested. In 1899, after the vicar had disenfranchised several persons on the grounds that 'they had not subscribed to the churchyard fund', the selection result was close when Joshua Valentine Proctor won by 23 votes to Robert Graham's 22. The wardens then stipulated that Joshua's term should be limited so 'as to act as a check to a tendency to overcharge at funerals'. Joshua managed to hold the job until 1906 when after 'complaints being made of misbehaviour' he was given a month's notice whereupon 'he tendered his resignation immidiately'.[13] A sad event occurred in 1900 when a temporary sexton the father of eleven children committed suicide in a shed in the corner of the yard,[14]

## Extension of the Yard

The yard was extended in 1871 and 1900 making it about four acres in area. Judging from the voluminous correspondence, committee minutes and the sales contract, a copy of which ran into six sides in the vestry book (space sufficient for about ten years' normal entries) the negotiations for the 1871 extension were extremely complicated. They were also prolonged as the wardens first approached the Misses Burrow, who owned most of the land required behind Heversham Cottage, in 1868. Before selling the Burrows required compensation in the form of land which belonged to the Dallam estate. In addition some of the Dallam land was required for the Churchyard. George Wilson of Dallam Tower was prepared to sell to the wardens but was more tardy about selling to the Burrows. Eventually three contracts transferring land from the Burrows and from Wilson to the Church and from Wilson to the Burrows were worked out and three quarters of an acre was obtained by the churchwardens for £300. The cost was met by £160 from the burial fund, from £100 raised by a church rate of 2d. in the pound and £40 by subscriptions collected by the Burial Ground Committee. The wardens also had to pay for grubbing out the old and for the erection of new fences round both the new yard and the Burrows new paddock which lay to the east of the cottage.

In 1900 a triangular plot was obtained at the eastern end of the yard where most twentieth century burials have taken place. Again land had to be obtained from the Burrows (whose title to the property was at one stage questioned) and from Mr. (later Sir) Maurice Bromley Wilson of Dallam Tower. Moreover, the problem of a customary right of way from Woodhouse Lane across the land was a further complication. It was decided that this was not a public right of way in the same way that the footpath running from the Lychgate northwards to the gate onto Heversham Head. This latter path dated at least from the foundation in 1613 of Heversham Grammar School to whose original building it led. At first in 1900 it was decided to open the Woodhouse Lane Gate to the customary path only on 'Sundays from 10.00 to 12.30, or 1.00'. However, it was agreed in 1901 that the gate would be opened at anytime subject to the discretion of the churchwardens and 'that it be part of the caretaker's duty to attend to this matter'.[15]

A line of plane trees was planted in c.1902 along the lane wall in the new yard and also two yews on each side of the path near the gate. The yews had reached 60 feet high by 1982. Having become an ugly tangle the plane trees were replaced at the expense of Mrs. Ellwood of Horncop in 1947 by flowering trees including several spectacularly florid cherries.[16]

Regrettably the mid-twentieth century fashion of putting kerbs round graves caused the new part of the yard to become the most untidy as the scythe or mower were impeded severely. Accordingly in c.1970 it was resolved that future memorials should consist of head stones only. Although first suggested in 1939 tarmacadam has not been applied to the yard paths which from the eighteenth century have been of gravel. In 1943 Mrs. Macleod, Vice Chairman of the P.C.C., provided the teak garden seat for the yard which was placed by the south-east door,[17] and in 1982 another seat was placed in the north-eastern yard to the memory of Ian Entwistle.

In 1975 the yard was the subject of a fierce controversy after the judge in the Best Kept Village Competition (in which Heversham had come second in the large village class) said that the church grounds were 'not worthy' of Heversham. He went on to suggest that the grave stones be placed against the boundary walls to provide an 'excellent village green'.[18] Letters in the press followed when it was made clear that Heversham parishioners would regard such a change of use of ground hallowed by possibly twelve centuries of Christian burial as an act of desecration. Stung by the criticism, greater efforts were made including voluntary boon days and by the standards of most large yards the condition improved. Again, however, in 1982 the competition judges criticized the state of the yard noting especially three milk bottles by the door, unsightly dustbins and that mown grass had not been raked up.[19]

## Vandalism!

In 1919 having survived the holocaust of the Great War the parishioners switched their sense

*Fragment of arm of Anglian Cross embedded in wall below window. The War Memorial was based on the design of the Anglian Cross.*

*War Memorial*

of horror from the huns to a 'child not passed 8 or 9' who had been responsible for breaking a marble cross. The vestry resolved 'to send a printed notice to every house in the parish urging all persons to respect the sanctity of the yard'.[20]

## The War Memorial

On the 23rd September 1919 an application was made for a faculty to erect the War Memorial Cross in the Churchyard.[21] This was unveiled by Canon Gilbert in a ceremony held before evening service on Easter Day 1920 'in the presence of a large gathering of parishioners and friends the Cross being draped with the Union Jack and wreaths of laurel and flowers, laid at the base'. Major Argles as 'churchwarden for Heversham with Milnthorpe briefly requested that the vicar and churchwardens of Heversham would accept the trust and charge of the memorial on behalf of the parishioners'. Canon Gilbert replied that 'for the honour of Westmorland he was proud to say that our boys were imbued with a spirit which was in no way behind the rest of the country. Heversham lads had come forward and taken their share.' The ceremony concluded with the congregation singing the hymn 'Jesus lives' and the National Anthem before going inside to hear the Canon preach from 'the last words' of Edith Cavell: 'We shall meet again'.

Designed by J.F.Curwen, the Cross is constructed of darley stone and stands 13 feet high on a stepped base. Its cost was 'entirely obtained by voluntary subscription amounting to £246.'[22]

On the north face went an inscription containing almost every Great War cliche except the 'un-Heversham' one of saving the world for democracy. 'To the memory of those who at the call of King and country left all that was dear to them, endured hardness, faced danger and finally passed out of the sight of men by the path of duty and self sacrifice giving up their own lives that others might live in freedom.'

As the shaft is narrow only the initials and surnames of the 17 victims are carved on the south side. They are: G.A.Wilson, J.Hamilton, T.Philipson, H.V.Shaw, J.E.Woof, J.Chamley, R.Smith, J.Atkinson, W.H.Ward, F.Baines, G.H.Proctor, E.Proctor, J.Proctor, J.Sisson, J.Moore, T.Dowker, J.B.Germaine. The full names, rank, decorations and place of death of the fallen are, however, engraved on brass plaques on the wooden cross (originally erected in the yard during the war) fixed inside the church on the south side of the tower arch. (Curiously on the inside cross Proctor is spelt with an 'e' while outside it is spelt with an 'o'.) Even in Lent flowers are placed weekly at the foot of both this and the Second World War Cross on the north side of the arch. In addition the vestry book lists the '106 men connected with Heversham Parish who served in the Great War 1914-1918'. Headed by Brigad.-Gen. W.G.Braithwaite D.M.G., D.S.O., Lieut. Sir Alan Desmond Bagot, Bart., R.H.G., and Major Sir Maurice Bromley-Wilson Bart., Notts. Yeom., there are 14 officers, 59 privates and a variety of other ranks including 'a wheeler' H.Kilshaw. They served in the full range of British regiments with individuals belonging to the Australian Imperial Force, Canadian Highlanders, the Canadian Corps, the South African Infantry and the American Army.

Though there were far fewer local fatalities in the Second World War than in the First a cruel sexual equality was achieved at Heversham for two of the four victims, Jean Strickland and Jean Binnie, were members of the Women's Forces. The men were W.Norman Smith and William G.Sisson.

### The Churchyards Monuments
There are about 650 tombstones surviving more or less intact in the Churchyard.[23] In 1886 Bellasis recorded some 270 monuments of which about 50 dated from before 1820.[24] Of the latter monuments about 360 were erected between 1886 and 1940 and 100 between 1940 and 1981, suggesting a decline in memorials by fifty per cent in the mid twentieth century compared to the period around the turn of the century. On the other hand in the earlier period most of the dead from Levens, Crosscrake and Milnthorpe were still buried at Heversham and there was no cremation. The first internment of ashes was in 1931.[25] By 1981 half the persons dying in Heversham were cremated but of those who were buried between

*Churchyard from the South*

1940 and 1981 three quarters were commemorated by a monument whereas in the nineteenth century less than half had a stone to mark their graves.

The oldest monuments are of sandstone and in the case of the altar tombs the inscriptions on the horizontal surfaces have worn considerably; fortunately in many cases sufficient lettering survives for the early tombs to be identified from those recorded by Bellasis.[26] Judging from inscriptions which are complete his records seem to be accurate. Unfortunately he does not include a plan and the sexton's plan kept in the vestry is neither complete nor correct. Approximately thirty of the monuments noted by Bellasis have either disappeared or are so eroded as to be unidentifiable. They include Nathaniel Bateman's tomb of 1832 which had the following inscription:

'Reader while poring o'er this clay
Know life is but a transient day
From death's cold grasp escape is vain
Eternity must o'er thee reign
Friends, relatives, once loved and kind
Mourn not, your stay is brief behind
As I, so you to dust must turn
And sleep awhile in death's cold urn
Be wise, prepare from grief refrain
The good but part to meet again.'[27]

Another missing tomb, to William Jackson late surgeon of Milnthorpe died 1831, had the epitaph which referred both to his profession and to his premature death:

'Stop for a moment youthful passers by
On this moment cast a serious eye
Tho now the rose of health
May pluck your cheek
And youthful vigour may your health
  bespeak
Yet think how soon like me you may
  become
In youth's fair prime the tenant of
  the tomb.'[28]

*Churchyard from the North*

For the purpose of providing a rough quide to graves mentioned below reference will be made to the churchyard as being in five parts: 1) the south yard being the area south of a line drawn along the south wall of the church extending as far as the eastern boundary wall near to the large beech tree 2) the northern yard being the roughly square area between the church and the Old School and including a corner near to the gate leading on to the Head 3) the east yard running parallel with the east side of the main pathway as far as the northern wall 4) the north east yard being the area immediately behind the Eagle and Child, Heversham Cottage and the adjacent paddock 5) the new yard being the triangular area abuting Woodhouse Lane with a contiguous rectangular area to the north-west.

The earliest dateable grave is probably the altar tomb immediately east of the church belonging to James Backhouse of Milnthorpe who died on 24th March 1727[29] There are several contemporary tombs including a flat stone by the pathway in the south yard of Robert Cornthwaite of Milnthorpe who was buried on 15th October 1736.[30] A few yards to its east is the altar tomb of William Birkhead of Kidside who died on 10th November 1727 aged 77 and of his wife Jane who died on 27th May 1744 aged 92.[31] To its south is the similar altar tomb of William Bare who died 10th June 1739 aged 22 which has the just traceable inscription:

'Remember Man as thou goest by
As thou art so once was I
As I am now so must thou be
Think on thy own mortality.'

In the northern yard sufficient words survive on the tomb of William Higgin died 16th November 1730 aged 71 which bore a similar inscription:

'Remember friend thou ... walks by
As thou art so once was I
As I am now so shall ...
Remember then that thou must die.'[33]

Above the inscription is a circular inset in which is a worn relief of a man's head adorned with an eighteenth century periwig.

In the eastern yard an older grave space is recorded in a stone inscribed 'Henry and Rebecca Smithers and decendants of Milnthorpe 1700-1862.' The gravestone and the masonry surrounding the twelve foot square plot date, however, from the nineteenth century.

Some of the early nineteenth century horizontal tombstones are extremely large. A single piece of slate measuring eight feet by five covers the tomb in the eastern yard of Thomas Wood Suart died April 2nd 1826 aged 36. Nearby slabs respectively six feet by nine and five feet by nine cover the graves of Thomas Braithwaite of Kendal who died February 24th 1822 and William Herd of Milnthorpe who died 19th April 1822. A similar stone on the grave of William Simpson died 29th December 1830 has now disintegrated sufficiently so that the stone and brick lined vault can be seen clearly. Just to its south a limestone slab measuring four and a half feet by eight feet which is six inches thick over the grave of Mary wife of John Scott who died 21st July 1863 has been upturned and twisted round by earth movement caused probably by the roots of the adjacent beech tree. The largest tomb of all is that of James Gandy died December 26th 1842 aged 21, his father James died August 24th 1850 aged 69 and mother Annis died April 12th 1858 aged 65 in the centre of northern yard which measures ten feet by twelve. These large mid nineteenth century tombs show the failure of attempts to limit their size in 1831 which followed complaints recorded in the vestry book that 'the churchyard had been very shamefully cut up by narrow wheeled carts in bringing into it sundry large monumental stones'.[34]

Fortunately, though many are large, most monuments are restrained and there are few examples of the more florid excesses of Victorian funeral art. There are only about a dozen chunks of salami like Shap granite and there is a happy absence of green chippings, draped urns or weeping anglels. The only figurative sculpture is a wooden crucifix, whose arms are now missing, marking the grave of Eleanor Broughham who died 9th April 1925. Perhaps the most ornate monument is that erected in the north-east yard to the memory of Enoch Knowles of Milnthorpe who died 9th September 1895 which consists of a marble anchor cross emerging from a craggy base with a 'chain' also in marble looped round the left arm of the cross. Next to it is a slightly more demure rustic cross, covered with marble roses, over the grave of William Dobson of Bela View Milnthorpe who died 1895. Another eleborate monument is a seven foot high marble wheel head cross decorated with an Anglian rope motive but including the Latin I.H.S. in the axis which is in the northern yard. The leaded inscription on the base reads in affectionate memory of Mary Amelia Tribe who died at Levens Hall 1884 aged 73 who for many years was the valued friend in the family of the late Robert Thompson Crayshay of Cyfarthfa South Wales. 'Strength and honour are her clothing, she shall rejoice in the time to come 'Prov. XXXI.25'. The grave is enclosed by sandstone pinnacles surmounted by crosses between which hang decorative chains. A century of weathering and growth of lichen and mosses have spread a chaste veil of greeny grey over the white glare of the marble so that the cross now harmonizes with the adjacent limestone boundary walls and slate monuments.

*The Chained Cross*

Practice, in any English University, at Manchester.

Similarly a group of marble crosses and tombs, including several to the Grundy family, by the path in the eastern yard, which stand out conspicuously on postcard photographs of c.1920 are now stained black. Across the path a spray of marble lilies on stone erected to the memory of Agnes Lilian Dobson who died 11th April 1904 are covered now by bright yellow lichen - a triumph of nature over artificiality.

Indeed the yard is full of natural beauty. Daffodil time is best when both the eye is charmed by a Wordsworthian host rustling across the hummocky turf and the ear by a squabbling bird cacophony emanating from the billowy firs, yews and cherries in the northern yard raucously punctured by the cawing tenants of the chestnut trees by the lychgate at the south entrance. No birds live in the gorgeous copper beech that over shadows the east window but at its base are a family of Rooks! James Rooke died December 13th 1863, his wife Jane died July 20th 1870 and his brood who died young, Thomas died aged 14 on 10th June 1850, John 12th July 1849 aged 8 years, Robert died 20th September 1844 aged 3 weeks and James, their grandson, who died 4th October 1868 aged 2 weeks.

Occasionally vegetation seems to have protected the monuments; a sycamore sapling, for example, has kept clean the historically interesting inscription on the slate altar tomb in the eastern yard which reads

'Here Lieth John Yeates esq. of Parkland Levens and formerly of Kirkland Kendal who died December 23rd 1847 aged 51. A mark of the esteem in which he was held by his fellow townsmen he was elected the first Mayor of the Ancient Borough of Kendal after the passing of the Municipal Reform Act. Also in Memory of Margaret his wife who died September 29th 1847 aged 45 years.'[35] ***

Under the beech at the east end of the church is the pyramid monument to the Rev. Dr. George Lawson (Vicar of Heversham 1797-1842). During the severe frost of December 1981 the slate cladding was shattered to reveal the monument's red-brick and plaster core. The inscription, which acknowledges the setting, can still be read:

'Inter arbores aliis profuturas quas A.D. 1800 posuit mortale fuit Georgii Lawson Ec(clesiae) hujas plus quadruginta annis vicarii, dehinc autem [36]·meliora petentis obiit A.D. 1842 Aetatis 77.'

(Among the trees which being for the future he planted in A.D. 1800 for others is the Mortal (body) of George Lawson Vicar of this church for more than 40 years, hereafter seeking better things died A.D. 1842 aged 77.)

Dr. Lawson's successor as vicar of Heversham Archdeacon Robert Wilson Evans who died 10th March 1866 lies in a slate altar tomb elevated above the pathway in the eastern yard. Interred with him are his father Dr. John Evans died 18th January 1846 aged 91 and his sisters Jane Amelia died 8th June 1862 aged 77, Georgina Elizabeth died 31st August 1863 aged 75 and Frances Louisa died March 10th 1866 aged 76. Canon Thomas Morrell Gilbert died 16th December 1928 aged 93 is buried with his wife Esther Anne died 21st August 1917 aged 79 in the new yard. Their memorial cross has now broken but the inscription recording Canon Gilbert's incumbency 1866-1921 and that he had been a scholar of Westminster and

Fellow of Trinity College survives. In the northern yard a simple granite stone marks the grave of Wilfred Alec Cleghorn vicar of Heversham from 1939 until his death at the age of 60 on 27th December 1955 and of his wife Jesse who died, aged 86, on March 10th 1978. To their memory, in 1980, four cherry trees were planted by the Parochial Church Council along the main pathway. In 1982 the ashes of Rev. Tom Martin (Vicar of Heversham 1964-1976) were interred in the lawn by the south east door which since 1975 has been reserved for cremated remains. The names of persons whose remains are interred there are inscribed in a book kept, since 1981, in a glass case in the chancel by the vestry door.

There are several other clerical graves in the yard. The oldest such grave is an altar tomb in the northern yard. Its sides have now collapsed but the inscription survives recording the missionary adventures of

'the Rev. John Langhorn who in 1786 crossed the Atlantic Ocean to Upper Canada where he continued 27 years as a missionary in the Society of the Propagation of the Gospel in Foreign parts. Finally he closed his steady life at Natland Beck, near Kendal May 15th 1817 Aged 73 years. And of Martha his sister who died February 21st 1828 Aged 75 Years. And of the Rev. John Corry who died April 17th 1828 Aged 44 years...'[36]. **

By the south east door lies Rev. John Fisher Audland D.D. who died May 3rd 1861, while his nephew, another Rev. John, died 17th July 1926 aged 72 is buried in the north-east yard. Nearby are the graves of Rev. George Paul Davies 1868-1918, his father-in-law George Masham Argles, Canon of York, 1842-1920 and of Rev.Arthur John Smith the inscription on whose tomb stone states that he was

'incumbent of Levens 1864-1912, born September 16th 1834 Died July 28th 1912. He preached unto them Jesus and the Resurrection Acts XVII. 18'.

The Rev. Smith's predecessor's tomb is in the eastern yard close to that of Dr. Lawson. It is inscribed

'Here rests the body of the Reverend William Stephens, first incumbent of the chapelry of Levens, of which he was the faithful paster for 37 years, he died on 22nd of June 1864 aged 78 years. 'Looking unto Jesus' Heb. XII. 2.'[37]. ***

Close to the northern boundary wall on a memorial cross to

'Elizabeth widow ot the late Rev. James Cheadle Vicar of Bingley, Yorkshire who died at Arnside on the 7th February 1871 aged 72,'

is the motto later adopted by the R.A.F. *per ardua ad astra* (For through endeavour to the stars).

In the eastern yard the inscription on the cross over the grave of William Crane M.A. died December 17th 1903 Rector of St.George's Hume faces west indicating that the tradition was followed that a clergyman is buried westward facing his congregation,  whereas the laity face east towards Zion. This latter custom has had the effect that a line of grave stones along the eastern side of the path in the new yard have their inscriptions facing away from the passer by, although some have a rather official looking surname inscribed on the back. One of these graves is that of Rev. James Godfrey Spenser Vicar of Broughton-in-Furness who died at Heversham of 6th February 1976 aged 62.

On only a relatively few other gravestones are the rank and occupations of the deceased recorded. There appears to be no titled people buried in the yard other than the two Levens baronets Sir Josceline Fitzroy Bagot 1855-1913 and Sir Alan Desmond Bagot died 1920. Their blue granite tombs are in the northern yard by the entrance to the Levens Chapel. Lady Bagot's inscription on her husbands tomb beginning 'To my beloved Josceline ...' was copied on their husband's graves by several other widows in the next decade or so.

Sir Josceline's epitaph records that he had been a Captain in the Grenadier Guards and Sir Alan's that he was Lieutenant Royal Horse Guards 1916-1920'.

Several other tombs record warriors. In the north-east yard a War Graves Department's portland stone tombstone is inscribed

'J.Proctor Royal Army Medical Corps 29th June 1918 aged 29 also Sergeant E.Proctor D.C.M. aged 32 Faithful unto Death'

while in the newer yard is a similar stone marked

'6918 Private J.Atkinson South Wales Borderers 22nd March 1918 aged 18'.

A small shap granite stone by the north-east gate bearing the ATS badge marks the grave of Jean Binnie who died of an illness contracted during the Second World War on May 1st 1948 aged 23. Across the path to the east there is no reference to his rank of Brigadier on the grave of Edward Gordon Audland who died 22nd October 1976 aged 79 but the stone bears the Audland crest of the oak leaves surrounding a Cross of St.John.

A reminder of the port of Milnthorpe occurs on a slate tomb by the pathway in the northern yard which is inscribed: 'Sacred to the memory of Margaret Relict of the late Thomas Nunns of Milnthorpe Mariner who departed this life April 21st 1824, aged 75 years[38]. Nearby is the grave of John Reed who died on 21st January 1850 aged 60 years which states that he was parish and vestry clerk of Heversham for 23 years[39]. Similarly a tombstone in the south yard records that Robert Bindloss who died 14th June, 1847 aged 71 years states that he was 'sexton of this Parish 26 years'.[40] Also in the south yard are the tombstones recording 'John Thompson, formerly Collector of Excise, Cambridge who died March 17th 1857 aged 80 years',[41] of Thomas Hudlestone of Milnthorpe for many years Court Bailiff to the Hon. Fulke Greville Howard who died May 2nd 1829 aged 78 years,[42] and of Thomas Turner died January 26th 1844 aged 60 years. For upwards of 15 years he discharged the duties of Postmaster of Burton with strictness and integrity.'[43]

There are several monuments to domestic servants. They include Alexander Forbes who died February 23rd 1861 whose memorial cross, in the northern yard, states that he was ' a native of Culloden in Scotland, for 51 years in the service of the family of Howard at Levens Hall, by whom he was beloved and respected'.[44] In the eastern yard the monument to Hannah Lowthian of Kendal who died February 22nd 1836 aged 77 records that she was a faithful servant in the family of the late Mr. Thomas Greenhow of Kendal for more than fifty years'.[45] An almost unique tribute to a member of a school's non-teaching staff occurs on the grave, in the northern yard, of Elizabeth Chell which states that for '15 years she was the faithful and valued Housekeeper of the Rev. Dr. Hart at the Grammar School. She died January 14th 1897 aged 45'.

In the northern yard the tombstone of Thomas Wilson died February 1894 states that he was a joiner while on an appropriately well carved and maintained latin cross George Jackson's (1906-67) trade of stonemason is recorded. Otherwise there are no references to practical occupations.

Other than clergy the largest occupation group recorded on the gravestones are doctors of medicine. In the eastern yard are the tombs of 'James Burrow, surgeon Prestwich who departed this life the 5th of December 1851 in the 42nd year of his age', and of Robert Wilson M.R.C.S. of Laburnum House Milnthorpe who died 16th December 1856 aged 42 years[46]. In the southern yard lies John Audland M.R.C.S. who died 1892, while in the new yard the graves of three doctors, Malcolm Macleod of Milnthorpe who died on 30th April 1932 aged 52, Thomas Taylor Surgeon of Halifax who died on December 7th 1925 aged 51 and William Edward Audland M.B.E. 'Knight of Justice of St John Born October 19th 1859 Died July 31st 1950. Side by side in the north-eastern corner of the northern yard lie a distinguished eye surgeon William Barrie Brownlie M.R.C.S who died 22nd September 1970 and Professor Patrick Sarsefield Byrne C.B.E. (died 25th February 1980) who was a medical practiner in Milnthorpe from 1936 to 1966 before occupying the first chair of General Practice, in any English University, at Manchester.

In the northern yard close to the pathway is the grave of a brewer and millowner William Tattersall who was probably the richest man buried in the yard as he left over half a million pounds in 1895. The lengthy account in the 'Westmorland Gazette' of Tattersall's funeral provides a vivid picture of the Victorian way of death at its most sombre and sumptious.

Although he lived for half the year at Quarry Bank, Blackburn close to the family brewery and mills, he died at St.Anthony's House on the 25th November 1895. Accordingly on the day of the funeral a cortege 'fully 200 strong' conveyed in over thirty carriages, preceded by the 'grammar boys' on foot, processed the half mile to the church where the coffin 'which was of oak magnificently furnished' was received by a dozen clergy. It was borne then to the chancel as Miss Germain played on the organ 'I know that My Redeemer liveth'. An hour later at the end of the service the 'Dead March in Saul' was played. At the graveside a number of Mr. Tattersall's aged pensioners were assembled and the spectacle generally was a very pathetic one. The sides of the grave were beautifully covered in with moss, ferns, lilies, orchids and chrysanthemums ... and as the solemn strains of the Dead March (played by a Blackburn brass band) drifted sadly across the old churchyard tears glistened in many an eye and Mr. Whiteley M.P.' (husband of the deceased's only daughter who had inherited nine tenths of the fortune) 'was apparently greatly affected. The wreaths were desposited to one side and literally covered six graves ... the magnificent blooms contrasting strongly with the humble grass grown mounds over which they were scattered'.[47]

This is in fact poetic license as there are older monuments close by including the grave of his fellow industrialist James Woods of Rochdale, who died September 18th 1867. His daughters Margaret, died October 7th 1898, and, Mary died June 18th 1904, (who donated the church bells) are buried here also. With William Tattersall lies his first wife Ann who died June 14th 1863 aged 30 years. Their stone is now cracked while that of his father who died 17th March 1863 aged 75 and brother who died 8th December 1856 aged 27 years, both of whom were called Benjamin, have now disintegrated. Yet the Tattersalls have a more durable memorial in the six Almshouses built and endowed by William in 1884 at the cost of £10,000 'for those who have once occupied better positions in life but such who have been reduced through circumstances over which they have no control'.[48] Their situation on the west side of Church Street has been the reason why that part of Milnthorpe Civil parish has remained part of Heversham's ecclesiastical parish. Traditionally the vicar of Heversham is a trustee of the Tattersall Almshouses and Heversham parishioners have priority of allocation; the reverse is the case with regard to the Bindloss Homes on the east side of Milnthorpe.

There are many monuments with interesting or poetic inscriptions. Since c. 1940 epitaphs have come to be restricted to names and dates with perhaps a short, often assertive (if theologically uncertain) phrase like 'at rest' or 're-united'. Reminders of the sentiments of earlier times are rare. The stone in the new yard, to Annie Hamilton Mason died 1941 and her husband Arthur Davenport Mason died 1953, however, is inscribed:

'The Lord watch between thee and me while we are absent one from another' and 'Death is the shedding of the blossom that the fruit may appear'.

There are few Latin inscriptions, and the only complete one is in the new yard. On a cross placed on the ground is inscribed: Ego Sum RESURRECTIO ET VITA, 'I am the Resurrection and the Life', while round the curb are the words:

Requiescante in Pace Memoriam Caroli Paston Crane Qui Obiit Die Januarii MCMXXXIX? Tuie Mariae Aliciae Carolinae Uxoris Eius Dilectissimae Ob Prid Id Ian MCMXLIV.

(Let me rest in peace. In memory of Charles Preson Crane who died on a day of January 1939 (?) Of his most delightful wife Mary Alice Caroline who died the day before the same (month) of January 1946.)

A few yards away the curb surrounding the grave of Jessie Brownson who died June 23rd 1957 aged 71, and George Leigh Brownson who died January 16th 1965 aged 81, is inscribed in the archaic forms, from Spensers 'Fairy Queen'.

'Sleepe after toyle, Port after storm. Ease after payne, Death after life does greatly please'.

Some of the older epitaphs are grimly enigmatic: thus the slate by the south door reads 'Near this place lies the Body of William Whalley late of Accrington in the County Palatine of Lancaster who departed this life 11th February MDCCLXXXVI (1786) aged LXV (65). What kind of man he was the last Day will discover'.[49] ***

To its east a sandstone tombstone is inscribed to 'James Hardman of Millthorp Mills, who departed this life 12th July MDCCLXXVI (1776) in the LXII (62nd) year of his age.

'Farewell vain world I've had enough of thee
Nor care I now what Thou canst say of Me
What I have done amiss take care to shun.
Here thus be warned before thy glass is run'.[50] **

Curiously in the north yard the verse on the tombstone of John Hunter of Sedgwick, who died March 2nd 1833 aged 37, has the same opening couplet but includes:

'Thy smiles I court not, nor thy frowns I fear,
My cares are past, my head lies quiet here'.[51] **

Equally grim are the words on the altar tomb in the south yard of William Docker who died on 28th November aged 58:

'All ye that come my tomb to see
When you read it pray think on me
Repent in time make no delay
I in my glory was snatched away'.[52] ***

Death's suddeness is also the theme on the epitaph, in the north west corner of the southern yard, to William Webster who died January 10th 1851 aged 92:

'To me't was given to die. to Thee't is giv'n
To live: Alas! one moment sets us ev'n
Mark! how impartial is the Will of Heav'n'.

A similar reminder is on the grave, by the north east corner of the church, of Anthony Gregg, died December 16th 1835 aged 64 and his wives Mary, died January 7th 1816 aged 43, and Elizabeth died August 8th 1862 aged 82:

'We rest beneath, in dust of death
His fatal dart we could not shun
Mortal! prepare, with earnest care,
Thy race, like ours, must soon be run'.[54] ***

A precise record of birth and death is recorded on the tombstone, in the east yard, of Hannah Greenhow which states that 'she was born at High House, Stainton, on Shrove Tuesday 1801, her sweet spirit departed heavenwards at early dawn on the 7th day of March 1875'.[55]

There are several monuments to death from drowning. In the north yard near the Gandy vault there is a sandstone cross set up 'by their schoolfellows to George Cowell of Lydgate aged 18, here buried Edmund J Goodwin of Manchester aged 19 and Richard T M Rigby of Chorley aged 15, drowned while bathing on the sands August 30th 1855'.[56] ***

The stone on the next grave but one tells more extravagantly the same sorry story:

'Here lies the remains of Thomas Barker who was drowned in crossing Milnthorpe sands on the 21st June 1815. Interred July 8th aged 18. He was the third son of Daye and Elizabeth Barker of Low Wood in the Parish of Cartmel. Amiable lamented youth: Heaven endowed thee with a strong comprehensive mind, and a guileless simplicity of Disposition. In thee we thought to have seen the Man of Worth but thy course was brought to a sudden Period by Him whose Decrees are sometimes insemlable yet ever merciful. What is our consolation? Even the exalted Hope of Immortality through Jesus Christ.'[57] ***

Perhaps the most tragic story is revealed (rather confusingly) on the altar tomb in the south yard to:

'Jane the loving and beloved wife of Mr. John Dickinson of Milnthorpe. She departed this life April MDCCLXX (1770) aged 43 years. As also Four Children Agnes 9th December 1763, Richard 12 August 1767, Elizabeth 25th March 1768, Birkbeck 10th August 1770. Drowned in bathing aged 1½ years, 6 years, 14 days, 11 years, (respectively). Mr. John Dickinson, Husband and Father of the above died August the 10th MDCCLXXIII (1783), Aged 62 years.'[58] ••

Nearby on the Scott tomb is a record of a more common domestic tragedy:

'Elizabeth wife of Joseph Singleton of Lancaster died in childbed 10th August 1783 aged 39 years ... also her infant son Joseph who left this world seven weeks after his fatal birth.'[59] •••

Also in south yard the epitaph to Thomas Briggs died aged seven 23rd March 1826 reads:

'the opening buds of youth, manhoods blooming prime Death withers by his blast. The fullblown flowers of age are culled by time at last.'[60] ••

Longer verses proclaim the same theme on the Holme family's altar tomb close to the pathway in the northern yard:

'Sacred to the memory of Robert Holme third son of Bryan and Mary Holme of Ninezergh in this Parish who died 30th July 1830 aged 18 years.

Grieve not that early death consign'd

My body to the grave;

The stroke in mercy was design'd

From future ills to save

Rejoice that when time's weary bound

No more confines this clay

The soul immortal will be found

In realms of endless day.'

His sorrowing Parents caused this stone to be erected to record the loss of a dutiful and affectionate son. Sacred also to the memory of John Holme son of Bryan and Mary Holme of Ninezergh who died 11th January 1836 aged 33. He left a widow and two infant children to deplore his loss. Tho' in the prime of life his work was done. Heaven so approved and blest, And took his soul to everlasting rest, Weep not for those who live an endless day, But bless the Hand that gives and takes away ...'[61] ••

A longer catalogue of child mortality is shown on a tombstone in the northern yard:

'Sacred to the memory of Elizabeth, infant Daughter of John and Maria Whittam of Milnthorpe who died December 29th 1835 And of Jane their Daughter who died May 10th 1837 Aged 4 years and 4 months. Also of James their son who died July 10th 1842 aged 5 years and 6 months. And of Mary Ann Whittam Daughter of the above who died September the 9th 1851 aged 5 years and 5 months. Also of Isabella Whittam who died August 30th 1853 Aged 5 years 3 months'.[62]••

A mother's farewell is inscribed on a grave in the northern yard belonging to Ann wife of John Gerrard of Milnthorpe who died 12th February 1799 Aged 45.

'She was A tender loving Wife, And an Indulgent Parent.

Weep not for me my children dear,

I am not dead, but sleepeth here,

Our time flies swift and soon will be,

That you and all must follow me.'

A lament for both parents is on an altar tomb nearby:[63] 'In memory of William Shaw of Milnthorpe who died May 14th 1855 aged 63 years:

A faithful friend a husband dear

A tender father lieth here,

Great was the loss we did sustain

But hope through Christ to meet again

Also of Elizabeth his widow who died October 13th 1867 aged 75 years

Weep not for me, my race is run

It was the Lord, His will be done.'[64] ***

Another tribute to a father is to John Stuart of Aynside near Cartmel (died March 4th 1845 aged 58) who is buried with three infant sons in the northern yard:

'Rest from thy toil, thy life of care is o'er

Rest with thy children dear from sorrow free

On earth, through cold and heat thou now no more

A way worn weary wanderer shalt be

Thy Partner yet surviving mourns her fate,

Unaided by thy help she still must roam

Hoping erelong to quit this toilsome state

And join thee in thy silent peaceful home.

Also Ann Stuart who died December 10th 1866 aged 80 years.' So she had a wait of 21 years![65] **

A similar theme is inscribed on the tomb, in the south yard, of 'Joseph Noble who departed this life 10th of July 1782 aged 62. He was kind friend, a tender Father, a loving Husband his Wife hath placed this stone over him from a grateful remembrance of their past love.

'O! cruel Death that wou'd no longer spare

Moving Husband, tender partner dear, Great is the loss to me now left behind

But I'm in hope eternal Joy he'll find.'[66]

A pun as well as simplistic sentiment and rhyme are attempted on the epitaph on the tomb, in the north yard, to Warham Jemmett Browne Esq. who died December 31st 1861 at Heversham House aged 79 years ...

'Another Gem in the Saviour's Crown

Another Star in Heaven.'[67]

Britain's imperial past is echoed in several inscriptions. Under a yew in the new yard lies Mary Mesner died 16th September 1920 aged 53, wife Charles Mesner of Hong Kong. On a cross in the north eastern yard is recorded the death of James Eldest son of Alfred and Mary Grundy, June 7th 1882 at Yokohama Japan aged 35 years.' Nearby close to the gate an inscription in bronze running along the high curb bordering the Swindlehurst family grave tells of the fruitful journeys of Jane Swindlehurst who (with her husband Henry 1820-1895) in 1855 'sailed round Cape Horn with three children and after visiting the coast of Peru' retuned in 1859 with five children; Mary and Juanita having been born at Valparaiso to Hincaster House where 'she bore a short but severe illness with exemplary resignation until on the 22nd August 1883 the Lord took her into Everlasting rest.'

The longest journey a corpse has made to Heversham must be that (recorded on a cross surmounting a large vault in the north east yard,) of Lt. Col. Alfred Dixon R.H.A. died at Kasauli India 16th May 1882 brought here 2nd February 1884.'

Finally, the tombstone, by the Lychgate in the south yard, of Esther the beloved wife of Paul Derome who departed this life October 23rd 1866 in the 59th year of her age' tells how she did not leave Heversham according to her own plan:

'It was on the eve of leaving

This native home of mine

To join a loving son

In a far distant clime

But by death was overtaken

My race of life was run,

It was God's will that I should go,

So farewell, farewell, dear son.'[68]

## Notes and References to Sources  Chapter VIII

1. Curwen History of Heversham with Milnthorpe p.22
2. see above
3. Memories Mrs. M.Tyson and others.
4. John and Marie Byrne d. 1962 and 1967
5. Vestry book (H)
6. Ibid
7. Westmorland Gazette 19 February 1895
8. Vestry Book (H)
9. In possession of Mr. H.Kilnshaw.
10. Book of Accounts (H)
11. Vestry Book (H)
12. Ibid
13. Ibid
14. Westmorland Gazette 1900
15. Vestry Book (H)
16. P.C.C. Minutes.
17. Ibid
18. Westmorland Gazette 12 August 1975.
19. Westmorland Gazette 13 August 1982.
0. Vestry Book (H)
21. CRO(K) WPR/8
22. Westmorland Gazette April 1920
23. Survey made by author August 1975, checked August 1982.
24. Bellasis
25. Burial Register (H)
26. Monuments in good condition are marked ***. Reasonable (most of inscription) legible **. Poor, damaged monument; inscription just discernible for identification in Bellasis *.
27. Bellasis ref. to Heversham are contained in Westmorland Church Notes. Specific references to graves are:
27. p.241-242
28. p.260.

## CHAPTER IX

# Parish and Church Government the Churchwardens and the Council of Twenty-Four

The Memorandum which recorded the fire of 1601[1] was mainly concerned with the ancient administrative structure of the parish as recalled by the oldest inhabitants. Their testimony was taken in 1622 forty years or so after the drawing up of a formal agreement which had been destroyed in the fire. As seen by the number of Churchwardens and Swornmen who could only make their remarks in the Book of Accounts, early seventeenth century society was largely illiterate. Therefore, the memorandum illustrates also the difficulties which rose when a vital document had been lost and a copy had not been made.

## The Post-Fire Memorandum

After the preamble recalling how 'all other things were perished' in the fire the memorandum continues:

'Concerning which things there was an Awarde indented the date wherof we have not in perfect memory, yet we thinke that it was aboute the yeare of Christe 1580 Maide betweene the Inhabitants of Crostwhat and Lithe being a hamlet of the same Parishe, on there partie and the Inhabitants of the other hamlets of the sid Parishe on the other partie Awarded by the right worshipfull Sir Thomas Boynton knight, and Rowland Phillipson Esqre touching certain Questions, Artickles, suites & Controversies then depending Amongst them. The articles whereof we whose names are hereunto subscribed, thought meet and convenient to expresse and sett down so neare as our memories doo extende unto. First ordered and awarded that the said Inhabitants of Crostwhat and Lythe by their Churchwardens and swornmen shall yearly upon New Years even make their accomptes and Reconings at Hevsham churche for all matters and receipted for the benefite of the said churche and yearly pay suche summes of money as shall fall dewe to the Churche to the other Churche- wardens of Heversham And allso shall pay towardes the stipend and wages of the Parishe Clerke of Heversham yearly on New Yeares even, the somme of 17s. And also shall pay for every Corpes being buried above the Queare wall at Crostwhat 2 shillings and threepence And for every Corpse being buried beneathe the Queare wall 20 pence Allso ordered and Awarded, that when anie Questions Quilibet an proportion shall be born and imposed for the necessary reparacions of the Churche of Heversham, the said inhabitants of Croswhat and Lithe shall answere beare and paie a full quarter or fourthe parte of the same, so oft as need shall requyre. Allso ordered and awarded, that the said inhabitants of Croswhat and Lithe shall appoint and name two sufficient men in their hamlets to serve as churchwardens at Heversham church yearly and six others to be sworn as assistants to make upp the number of twenty-four sworne men. And the said Churchwardens and sworne men to joine with the other churchwardens and sworne men of the said Parishe in all things needful and necessary for the said churche and all waies to be appointed on Newe Years Even, and to take those oathes on the fifthe day of January, being the Twelth even, at the said Churche of Heversham accordingly as hathbeen accustomed, and accordinge to the intent and meaninge of the said Award. And because the said Inhabitants of Crostwhat and Lythe do say and alledge that their Award cannot be founde, and our Awarde was consumed with fyre we thought very meet to declare our knowledge touching the same. And in testimony wherof our Names are herunto subscribed the Fifth day of January.

1622 Perused and Redde divers and sundry tymes
By me Thomas Parke'.

Ane same Awarde was seene and redde unto these which are yet livinge Vizt Peter Smythe. Richard Gibson, Walter Levens, Richard Preston, Richard Banks, Richard

Nicolson, Roger Lyndeth and others.[2]

The Council of Twenty-Four was also known as the 'Marksmen', a Teutonic derivation, which was probably a descendent of the Anglo-Saxon village assembly as was also the Grand Jury.[3] By 1601 the Twenty-Four were concerned primarily with worship, church repairs and finance but a number of civil functions were exercised by them until the local government reforms of the nineteenth century.

### The Oaths

Their Book of Accounts which begins immediately after the fire is a particularly rich and valuable source for the social as well as religious history of the parish. It records in the seventeenth century the oaths of the church wardens and sidesmen that continued to be administered in more or less the same form until modern times:

'You shall take upon you the office of Churchwarden and, to the utmost of your power, shall faithfully and truly execute the same. You shall carefully with all your endeavours seek to maintain the good and benefit of this church and observe and keep all such orders, as hereto fore have been in force. And according to former order, at the year's end you shall give up a true and perfect account of all your expenses and receipts whatsoever,

As God help you'.

'You shall take upon you the office of Sidesmen, and at all times upon lawful warning given shall assist the Church wardens in any thing, and upon any occasions which they make for the good and benefit of the church

So help you God'.[4]

The Churchwardens and Swornmen, or Sidesmen, were from the mid-seventeenth century chosen at the annual vestry meeting held on either Easter Monday or Easter Tuesday. Sometimes a Michaelmas meeting was held in addition to special meetings to discuss repairs. At the Michaelmas meeting, on 20th September 1603, it was decided to impose fines for not attending meetings: 'Agreed by the Churchwardens and 24 this year, that whatsoever being sworn for the Churche shall not absent himself at any meeting for the business of the Church having notice, shall forefeit for every default 12d. except (on) lawful business'.[5]

Those attending were supplied with ale and they could claim expenses. In the early eighteenth century exorbitant expenses were recorded. For example the 'Easter Munday' expenses of 1720 and 1721 were respectively £2.8s.6d and £2.1s.5d, while expenses at an irregular meeting held 'when the 24 met to consider what was necessary for repairs to the Church were 19s.6d. This was at a time when a quart of ale cost 2d. The work decided on was scarcely more expensive and included 'flags for the Church door' 4s.9d... 'Henry Hudson 3 days work 3s'... 'Chris. Parker's bill for new glass 10s.10d' and a load of 'gravel' from Kendal 1s.[6]                    1s.[6]

*The 15th Century
Vestry Door*

93

A scale of maximum expenditure was eventually fixed on December 17th 1722:

'Memorandum the day and year above written. We the twenty four men of the Parish of Heversham, to fix and settle the charges and expenses of public meeting relating to Church affaires and likewise to put an end to some former diffrences that lately arose concerning the said Expenses, do now Unanimously agree, that for the future at all meetings, when it shall be thought necessary for the twenty four men to meet, there shall be an allowance of six pence per man, for the Churchwardens and twenty four men: or for as many of the Churchwardens and twenty four men as shall at such meetings attend - And likewise if there shall be occasion for any necessary repairs that the agreements be made at some of the public meetings, and attested by so many of the twenty four men as are then present: And likewise we agree that at the visitation the old and new Churchwardens and Parish Clerk shall have an allowance of twelve pence per man and no more - as witness all our hands

| | | |
|---|---|---|
| James Parke | Wm. Johnson | Rich Lancaster |
| Ja. Backhouse | Robert Moore | John Knipe |
| Geo. Croft | John Hodgson | James Scott |
| Nick Robinson | Edward Backhouse | Chris. Cowper.[7] |
| Chris Ffletcher | Wm. Watson | Thomas Harrison (?) |
| | John·Preston | Nichlos Dickson (?) |
| | Tho. Robinson | |
| | Tho. Preston | |
| | Matthew Willson | |
| | James Borrow | |
| | Rich. Dowker | |

The intention of the memorandum seems to have been followed for the 'Easter Munday' expenses of 1723 amounted to only 12s. Nevertheless special meetings to discuss maintenance continued. Thus in 1725 are recorded 'Expenses when the 24 met to consider what money was necessary to be raised and to bargain with the workman for Roughcasting the Church Steeple Inside and Outside 16s'. For the work itself Robert Bindloss was paid in 1726 £14.00. Typical subsequent expenses were: 1726, 'Expenses total on Easter Monday at Roger Prestons 18s.00' '1727, given Thomas Ffischer and four other Crosthwaite men 3s' ... 1755, To Crosthwaite men for their Expenses on Easter Monday 2s.6d, paid 17 of this side of the Moss for their expenses 8s.6d ... 1804, Churchwardens Eating and Ale £1.5.8d, Horses Hay of 6d.4s, Dr.Lawsons' (the vicar) dinner 2s.d. and 1814, 'Wine and Liquer' on Easter Monday £1.5s.1d'[8]

### The Churchwardens

In 1601 the Churchwardens were chosen for the five hamlets: Heversham, Levens, Stainton, Preston Richard and Crosthwaite and Lyth. Milnthorpe was substituted for Heversham in 1670 though Churchwardens continued to be chosen from Heversham to represent both places. In 1827 this area was re-named 'Heversham and Milnthorpe' or 'Heversham with Milnthorpe'. At about the same time the former hamlets were called townships. From 1827 the Levens Churchwardens were joined by wardens from Hincaster and Sedgwick and the office appears to have rotated amongst representatives of these townships. In 1916 Sedgwick ceased to be represented as by that time it formed (with Stainton) part of the independent parish of Crosscrake. Nominally Levens and Milnthorpe continued to have a Churchwarden until the retirement of Canon Gilbert in 1921, after which time the separation of these areas from Heversham was acknowledged formally. From then on the Churchwardens have been elected to represent the 'districts' of Heversham, Hincaster and Preston Richard although representatives do not need to live in their particular district. Preston Richard is almost an anomaly as much of the hamlet's former area is part of Preston Patrick. Hincaster, though an independent Civil Parish, is entirely within the ecclesiastical parish of Heversham.

Churchwardens for Crosthwaite and Lyth are not recorded for 1628, 1629, 1636, 1657, 1672-75, 1679, 1745-50, or between 1753-1823. They are then recorded until 1865 when Crosthwaite and Lyth became independent.

Generally there were two Churchwardens for Crosthwaite and Lyth and one for each of the other four places. There are variations in the traditional representation during the *Interregnum* c.1640-1660 with two Churchwardens for each hamlet and occasionally three for Crosthwaite and Lyth. Two Churchwardens are also recorded for all hamlets in 1701-1705. There are no entries of any kind for 1648, 1649 or 1650 and the names of Churchwardens were omitted in 1697.

Until the early nineteenth century it was rare for the office of Churchwarden to be held by the same person in successive years. Churchwardens were often chosen in rotation from among occupants of certain properties, many of which are named. Some of these occur regularly including Greenside, Halforth (Hayforde), Mabbin Hall, Old Hall and Parkhead. Others like 'the cotton factory' which Thomas Howson of Stainton represented in 1804 have disappeared or like 'Pissmire Hill' at Barrows Green, represented by John Dawson in 1789, have been renamed. From about 1730 it became common for the landlord or tenant of a property, whose turn it was to provide a churchwarden, to nominate a substitute to fill the office. This is recorded in various ways e.g. 1730 'Thomas Turner for Widow Wilson's Estate,' 1734 'Edward Backhouse hired with Thomas Scott' and 1789 'John Wakefield's Estate at Sedgwick John Adisson serves'.

As in the case of names in the Parish Register allowance has to be made for variation in spelling e.g. Brigges/Briggs, Cock/Cork, Cornthwhait/Cornthwaite, Garnett/Garnitt/Garnott, Hodshon/Hodgson, Parke/Parker and for different families with the same common surname especially Atkinson and Wilson. Even so the recurrance of surnames (sometimes with the same Christian names) over several generations, indicates the retention by the same families of the status of landowner, yeoman or substantial tenant from whose ranks Churchwardens invariably were drawn until the twentieth century. Thus the Preston family provided 41 wardens between 1602-1834, the Parke(r)s 33 between 1605-1854, Cornthwaites 24 between 1625-1819. Backhouses 18 between 1604-1765 and Bensons 15 between 1601 and 1828. Some families, while appearing regularly in the lists of 24 sworn men, only rarely achieved the status of Churchwarden. For example the Audlands provided only 9 Church-wardens in the seventeenth and eighteenth centuries. The Audland's non-appearance in the churchwardens list in the early and mid nineteenth century was caused by social advancement rather than decline for members of the family entered the Church and learned professions which took them away from the area until retirement. It was after he retired that Dr. John Audland was continuously Churchwarden from 1879 to 1891. Similarly the Pricketts, a family like the Audlands still resident in the area, only provided wardens in 1601, 1742, 1813, 1899, 1900 and 1901. Some fairly notable local families only provided one Churchwarden throughout the period. An example is Simon Washington Churchwarden for Crosthwaite and Lyth in 1693. He was reputedly a colateral descendent of the same ancestors as President George Washington.

By the same criteria the Churchwardens lists reflect the social decline or disappearance of a family. Thus the Brigge and Cock families provided respectively 16 and 11 churchwardens in the seventeenth century but only one in the eighteenth century.

During the nineteenth and twentieth centuries Churchwardens frequently served in successive years and, moreover, often came from the same family. Thus for Crosthwaite and Lyth Robinson, John and James Cartmel were Churchwardens between 1823 and 1848 and William Simpson and John Dixon were Churchwardens respectively between 1847-1862 and 1851-1865. Between 1866 and 1900 William W.Rutledge (or Ruttlidge) was churchwarden for Preston Richard. He was succeeded by Thomas Inman who held the office until 1915. Other long serving Churchwardens in recent times have included Thomas Atkinson Argles 1892-1923, Henry Sisson 1924-1938 and Fred Astley 1929-1951. Between 1965 and 1979 the three Churchwardens were continuously Norman George Kilshaw, John Thompson Sowerby and William Brockbank Dawson.[4] Since the Second World War the disappearance of paid functionaries like the Clerk and Sexton has meant that additional duties have devolved upon the Churchwardens, especially in making necessary arrangements for day-time weekly activites including funerals. As most members of the congregation have their day time occupation out of the village it has become convenient for the Churchwardens to be retired people and, indeed, most post-war holders of the office have been senior citizens. Fortunately in all cases the duties have been carried out with vigour as well as dedication. In 1983 the Churchwardens were Norman George Kilshaw, John Thompson Sowerby and Malcolm Sisson - each of whose father had previously held the office. So far there has been no female Churchwarden though lady sidesmen (not 'sidespersons') have been appointed.[9]

## The Parochial Church Council

One of the major changes in church organisation during the twentieth century was the introduction of Parochial Church Councils, which took over most of the responsibility of the vestry meetings. At Heversham there appears to have been no formal inauguration of a Parochial Church Council. In 1911 a member of 'lay communicants' met to choose representatives to the Rurideaconal meetings and an annual register of 'signatories in connexion with the status of Lay Communicants' was made from then on.[10] The first official meeting was on 5th January 1920 when Canon Gilbert stated that although the duties and powers of a P.C.C. were 'still to a great extent undefined it was possible to meet for purposes of consultation about the spiritual good of the parish' - especially as 'followers of Satan were active enough and the followers of Christ should be active too.' He knew of 'several who seldom or never come to church and more who never attend Holy Communion.'[11] For the first four meetings worship was the major item on the agenda. There was discussion as to whether the litany should be said or sung more often, whether there should be a course of sermons on spiritual needs and whether 'something should be done to make the farm lads feel they were not forgotten by having once a month a special service for them.'[12] In fact the litany was omitted from Holy Communion in 1922, special 'spiritual' sermons were dropped 'as scarcely going to the root of the matter' while there is no record of separate provision being made for 'farm lads', nor of their being consulted about the proposal. Unease was also voiced about the 'habit of non-communicants leaving before the consecration' and it was decided to hold a midday celebration every second Sunday when there would be a 'brief' sermon and only three hyms at Matins.

In 1922 it was laid down that Persons over 18 could be on the Electoral Roll provided they were 'active communicants', which the council agreed should be taken to mean those 'who (unless prevented by illness) had received Holy Communion not more than a year ago.' This mild condition was, however, often broken and several council members were not even confirmed. Unitl the Second World War there were fewer than a hundred names on the Electoral Roll. After a recruiting drive, the number reached 253 in 1949 but dropped to 232 in 1966. In the 1920's there were only six councillors plus three wardens. In the 1930's the number was about 12, in 1940 18 and from 1970 24. At first, following the precedent of the old churchwardens, meetings took place only at Easter, Whitsun, Harvest and Christmas. They became bimonthly by 1939 and since the 1960's have been held every month except August - probably more a reflection of increased bureaucracy rather than of religious fervour.

Women have always been well represented. In 1922 Misses Hilda and Sybil Austin were members of the first properly constituted council. Often there have been more women than men and in 1942 12 out of 14 ex-officio members were women. Presumably at this date the men were pre-occupied by the war. Apart from this between 1939 and 1945 the P.C.C. minutes hardly refer to the supreme cataclysm of the twentieth century and show instead peacetime and peaceable concern with the minutiae of money matters and maintenance. In 1940, however, it was agreed that the 'church tower be left unlocked at night in case of incendiary bombs and that Messrs. Allen, Varley, P.Tyson would act as bell ringers if an emergency made ringers necessary'. It was suggested that further efforts be made towards demolishing ugly, iron railing in the church-yard.' These were taken away in 1943 when the P.C.C. received £6 for the scrap.[13]

The bells were rung to celebrate El Alamein in 1942 and ringing every Sunday was resumed from July 1944. Although the church lacked blackout Evensong continued and in the service register the Reverend Cleghorn recorded the time as being 6.30 p.m. even in winter when all visible light should have been extinguished. However some parishioners recall that services were held in the afternoon in winter.[14] With the exception of the suggestion which was not carried through that the 'Saxon cross be put inside the church for the duration' no other precautions were made other than the purchase of a fire extinguisher.[15]

Although the Reverend Ellis introduced opening and closing prayers at meetings in 1922, discussion of spiritual matters by the P.C.C. has been almost totally eclipsed by the dark shadow of finance, repairs (especially of the organ), the churchyard which was never considered to be in a satisfactory state, and additions to fabric. Reference to worship has taken the form of complaints that the congregation was 'too feeble in singing',[16] that the 'choir did not give sufficient lead', that services were lacking in variety or were too long and that the Grammar School Boys did not take part or did not behave properly.

Liturgical differences were mild. The controversy associated with the adoption of the Revised Prayer Book by Convocation in 1928 and its rejection by the non-Anglican majority in the House of Commons was debated at a special P.C.C. meeting on 14th November 1929. After it had been ascertained that the Bishop had sanctioned the 1928 book it was decided to use it for Matins and Evensong but to follow the Old Form at 8.30 Holy Communion. A similar compromise was made in 1979 when the P.C.C. agreed, rather tardily, to the introduction of Series Three Family Communion. This followed a call by the vicar for 'spiritual awareness in Heversham' and for the P.C.C. to recognise that 'it was in a missionary situation with a need to explore types of service needed for a complete family of worship'. Taking up the call that 'the spiritual side of our democracy needed always to come first', the P.C.C. decided to ask for views on services from everyone on the Electoral Roll. There were 50 replies and of these 23 were for the 1662 Book of Common Prayer, 24 in favour of Series III and 2 said they would agree to Series III if others did; one did not know. A very Anglican compromise was worked out with the 1662 Holy Communion at 8 a.m. and at Matins held once a month with Series III at other services, including Family Communion on the second and fourth Sundays.[17]

Evensong at 6.30 p.m. was dealt a blow by the television series of the 'Forsyte Saga'[18] in 1968-69 but continued until the three-day-week heating restriction of 1974 led to its being abandoned. Musical evening services instead were held occasionally including 'Songs of praise services' at which hymns requested by sections of the congregation e.g. Mothers Union, Bellringers, were sung.

## THE PARISH REGISTER
### The Older Register c.1601-1800

The Heversham parish registers provide invaluable material for the local and family historian as well as being indispensable to the demographer. Any register kept in accordance with the ordinance of Thomas Cromwell of 1538 must have been burnt in the fire of 1601. As the parish chest in the vestry, the normal home for documents, survived they must have been kept in the main body of the Church at the time of the disaster. Thus the earliest entry is the baptism of 'Jacobus fil Jarasi Hind' on 6 September 1601.[19] There is then a gap until 1605, when the baptism is recorded of 'Richard fil Gulielmus Holme de Mylethrop'. The marriage entries start with Thomas Benson to Agnes Clovely on 28 June 1605 and the burial entries with Margaret wife of Robert Bell on 7 September 1605.

Until the Gregorian calendar was adopted in 1752 the register kept to the old style Julian year with New Year's Day being on 25th March. There are many gaps in the register and there is no regular detailed form of registration until 1780, the longest gap is of 10 years missing after 1667 and unfortunately the bishop's transcripts (contemporary copies of parish register entries sent to the diocesan registry each year) are missing also from 1667 to 1697 except for 1676, 1682 and 1690. Entries are relatively few during the Civil War and Commonwealth periods and between 1648 and 1660 less than six marriages are recorded each year compared with an average of 14 marriages annually between 1605 an 1640 and 12 annually in the 1660's. Only about 12 baptisms per year are registered between 1645 and 1660 compared with around 40 per annum in the 1630's. Perhaps the abolition of the Church of England during the Interregnum contributed to the reduction. However, as there is no general evidence of a fall in the death rate in the 1650's the register's annual average of about 20 burials during that decade compared with twice that number in the 1630's and 1660's must be the result of bad book-keeping during the incumbencies of the Presbyterians Samuel Cole, Richard Tatham and John Wallace.

The original registers are in a very poor condition and many entries are illegible. Fortunately there is a beautifully written parchment copy compiled in 1780 by John Preston of 'all that can be found or is legible of the old register'. There is also a copy of this transcription made in exercise books in the 1940's.

In the early 17th century entries are made in 'dog latin' e.g. May 1618 'Elizabetha filia supposita (supposed daughter) Thomae Benson jurioris'. English is used from c.1625 e.g. 'Edward and Margaret twinnes children of John Preston' until the incumbency of Thomas Bigge (1638-1645). He (or his clerk) tried his hand at fairly elaborate Latin and frequently dated entries by saints' days such as 'In festo Michaelis'. From the Interregnum onwards, entries are in English except around 1710 when the registers are embroidered with such terms as 'Pater familias', 'adoloscentula', Juvenis', 'infans' and, in the sole reference to health, 'idiota' noted after the burial entry of John Crossfield in 1712. Quaint English terms like 'sojourner', 'wench' and 'bastard' (instead of spurious or supposed child) also appear as in 1711 'William a bastard born by Moll Holme'. The death of the clerk is recorded on February 13th 1723 'John Croft who had been clerk of ye parrishe upwards 50 years'.

*Translation of a page from the Church wardens Accounts of 1603 opposite.*

*Edward Willson (righthand collumn) Was the founder of Heversham Grammar School.*

*September 20 1603*
*Agreed by the churchwardens and 24 this*
*year that whosoever being sworn for the*
*churche shall not absent himself at any meeting*
*for the business of the church having*
*notice, shall forfeit for every default 12d. except (on)*
*lawful business.*

| **Churchwardens** | **The 24** | |
|---|---|---|
| *Edward Saul* | *Peter Smythe* | P |
| *Gervase Gill* | *Richard Gibson* | |
| *John William* | *Christopher Fletcher* | |
| *Roger Cragge* + | *Edward Willson* | EW |
| | *Nicholas Benson* | |
| | *Jeffrey Parke* | IP |
| *Anthony Ayray* | *Christopher Bindloss* | |
| *Edward Gyll* | *Arthur Willisson* | |
| *Richard Holme* | *Allan Prickett* | |
| *Thomas Brigge* TB | *Rowland Greenhowe* | |
| *Thomas Parke* | *William Birkett* | |
| | *Walter Sympson* | |
| *The Order above said to stand* | *Richard Speight* | |
| *in full force from tyme to tyme* | *Edward Willson* | |
| *hereafter so that every sworn man* | *Richard Banks* | |
| *have warning from the churchwardens* | *Walter Preston* | |
| *of every hamlett besides open warnings* | *Thomas Benson* | |
| *in the Churche.* | *Edward Fingis* | |

*Walter Barkehouse* <

*29th day of Mai 1604*
*Mem the dai and yeare above written of the Composition*
*touchine the Chappelle of Crosthwaite was read openly in the Parish*
*Church of Heversham at the High altar according to the dir*
*-ection of the same composition which day above said was*
*Tuesday in Whitsuntide Week.*

September 21, 1603

Agreed by the Churchwardens &c. this
yeare, that whosoever being a Townesman be
tause of penalty, absent him selfe at any meetinge
for the busines of the Church havinge notice shall
forfeit for everie defaulte iiijd except
lawfull busines

Churchwardens                    xxmj li

Edward Sewell                    Peter Smith
Ferbisse Hill                    Richard Gibson
John Wilson                      Chrofer Aldersey
Roger Gregge                     Edmund Wilson
                                 Richard Obenson
                                 Roger paull
                                 Chrofer Rynoldes
                                 Arthur Williamson
Anthony Ryans                    Alton Curbett
Edward Syll                      Rowland Swanesford
Richard Holme                    William Rynkill
Thomas Brigge                    Walter Symson
                                 Richard Spencer
Thomas parke                     Edward Watson
                                 Richard Bamde
                                 Walter Prestwid
                                 Thomas Benson
The order aforesaid to stand    Edward Fifre
in full force by the         
herafter at their enter ground   Walter Barke
Johm theis meetinge a deferring
this Presoden of theis Paule the
keeped open meetinge in the 
church

The xxix daie of May 1604
Md that the deane and chapter of theis Compa shire
townshipe the Harvest of Crossmills vee will uphold
in their giste of theis of Overston at the gyste
illowe, the mill theis the Ill directions of theis Compa
in their daie at the same have sett it in the same use

Spelling lacks standardisation so that it is hard to decide whether similar names refer to the same or different families. Examples include Ayray and Airie, Crag and Craig, Helme and Holme (e's and o's also look alike in most hands), Ionson and Johnson and Nelson and Nealson.

Place names are appended to some entries perhaps to distinguish between families with the same name. Their spelling is equally varied. Examples with date of registration include: Augethwaite 1620, Aukenthwaite 1641, Aukinthwaite 1641, Ayekenthart 1662; Beathwat Green 1640, Burchwayt Greene 1641, Bethet Greene 1660, Bethel Greene 1680; Deepthwaite 1661, Depthaite 1665, Thendmor 1630, Eane Moore 1646, Fowleshate 1666, Hayforde 1630, Hollforde 1693, Hayford 1780, Leasegill 1611, Leesfill 1621, Eversame 1630, Heaversame 1643, Heversame 1663, Myllthrope 1669, Milnthrop 1642, Millthrop 1661, Milthrop 1713, Milnthorpe 1732, Ninzerge 1665, Ninesergh 1697, Siggswicke 1632, Sigiswicke 1664, Sidgwicke 1682, Stayton 1624, Stainetone 1630.

Addresses were not required until the nineteenth century. Even so a number of houses and farmsteads are named in the registers before 1640. They include Crag Yeat (Ackenthwaite) Hallford or Halforth (Heversham), Holmskells (Endmoor) Johnskells (Lythe), Mabbin Hall (Hincaster), Lawrence House (Levens) Mosside (Heversham), Plummestre - Plumtree - Bank (Heversham) and Parkhouse (Heversham). Evidence of earlier settlement patterns is indicated by the frequent references to hamlets that are relatively small in the twentieth century such as Halfpenny Greene (or Halfpenny Pastures) and Deepthwaite (or Deepthwaite Bridge) and Deer Park. Two places are recorded which no longer exist, namely Scout Bank which was west of Milnthorpe near the Bela and Wellheads north-east of Hincaster.

In the seventeenth century entries for Beathwaite Green (Levens) and Hincaster are as common as for Milnthorpe. From 1740 Milnthorpe becomes by far the most commonly recorded place.

## Occupations

Except between 1718 and 1735, occupations are not registered until c.1780. Only the extremes of rank are mentioned e.g. 1609 'Alice daughter of Thomas Cooke a poorman' and 'an infant borne of a poor wenche in Brigstear'. The subjects of the church's finest monument are given full social status in the burial register for 1626: 'Jan 23 Dorothye wife of Sir Henrye Bellingham Kt. Baronett'. The male Wilsons of Nether Levens and, later, of Dallam receive a 'Mr' as do also the Prestons and Backhouses, the clergy and customs officers of the port of Milnthopre e.g. 1711 'Christopher, son of Mr Clarke officer in Millthropp' and in 1721 'James son of Mr William Clarke officer in excise Ackenthwaite'. Esquire was not appended until the eighteenth century.

Between 1718 and 1735 some occupations are recorded. More jobs were registered in 1719 than in any other year. The occupations of 33 out of 45 fathers, recorded in the Baptism registers in that year, are given. They are: 17 yeomen, 5 plebains, 1 esq., 1 Taylor (sic), 1 labourer, 1 traveller, 1 carrier, 1 Blacksmith, 1 whitesmith, 1 maltster, 1 housecarpenter, and two peddlars. In 1735 the baptism of Samuel son of Thomas Cornthwaite, 'a dancing master', was registered.

In the middle of the eighteenth century only four burial entries provide detailed information: 1735 The Reverend Thomas Watson formerly schoolmaster of Heversham, 1758 Henry Hudson Sexton at Heversham for 57 years, 1765 Mr Chris. Hall M.A., Senior Fellow of Queen's College Oxford, and 1767 Reverend Anthony Watson curate of Kendall Chappell.

From 1780 the entries are given under the seven headings (1) Christian Name (2) Surname (3) Abode (4) Profession or descent (5) Where died (6) Age (7) Destemper (Cause of death). Marriage registers required occupation of the groom, abode, ranks/occupations of the father, and ages of bride and groom. Occupation columns were left blank in many instances but neverthless it is possible to discern some trends in employment. Throughout the late eighteenth and nineteenth centuries most occupations were agricultural being registered as 'yeoman', 'farmer', 'labourer' and 'husbandman' - never as 'shepherd' or 'cowman', etc. By the turn of the eighteenth century most occupations for Milnthorpe reflect the local mini-industrial revolution: for 1798 the register records 3 twine spinners, 1 whitesmith, 2 blacksmiths, 3 paper makers, 1 cotton spinner, 1 cordwainer, 1 carrier, and 1 powderman. The number of mariners registered is greatest in the period 1800-1820 but never exceeds three per annum.

## Christian Names

The registers provide evidence as to the popularity and changes in fashion of Christian names. Throughout the seventeenth and eighteenth centuries Thomas was the most popular male name followed closely by John and William; Henry, Brian, Roger, Geoffrey - or Jeffrey - and Giles also occur regularly. Though the parish was Royalist in sympathy the Stuart names of Charles and James are rare. In 1679, however, one Mr Toogood who had the republican name of Oliver had his son named (after the second Protector?) Richard.

Among female names; Agnes was by far the most popular in the early seventeeth century being the name of seven out of sixteen brides in 1606 while Anne, Isobel and Margaret were the next most common names. Many girls were named after the Virgin Queen but only one, in this anto-popery era, bore the name of the Virgin Mary. After 1720 Mary became the fourth most common name after Anne, Margaret and Elizabeth, followed by Ellen, Hannah, Agnes and Jane.

## Old Families

To the family historian the recurrence of surnames is a useful guide. Many surnames registered in the first decade of the seventeenth century were common in the parish three centuries later. They include: Ashburner, Audland, Beck, Backhouse, Chambers, Gibson, Cornthwaite, Diconson (Dickenson), Garnett, Nelson, Pearson, Saul and Wilson. The latter name is the most freqently registered. Even in the seventeeth century it was held by at least six families as well as by the squire of Nether Levens and Dallam. Many families chose the same Christian name from generation to generation. The first of many John Fawcettes occurs in 1612, the first George Atkinson in 1627 and the first William Scott in 1617. In the century between 1720 and 1820, the most common surnames are Cragg (or Craig), Beck, Burrow (or Barrow), Hall, Woodburn and Wilson. Shaws, Clarks and Mashiters which are numerous in the twentieth century are not common before 1800. There was apparently only one or two Clark families between 1650-1750 while the first Shaw does not occur until 1781 with the registration of the baptism of William son of John Shaw. The record of John's death in 1783 states that he died in the Workhouse and was formerly a dragoon.

The earliest reference to a poor house in Milnthorpe occurs in 1736 in the registration of the burial of Mary Mills. In 1740 the burial register states that Barbara Sanderson came from the workhouse at Sedgwick.

Because of the many inconsistencies and ommissions a detailed demographic study based on the Heversham registers cannot be made in a general history. However, a superficial impression of some population trends and mortality can be noted. In the seventeenth century the average annual death rate was about forty. There were fewer baptisms which numbered about 35 per annum. Many burials are registered of still born or non-baptised babies e.g. 1618 'two abortive children a boy and a woman child' and 'Puer abortinus a child of Willam Prestons non baptisatus'. Probably, therefore, birth and death rates were roughly equal at this period. About a third of all deaths were of infants and minors with occasional peaks as in 1637 when 19 out of 37 deaths were of children.

## The Plague

The highest number of deaths registered in one year was 157 in 1623. Allowing for the usual slight increase during the winter months the deaths are distributed fairly evenly throughout the fatal year: 12 in April, 14 in May, 8 in June, 9 in July, 12 in August, 10 in September, 18 in October, 16 in November, 17 in December, 16 in January, 18 in February and 9 in March. The absence of a significant peak especially during the hottest months would rule out an epedemic like bubonic plague, nor are there any records of famine. Whatever the cause this was, probably, Heversham's worst natural disaster.[19A]

The next worst year was 1746 when 27 children died in Milnthorpe. As 21 of the deaths occurred between September 11 and December 20 an epedemic of perhaps smallpox could have been the cause.

Twins, registered about once every three years seem to have been in the same ratio as in the twentieth century of one set of twins to every hundred single births. No multiple births are registered at all.

Illegitimate births were registered in virtually every year. There was a slight rise in bastards in the early eighteenth century but generally the rate was about four per cent of the total.

Only a little evidence about religion is provided in the registers. The earlier registers show that many children were baptised at one time. On 7th June 1613, for example, eight babies were baptised. Later in the century individual baptism became common. An assiduous clerk in the 1730's noted the age of infants showing that baptism invariably occurred within a month of birth.

There were, however, a few adult baptisms as in 1747 'Wm. Fisher of Deepthwaite Bridge aged 23 years'. In 1793 the baptism is registered of John Burrall aged 22 who was 'born in Whydah in Africa'. Possibly he was a negro slave brought to the parish by one of Milnthorpe's sea captains such as Joseph Fayrer.

The Society of Friends was the only sect whose members were not buried in the churchyard as they had their own burial ground at Preston Richard accounting for such registrations as that in 1700 of 'Margaret Pearson buried among the Quakers'. In the mid-eighteenth century several Roman Catholic burials are recorded including: 1743 William Hughes a traveller, 1745 Sarah Stockdale of Beathwaite Green, 1747 Dorothy wife of Richard Johnson and 1759 James Cook. Although by that time Papist priests were tolerated and a private Requiem Mass would probably have been allowed the internment would have been conducted by the vicar using the Protestant burial rite as by law established.

Apart from the Quakers there were other Dissenters in the parish and there were conventicles at Ackenthwaite and Stainton in the eighteenth century. No reference is made in the burial or in the marriage registers to them. There are however, a couple of references to non-Anglican baptisms: 1742 'Walter son of Robert and Elizabeth Atkinson Presbyterian Minister baptised by Mr. David Murray a Presbyterian minister' and in 1747 'Robert son of Mr. Robert Bradley Nether Levens christened by Dr. Rothersham a Dissenting Minister.'

In the older registers accidents are the only cause of death registered e.g. 1732 'Edward Pastner and William Clark both drowned together'. After 1780 the 'distemper' causing death was recorded. What constituted a distemper was often vague or unscientific e.g. between 1796 and 1809 seventeen children died of convulsions, six of worms, four of 'teeth' and one John son of Thomas Beck died in 1803 aged three weeks of the 'decline'. In 1808 'water in ye brain' killed Henry son of Henry Tindal 'of the British West Indies' aged 9 years and Thomas son of Thomas Camm aged 7 years.

In the same period consumption was the commonest cause of death accounting for 58 fatalities followed by smallpox which claimed 48 victims. 'Old age' was registered as the cause of death for anyone over 69 years and often younger as in the case of Jane Smith who died in 1803 aged 53!

Accidental deaths noted in the fuller registers include: 'Robert Haresnape perished in ye snow on the north side of Heversham Head aged 81' in 1784; 'William Mills Glazier drowned in 1803; and Robert son of William Garnett aged 2 years in a well drowned' in 1803.

Before 1780 extreme old age is recorded e.g. 1747 Jane Woodburn 94, 1756 Margaret Dickinson 'from the Workhouse' 97, and 1762 Margaret Wilson from Underbarrow aged 101 years. After 1780 only one centenarian appears in the burial registers 'Christian wife of Robert Easington of Beathwaite Green aged 100'. Nonagenarians registered include: 1785

William Cragg 90, 1793 Thomas Crompton 90, 1796 Isobel Cragg 90, 1803 William Audland 92, 1803 William Fisher 91, 1807 John Jennings 92 and 1808 Richard Blakehow 92. The highest age in the registers occurs in 1694 with the burial of Mr. Thomas Benson aged 103. It is possible that he was the same Thomas who married Agnes Clovelly in 1605 (such a young marriage was legal and not unusual) and who fathered a bastard called Elizabeth in 1618. If so he was a quick starter and a late finisher.

**The Newer Registers from 1810**
The burial and baptism registers from June 1810 to 1917/18 are contained in a huge leather bound volume some 18 inches wide by 2½ feet long and six inches thick which is kept in the vestry. Entries are from all parts of the parish except Crosthwaite and Lythe which had its own register from the sixteenth century. Copies of parts of the Crosthwaite registers are, however, in the Heversham archives. In the main register Crosscrake entries are put under a separate heading as are Levens' baptisms afer Levens church was consecrated in 1828. No distinction is made for Levens' burials. The Levens' entries cease in c.1910-11 when its parish became fully independent. From 1840 to the end of the volume Milnthorpe burials as well as baptisms are listed under separate headings. From the middle of the nineteenth century workhouse or 'Union' baptisms and burials are also registered separately. Apparently several years of workhouse registrations were written in at a time and odd spaces were used.

The 1811 burial register records the following 'distempers': Old Age 9, Water in ye brain 2, Whooping Cough 4, Consumption 4, Convulsions 1, Decline 3, Complaints in the Bowell 2, Infancy 4, Tooth fever 1, Fever 1, Decay of the liver 1, Weakness 1, Rheumatism 1, Weaning 1, Stroke 1, and suffocated in a limekiln 2. The last two deaths were of Robert Bindloss aged 20 years and James Atkinson aged 34 years of Greenside.

The 1901 workhouse entries have been missed out. As there were at least half a dozen pauper funerals and baptisms annually in the late 1890's and 1900's the possibility of there being no workhouse deaths or births in 1901 can be precluded.

Terminology and spelling are almost modern. 'Illegitimate' or natural child is used instead of the earlier 'spurious' or 'bastard'. 'Pauper' is used only to describe workhouse burials and unmarried mothers from that institution are described simply as 'singlewoman' or occasionally 'servant'. Ninety per cent of workhouse babies were illegitimate compared with an average of about 5% for the rest of the parish. This was slightly higher than in the eighteenth century - perhaps a result of a decline in miscarriages and infant mortality rather that of an increase in immorality. Names of 'supposed fathers' of illegitimate children weie not recorded after 1810.

In the early nineteenth century an ambitious attempt to record more personal information in the registers was made, The baptism registers required date of birth, father's occupation, abode, seniority of child in the family (the highest number registered was seven) and mother's descent (i.e. her father's name and occupation) as well as the child's name, and the date and name of the officiating minister at the christening. From 1817 the mother's descent and seniority columns were left blank.

The occupations registered in the late eighteenth century indicate industrial and commercial types of employment of Milnthorpe fathers compared to those from other parts of the parish. In 1821 Milnthorpe jobs included 1 twine weaver, 1 shopkeeper, 1 blacksmith, 1 spirit merchant, 1 carrier, 2 paper makers, 1 school master, 1 nailer, 4 weavers, 1 cordwainer, 1 mechanic, 2 carpenters, 2 husbandmen and 2 labourers. The last two occupations were followed by about half of the fathers from Heversham and Levens. A generation later in 1865 sixteen occupations ranging from veterinary surgeon to limekiln burner were undertaken by 24 Milnthorpe fathers whereas six out of 14 Levens fathers were farm labourers; four of the rest were servants. The register for 1901 shows the father's occupations for each of the parish's three main townships as:

**Milnthorpe:** 1 coachman, 1 porter, 1 railway signalman, 2 comb-makers, 1 postman, 1 farmer, 2 stone-masons, 1 gardener, 1 land agent, 1 coal agent, 1 carrier, 1 foreman builder, 1 cabinet maker, 1 'man servant at the Grammar School' and 3 labourers.

**Heversham**: 1 servant, 1 gentleman, 2 gardeners, 1 ganger, 1 farmer, 1 joiner, 1 publican, 1 licensed victualler, 1 workman and 5 labourers.

**Levens**: 3 joiners, 2 farmers, 1 farm bailiff, 1 policeman, 1 publican and six labourers.

Thus it seems that despite Heversham and Levens having several grander residences they were the more plebian townships in the nineteenth century. This social pattern changed completely in the next eighty years which saw Heversham and Levens expand into large bourgeois retirement villages with Milnthorpe remaining substantially a working class community.

### Place Names
The nineteenth century registers show that spelling had become standardised and that the forms used were generally the same as in the late twentieth century. Exceptions were Arnisteade (1821) for Arnside, Sidgwicke for Sedgwick until c.1861 and the interchangeable use of Milthrop, Milnthorp and Milnthorpe until 1870 when the modern usage appears in all registrations.

### Christian Names
Christian names registered show that fashions for boys' names remained stable with John, William and Thomas still appearing several times each year and with almost annual entries of Richard and Robert. Biblical e.g. Samuel, and obviously Victorian names e.g. Albert, are rare. In female names fashions were less conservative. In 1821 Margaret and Mary were names of 9 mothers and there were 5 Elizabeths, Bettys and Janes accounting for half the females registered. A generation later in 1861 Jane was the most common name but Clara, Sarah and Hannah were more popular than Margaret or Elizabeth. From the 1860's onwards about half the babies were given two names of which one was invariably that of a parent.

### Aged Death
The registers show that nineteenth century clergy were kept busy with burials. There were 38 burials in 1811, 54 in 1831, 56 in 1864 and 38 in 1901. In contrast between 1931 and 1979 the average annual number of burials was about 10. Improved medical and social conditions are reflected in the decline of infant mortality (i.e. deaths below the age of 4) from 14 out of 54 burials in 1831, 7 out of 56 in 1865 and 2 out of 38 in 1901. The figures for child deaths (5 to 12 years) were 5 in 1831, 1 in 1861 and 2 in 1901. 1879 was the peak year for the infant and child deaths for 20 burials of minors were recorded, about a third of the total. Excluding infant and child deaths (0 to 12) the average ages of burials were: 54 in 1831, 62 in 1861 and 64 in 1901. Examples of extreme old age include: 1811 Isabella Strickland 94, 1817 Mary Mcliver 94, 1828 Alan Rowell 98, 1848 Robert Moncrief 94, 1850 Baryillai Hernshaw 96, 1861 Elizabeth Penny 98, 1862 Jane Wilson 99, 1867 Francis Bowen 97 and 1861 John Farrer 96. The only centenarian recorded is Ann Gibson of Levens who was buried on 31st January 1900 aged 101. However, one other centenarian is known to have lived in the parish at Hincaster. He was James Cunningham 'Old Jemmy' formerly a canal labourer or 'navigator' whose hundredth birthday was reported in the 'Westmorland Gazette' on 21st August 1880. As he was Irish and probably a Roman Catholic he must have been buried elsewhere assuming he died in the parish. In recent times the oldest age reached by a parishioner was achieved by John Handley of Heversham Hall. A wholehearted servant of the church and a churchwarden he died aged 97 in 1970.

### The Marriage Register
There are three registers covering the period 1813-1958. Until 1836 the only information required was the date of the ceremony and names of the bride and groom, the two witnesses and the officiating minister. From the passing of the Registration of Marriages Act in 1837 the ages of bride and groom and their fathers' rank or occupation was required. Until 1873 only 'minor' or 'full age' is recorded. After that time evidence of average age of marriages can be determined. In 1873 the average age for grooms was 28 and brides 20. The corresponding figures at intervals of a decade are:

1883: 25 and 25. 1983: 31 and 27. 1903: 31 and 27. 1913: 36 and 32. 1923: 26 and 32. 1933: 27 and 29. 1943: 36 and 30. 1953: 23 and 22. 1963: 22 and 23. 1973: 24 and 23.

The higher ages for the earlier decades is partly accounted for by marriage of widows and widowers. For first marriages the average age was two or three years younger than the average noted. There were 8 marriages in 1873, 6 in 1883, 10 in 1893, 4 in 1903, 4 in 1913, 3 in 1923, 3 in 1933 2 in 1943, 7 in 1953 and 3 in 1963, and 3 in 1973.

The decline in marriages in the first half of the twentieth century reflects the social change following the settlement in the village of a high proportion of retired people whose children were either married or lived away. The marriage register also shows the increase of literacy during the nineteenth century. In 1813 7 grooms and 10 brides out of a total of 17 marriages could not write their signatures and therefore instead made their mark - usually a cross. in 1834 there were 6 illiterate grooms and also 6 illiterate brides out of 21 marriages. The figures for the next four decades are:

    1833 illiterate grooms 3, brides 7, out of 24;

    1843 illiterate grooms 3, brides 3, out of 18;

    1853 illiterate grooms 1, brides 2 out of 20;

    1863 illiterate grooms 3, brides 2, out of 16.

In 1873 all brides and grooms could write their names. Thereafter there were only four cases of illiteracy (3 brides and 1 groom), the last occasion being in 1899.

**Re-organisation of Finances and the Sale of the Glebeland**
**circa. 1921-1948**
During the incumbencies of the Rev. E.R.Ellis 1921-1939 and the Rev. W.A.Cleghorn 1939-1955 the finances of the living were re-organised. Between 1922 and 1948 over 600 acres of Glebeland spread over the whole parish and including valuable holdings at Endmoor, Barrows Green, Sampool and Heversham Marsh were sold leaving only a fifty acre allotment at Crosthwaite which still officially belonged to the living in 1983. The cause for adandonment of the landed endowment of the church (what dated back to its very foundation) was an agricultural depression combined with the growth of deceptively easier and more profitable forms of investment. The mid-nineteenth century depression was not as severe in a mixed farming area like Westmorland than it was in the areas of grain production. Nevertheless the returns of the Heversham glebe dropped from £700 gross (net £515.) in 1862 to £615. gross (net £460.) in 1914.

Some land was sold by Canon Gilbert. The first sale of a field in Endmoor in 1892 was encouraging. Messrs. Talbot Rheam and Webster, the solicitors, expected only about £90. Canon Gilbert suggested £100 - so the solicitors asked £120 (40 years' rental) and to their surprise got it. A letter survives in which Canon Gilbert wondered whether it was ethical to accept such a sum. In fact he did so. The £120 was invested in 3% India stock.[20] In 1912 J.C.Hamilton paid £66. 3s. 0½d. for a plot in Heversham which sum was invested in 3½% London County stock. About four acres of awkward fields around the cross roads at Milton Moor were sold in 1919 to Thomas Inman for £84. This was invested in the unprecedentedly high 5% War Loan which subsequently was reduced to 4% Funding Stock without loss of income.[21]

Canon Gilbert's retirement in 1921 prompted the first important sales of land. The post war depression had hit agricultural rents but war-time profits meant that the tenant farmers were in a position to purchase. Moreover, the living needed ready cash to meet the cost, estimated by the surveyor, J.F.Curwen, at £427.10s.9d. for delapidations to the vicarage and farm property. Properly the sum should have been met by Canon Gilbert but after his 55 years of service to the parish neither the wardens nor the ecclesiastical commissioners felt able to insist on payment.

Although in his delapidation report J.F.Curwen stated that 'most of the field gates were in a deplorable condition' the land was well-farmed and he felt bound to record that a severe sea storm (1907) which burst and destroyed the river embankments (at Sampool and College Green) put the vicar to exceptional expense; that to somewhat recompense the tenants the farms have been let at very low rental; that the farmers have since reaped considerable fortune from the land. I am convinced that the land could be sold very readily and that the condition it is now in without very appreciable reduction; that the value of the living would be greatly enhanced; and that if this could be accomplished at once the late vicar might well be spared the expense of making good the defects.'[22]

So, partly out of kindness to Canon Gilbert, the sales began. Trinity College put up a mild protest about a £1 fine on part of the marsh land which the 'been mentioned in the Beaumont Survey of 1563 the first survey made after the rectory was given to the College by Queen Mary, and had been paid ever since.' After a commutation had been paid for the £1 fine 57 acres 1 rood and 8 perches of the marsh farm estate was sold to John Handley for £1,800. With other monies this was brought up to £1,967 and invested in 4% stock. In 1932 land at Endmoor was sold to the Territorial Army Association for £53. 7s. 8d. and in 1939 the Helm allotment at Barrows Green was sold for £900.

From 1939 income from the glebe was paid directly to the Church Commissioners who sent a quarterly cheque to the vicar thereby releasing him from much paper work. The Rev.Cleghorn, however, did negotiate himself for the sale of £100 of standing timber from the glebe in 1940.

Fate decreed that 1943, perhaps the worst possible time, was the year when 400 acres, the bulk of the glebe, was sold. The war-time shortages of capital meant that prices were depressed and, for example, J.Handley obtained 36.4 acres on Heversham Head for £600 while J.Fawcett and Sons obtained 22 acres on the marsh for £202. 10s. The approximate sum of £8,000 raised altogether by the sales was then invested in 3% National Savings Bonds.

In 1948 £3,820 net profit from the sale of the vicarage and a small part of the remaining glebe to the Drew family and Lord Rathdonnel was invested mainly in 2½% Treasury Stock. Even by 1948 the sanguine hope of J.F.Curwen in 1921 that the 'value of the living would be greatly enhanced' had not been realised. The Crockford's Report of the Heversham living for 1948 was: Queen Anne's Bounty: £8., Glebe: £6., Ecclesiastical Commissioners: £513., Fees: £3., Easter Offering : £29., Other sources: £150., Gross Income £765. Net Income £486.[23]

A rough estimate of the 1982 value of the former glebe land was over a million pounds and the probable income would have been between £18,000. and £20,000. - about three times the stipend paid to the vicar from central funds.[24]

### Church Finance in the Nineteenth and Twentieth Centuries

The major source of church income from the seventeenth century until 1875 was the church rate which was levied on all non-pauper households in the parish. It was based on annual assessment, abbreviated in the records as the 'cess'. In 1822, following the dispute with Crosthwaite, it was stipulated that the rates were to be at 'two double cesses viz Milnthorpe £10, Levens £12, Preston Richard £7, Stainton £7 and Crosthwaite £12.' Crosthwaite had to pay a fixed fee of 15s. towards the clerk's salary while the other townships had to pay in proportion to the general rate which in 1830 was calculated as Milnthorpe £2. 1s. 8d., Levens £2. 10s. 0d., Stainton £1. 9s. 2d. and Preston Richard £1. 9s. 2d. making £8. 5s. in all. Beginning in 1815, £1. 15s. was taken annually out of the churchyard account to bring the clerk's salary up to £10. In 1866 the old 'cess' was replaced by a rate of a farthing in the pound based on property values.[26] There seems to be no record of any opposition to the payment of church rates from the very small number of non-conformists in the parish. Rather it seems to have been the difficulty in assessing the collecting the rates that led to their abolition in 1875. Moveover at that time there were many landowners and other wealthy inhabitants of the parish able and willing to make substantial donations to church funds.

After the commutation of the tithes in the 'Inclosure Act of 1803', neither the Rector (Trinity

College) nor the vicar received a tithe income from most of the parish. However, it appears that until the general Tithes Act of 1936 Crosthwaite landowners were required to pay tithes to Trinity College, which donated a proportion to the maintenance of the chancel. In 1950 the Senior Bursar of the College restated that the College had always accepted responsibility for 'repairs to Heversham chancel and had insured it'.[27] He also suggested that the Crosthwaite commutation money be paid to the Diocesan Board of Finance and that the interest 'pay for chancel maintenance and insurance.' Accordingly in 1953 £560 was received to be 'invested for structural repairs to the church'.[23] There is no record that Trinity College has repealed or cancelled its obligation to contribute to the maintenance of the chancel from the income derived from awards made elsewhere in the parish in the 'Inclosure Act'.

Following the abolition of church rates at Heversham in 1875 a subscription scheme was introduced in the parish. Until the First World War moderate sums contributed by the gentry are recorded separately. In 1912, which was a typical year, the vicar, Canon Gilbert, and T.A.Argles of Eversley each contributed eight guineas and Captain Bagot, of Levens Hall, J.S.Gandy of Heaves, C.Walker of Bettargh Holt and H.H.Austen of Heversham House each subscribed five pounds.

Lesser subscriptions called 'book money' were collected twice a year by the church wardens and clerk until after the Second World War. Despite inflation these remained stable until 1940: Hincaster and Preston Richard produced about £7 annually from 1875 and Heversham about £24. There was a brief overall increase to nearly £50 soon after the induction of the Reverend Ellis in 1921 but this total declined to £19 by 1948 when a Gift Day was substituted. Unfortunately the first Gift Day figure of £187 was never again reached although it topped £150 in most years.[24]

By 1948 collections during services had become a major source of income. Until the late nineteenth century collections were made only at communion, which was celebrated only five times a year until the 1860's, increasing gradually to a weekly 8 a.m. Holy Communion by 1880. Traditionally communion money was spent on bread doled out to widows and old folk at the end of morning service, from bread shelves opposite the main door. It is recalled that the recipients brought with them a pillow case in which to carry the bread home. By c.1860 the Bread Fund was provided from interest on the accumulation of communion money amounting to about £77 and from £200 taken from a bequest of 'Robert Johnson of Kennington Place esq.,' who in his will dated 31st August 1802 directed that £361.3s.6d be invested in 3% bank stock the interest whereby to be divided amongst the Poor Persons of Heversham and Leasgill only firstly deducting thereout annually one guinea for the vicar of Heversham upon his preaching a Charity Sermon'. The sermon was preached on the first Sunday in January. A board recording the bequest was for long on the baptistry wall next to the bread shelves but is now stored in the Dallam Chapel. By 1939 only £1.9s.1d was spent a year on this charity and the P.C.C. agreed that 'as there are no suitable recipients for the bread charity Mr Tyson should ask Mrs Duncan (the shop keeper) to discontinue supplying the bread and that the accruing money should be saved for future use'. In 1948, bread was supplied to Mrs Allen and Mrs Kitching but thereafter bread funds were amalgamated with the consolidated charity fund.

There were regular surpluses from the charity accounts for most of the nineteenth and twentieth centuries. Until 1867 Crosthwaite Communion money was put in the same fund as that of the parish church and the Crosthwaite chapelry then received a quarter of the whole, which averaged about £3.10s per annum. No separate collection or provision was made for Crosscrake where, in any case, celebrations were rare until c.1850.

At the turn of the eighteenth century there were surpluses also from communion money at Heversham and in 1793 some of it was used to augment the Woodhouse charity. A further £50 was lent on interest to Christopher Fletcher who sold the bond to C.Bindloss from whom it was redeemed in 1813 'when the church was new floored and pewed'.[26]

In 1867 it was decided at a combined parish meeting held at Milnthorpe to discontinue a general allocation of communion money. As compensation for any loss the interest from £50 was allocated to Crosthwaite.

Until the late nineteenth century one of the Churchwarden's main duties was awarding Apprenticeship Money to Masters indenturing poor boys from the various townships in the parish. This was based on a rota: Milnthorpe boys were eligible annually, Levens boys two years in three and boys from Preston Richard, Sedgwick, Hincaster, Stainton and Heversham every third year. In the late eighteenth and early nineteenth centuries Apprenticeship money was itemised in the accounts. Between 1776 and 1786 it amounted to £1.8s.6d for each of the three eligible townships; from 1786-1799 it was £1.2s.6d p.a. and from 1802-1806 it was £1.14s.7d p.a. Thereafter references are sporadic and are for varying sums e.g., £3.0s.11¼ was paid out in 1815.

During Canon Gilbert's incumbency collections were started at morning service and by 1900 amounted to £100 per annum. This figure remained steady until 1930 when it began to rise to £318 in 1939, £505 in 1955 and -682 in 1959.

Largely through the instigation of the vicar, Canon Stanley Lane, the Friends of Heversham Scheme was devised in 1957 to coordinate free-will offerings from parishioners in the form of covenants, collected via bankers orders or dated envelopes from which a tax rebate was obtainable. The response was excellent. Every household in the parish was visited by the church wardens or members of the Men's Working Committee with the result that 253 out of 446 inhabitants had 'promised suppoort amounting to £1,014.4s.0d per annum which represented help from all the houses in the parish. The whole endeavour had only cost £7.10s.0d for printing, stationery and postages.'[33.] Over the next ten years, the Friends' contribution kept pace with inflation but in the 1970's there was a relative decline as the 1978 figure was only about £2,000.

### Expenditure

During the last 150 years there have been a number of regular expenses.[43] Of these, salaries remained almost stable. For example the clerk was paid £10 per annum from c.1815 until the death of the last holder of the office, Robert Squire, in 1956. Similarly the organist received £35 per annum from 1855 until 1950 when there was a rise to £50 and the bellringers' fees varied only between £23 to £25 for over a century. In the 1960's, ringing costs were reduced to £10-£15 per annum when the number of bell ringers declined. The full team of ringers formed after the repairs to the peal in 1979 provides its services free except for weddings. Cleaning costs have always been low: the cleaner's salary was £10 per annum until 1939 when Miss Mary Proctor received an increase to £13.10s and this rose to £25.10s in 1955. By 1965 church cleaners were paid £39.15s and in 1978 £78. Difficulties in finding a replacement for the cleaner when she retired in 1980 led to a rota of voluntary cleaners being drawn up. This removed a traditional and ever increasing expense while also providing an opportunity for practical service.

In contrast for the fall in the real cost of salaries, heating and lighting bills have kept pace with inflation. Before 1914 the cost of coke, carbide and 'making gas' came to less than £20. In 1923 the costs were £50 and in 1933 £60 but expenditure dropped to £40 per annum during the Second World War when, on account of black-out regulations, evening services were brought forward, apparently, to the afternoon and at 8 a.m. communion only the chancel lights were lit, obliging the communicants to sit together in the choir stalls. Representative post-war heating and lighting bills are £140 in 1960, £324 in 1970 and £570 in 1977.

### Charities and Missions

Few contributions were made directly to worthy causes from church funds in the early nineteenth century. However, the main local welfare agency was sponsored by the church. This was the St.Peter's Lodge of Oddfellows founded 1788, which survived until after the First World War. Ostensibly a Friendly Society collecting burial and health insurance, it was also a lively social organisation. Thus on New Year's Day 1844 150 people attended the Oddfellows ball at the 'Blue Bell' where between 8 p.m. and 4 a.m.

'they partook of an excellent tea, coffee and currant cake provided by the worthy Mrs White. This praiseworthy body of young men contributed to the proceeds of their purchased tickets which constitute the real part of their enjoyment to the want of others. They are giving to the fund for the relief of widows and orphans.'[35]

Also in 1849 the Oddfellows celebrated their 62nd Annual Meeting by processing to Milnthorpe where the grand provender of the association for twelve years, one Jeremiah Akister, was presented with a Bible. In 1871, at the annual Oddfellow's service held on the 3rd June, it was announced that 54 members had been paid 726 weeks' sick pay amounting to £254.6s.5d and that £24.10s had been donated towards funeral expenses.[36]

In the 1840's a Heversham Church Missionary Society was founded by the vicar, The Reverend Robert Wilson Evans and the Milnthorpe incumbent Nicholas Padwick. Monthly meetings were held in the Milnthorpe National School where, as well as 'singing beautiful missionary hymns',[37] members were addressed by visiting missionaries like the Reverend W.Smith from Benares, who was partly sponsored by the parish. After 1860 the Missionary Society seems to have been mainly attended by Milnthorpe people but Heversham continued to make financial contributions.

At the end of the nineteenth century, the number and variety of charities supported by the congregation had grown enormously. In the 1920's they were divided into five categories A to E. In 1924 Group A was for Central Church Funds and included 'Service Candidates Ordination Fund, Clergy Sustentation Fund and Kendal Rescue Work (prostitutes)' Group B comprised The National Society (Schools), the Church Army and the Mother's Union; Groups C and D were for missions including the Mission to the Jews, the Oxford Mission to Calcutta, the Cambridge Mission to Delhi, the Western Canada Mission, and the Melanesian Mission. Group E was for 'outside charitable objects' covering such diverse causes as the County Hospital Royal Agricultural Society, Japanese Distress, Easter Offering to the Vicar and the Flower Fund. In 1924, £169.8s.1d in all was given to charity and the figure thereafter was never less that £150 per annum.[38]

Although the grouping system was abandoned in 1935, many of the original causes continued to be supported; the Melanesian Mission received £5 annually until 1970 when donations to overseas ministry were amalgamated in a general contribution to Christian Aid. That contemporaries really did know of the geographical position of Melanesia is indicated by there being no contribution when the area was occupied by the Japanese.

With the coming of the Welfare State contributions to hospitals and the relief of basic poverty ceased, although evidence that charity could still be firmly based at home is indicated by a P.C.C. minute of the 1st May 1847 when it was agreed that 'the five shillings which had been earmarked for the Lord Mayor's Fund should be sent but that owing to the loss of livestock during snow and floods, the rest of the collection £23.3s.0d be sent to the National Farmers' Union.'[39]

## Living and Giving
The financial system devised at the inauguration of the Friends of Heversham scheme in 1957 was reasonably effective until 1980 when the church 'cost £7,388 to run and income from all sources was £6,915.' The deficit of £473 was met out of a small reserve fund. By far the largest item of expenditure was the 'Maintenance of the Ministry, quota, dioceson readers, parochial administration' contribution of £3,719 which rose to £5,159 in 1981. Also in 1980 it was estimated that there would be a decline from £4,149 in 1980 to £3,250 in 1981 in income from bankers orders caused mainly by death or removal of parishioners. Even with economies in the costs of cleaning, heating, repairs and church music it was feared that the 1981 deficit would be £2,509. There was also concern that no regular giving had been made to the 'less fortunate' although special collections had been made. As always there was a desire to encourage new residents and occasional worshippers to contribute to the upkeep and life of the church.

In an attempt to solve these problems the P.C.C. set up a sub-committee, under a lay chairman, to make detailed arrangements for a 'Living and Giving Campaign'. These included the circularising and visiting of every household in the parish and also of non-parochial worshippers. In October the campaign was launched at a Parish Dinner held at the Grammar School when the Rural Dean Canon Colin Stannard of Natland gave a short address on Christian Stewardship. Almost immediately a majority of those who belonged to the Friends of Heversham increased their contributions and many others joined the scheme. Six months later increases in the contributions on a regular basis had been such that the annual increase for each of the succeeding four years was estimated as being at £3,800 p.a. which represented an increase of over 66%.

There was an audible gasp of amazement from the congregation when in June 1982 the vicar announced (at Parish Communion) that a tax rebate of £1,400 had already been received. This encouraging financial position seemed to be an answer to the campaign prayer:

'lord God, you are the supreme owner of all that we have and are: give us grace so that the spending of our lives may be in accordance with you will, and wisdom so that we may use responsibility what you have entrusted to us, to the glory of your Name. Amen'.[40]

**Notes and References to Sources   Chapter IX**

1. See above Chapter III
2. The Book of Accounts CRO (K) WPR/8
3. C.W.A.A.S. Calverly
4. The Book of Accounts also recorded in The Vestry Book left in the Church.
5. The Book of Accounts
6. *Ibid*
7. *Ibid*
8. *Ibid*
9. All references to churchwardens are drawn from The Book of Accounts until 1828. After 1828 the source is The Vestry Book.
10. P.C.C. minutes kept in church vestry.
11. *Ibid*
12. *Ibid*
13. *Ibid*
14. Recollection
15. P.C.C. Minutes
16. *Ibid*
17. *Ibid*
18. Author's recollection.
19. CRO(K) WPR/8
19a. See C.W.A.A.S. XV Visitation of the Plague in Cumberland and Westmorland by Henry Barnes M.D. F.R.S.E. read at Ambleside. Sept. 4th. 1889.
20. see Crockfords Clerical Directory.
21. CRO(K) WPR/8
22. *Ibid*
23. *Ibid*
24. Estimate made by author on land values and rentals in South Cumbria in 1982. Income from £1m. invested elsewhere would be many times higher than an income from land.
25. Vestry Book (H).
26. *Ibid*
27. P.C.C. Minutes.
28. *Ibid*
29. Vestry Book.
30. P.C.C. Minutes.
31. CRO(K) WPR/8
32. CRO(K) WPR/8 Charities. Also noted on board in Church.
33. Information from Vestry Book (H) and P.C.C. minutes.
34. Westmorland Gazette (January 1844).
35. *Ibid* 1871.
36. *Ibid*
37. Vestry Book.
38. P.C.C. Minutes.
39. Information sent out as part of 'Living and Giving Campaign 1981.

# CHAPTER X

# Nineteenth and Twentieth Century Clergy
# (1797-1842)

### DR. LAWSON - An Inpecunious Parson
### Disputes over the Heversham Enclosure Act

George Lawson was presented to the vicarage of 'Eversham' on the 19th October 1797. Formerly a fellow of Trinity College, Cambridge, he was the only incumbent to hold a doctorate. Within a few years he was involved in a dispute with the owners of Levens Hall caused by the Heversham Enclosure and Commutation of Tithes Act.[1] As a result he was ruined financially and his reputation undermined.

The enclosure awards were assessed in 1803 by three commissioners: Johnathan Teal, Richard Clark and John Tatham. A notice was put up in the porch stating that the Enclosure Act would be 'to the general advantage not only to landlords but that the said ruinous mosses and waste grounds be divided, allotted and enclosed and all the lands in the said parish exonerated from payment of tithes'.[2] The vicar was, however, to keep the Easter dues of

> 'three farthings for every person above fifteen years of age and for mortuaries for every person dying and being at the time of death of the value of moveable goods of £40 or more ten shillings, for those (worth between £30 and £40.6s.8d. and those worth ten marks to £30.3s.6d These fees continued to be levied until 1860.'

He also got fees of 2s.6d for weddings, 1s for publishing banns, churchings and burials and 5s for marriages by licenses. But, the vicar's main income had come from tithes. By 1880 these were rarely paid in kind e.g. one calf in every ten, but had been commuted for cash. The Act gave land to the vicar and Trinity College (the owner of the Rectory) in enchange for their giving up the right to collect tithes. At the same time the land was re-allocated to form compact holdings, while the open grazing land, mainly on the mosses, was enclosed and drained.

At first glance the church and College did well out of the Act. The vicarage received 650 acres worth an estimated £450 per annum which was to be ring fenced by the parish.[3] Trinity College got 600 acres made up of an estate in Plumgarths in Strickland Ketel (Burnside), purchased by land owners who had not common land, and a share of the mosses and the ancient glebe. This was worth £600 per annum. The College sensibly let the land to tenant farmers and received an annual income from it more or less trouble free. The Vicar was neither so wise nor so fortunate. Long before the Enclosure Act received the Royal Assent of the Prince Regent on the 14th June 1815 (four days before Waterloo!) Dr.Lawson was in possession of much of the church land and, without any experience at all, he had embarked on large scale farming. To finance the enterprise he had borrowed £2,000 from Richard Bagot,[4] the Recorder of Kendal who was also the father of the Hon. Mary Howard, owner of Levens. As Levens

*Monument over grave of Dr. Lawson*

was a beneficiary of the Act it is possible that the loan was given to induce the vicar's consent to the Enclosure bill which could not have been enacted without the consent of the owner of four fifths of the land. Certainly there is no evidence that either the church or the College initiated the necessary legislation which as elsewhere was promoted by the lay owners of the great estates.

Even an experienced farmer would have found it difficult to farm the land awarded to the church. Most of it was scattered in smallish or isolated holdings. In Heversham the vicar received 43 acres on the Head and 58 acres, a mile away, on the marsh, with an outlying two acre field at the end of the lane leading to 'Hawforth'. Across the river he got 58 acres at Sampool but here the land required embankment and was split up by other holdings. Similarly on Lord's Plain two large allotments of 38 and 46 acres were divided by a 10 acre field owned by Charles Wilson. In contrast the Howards of Levens received a compact allotment of 156 acres on the plain. At Endmoor, Parsons Way, Hincaster and Rowell Green (Kidside) the church land was split up between the vicar and the College. The only large vicarage allotment more or less in a ring fence was 115 acres at Barrows Green but this was in the extreme north-east of the parish five miles from Heversham. The rest of the award was made up of small plots as, for example, four tiny fields at Milton Moor in the corners of the cross roads formed by the intersection of[5] the Deepthwaite-Wathsutton lane and the Milnthorpe-Crooklands road.

## Debt

Not surprisingly lacking experience, sufficient capital and with the costly tasks of clearing, draining and dividing the land, profits were not forthcoming and Dr. Lawson could not pay the interest on his loan from Mr. Bagot. Evidence of the bitterness of the resulting dispute is to be found in the Levens' archives. Thus in July 1811 the Levens' agent Mr. Digeon wrote to Richard Bagot stating that he had recovered a debt of £31.5s from Dr. Lawson but he had not got a 'farthing of interest' on the £2,000. On the other hand he had heard that Dr. Lawson and his brother 'have been borrowing from among the Jews in London at 15% which is paid quarterly and for which the Bailiffs are squatting in his house'. He concluded 'it would be best for the friends of his family if they took his concerns out of his hands...as...in my opinion he is no better than a swindler'.[6] In September the dispute waged even more furiously when according to the agent

> 'I met him on the road and he behaved in a most insolent manner to me and he had the impudence to dine at the venison feast on Monday (when) his goods and chattels were sold off to pay a debt and a hundred pounds ... in fact the bailiff is seldom from his doors. I have no pity on such a thoughtless extravagant fellow and if you do not stop me I shall certainly carry things to the utmost judgement'.[7]

By this time Dr.Lawson deprived of his stock and tackle had virtually no income with which to service his debts and he was forced to admit in a letter of the 20th September 1811 to Mrs. Howard that 'farming as you so rightly suggested is seldom a profitable concern to a clergyman and I find some satisfaction that it is drawing to a conclusion'.[8]

He then tried to supplement his income by teaching but failed to get a reference from the churchwardens who resolved that 'the Rev. Dr. Lawson is not considered by us to eligible as a school master of Heversham school'.[9] Clutching at straws he went on to claim 4% per annum for 1798 to 1805 from the old tithe on the Mill at Milnthorpe. This demand was called 'scurrilous' by Bagot as he had the signed receipt. Notwithstanding refusal of payment in 1805 ten years later Lawson was trying desperately to get '£24 to be paid in cash'[10] for the mill tithes. He was only saved from being forced to admit his error, or deception, by the opportune death of Richard Bagot in the same year. Perhaps it was to celebrate this salvation rather than the Battle of Waterloo that Dr. Lawson planted the chestnut trees in the churchyard in 1815 which are his chief memorial.[11]

Dr. Lawson never made up his quarrel with Levens. Even so he was able to induce other parishioners to contribute to a major church refurnishing scheme and at the end of his life he supported the foundation of the girls' and infants' school.[12] By the 1820's the glebe land

112

was all let to tenants and with the help of friends he was able to service his debt. Yet he was never able to pay his way. The 1841 census records only two indoor servants at the vicarage, and states that his younger daughter Tamar was a governess and lists the names of some fifteen girls who were being educated at a seminary established in the vicarage. Perhaps Dr. Lawson enjoyed female company for the epitaph on the large marble memorial scroll set on the chancel wall high above the vestry door reads 'The blessing of him that was ready to perish came upon him and he caused the widow's heart to sink with joy'.[13]

**ROBERT WILSON EVANS: 1842-1866**
**A Poetic Pastor**

'Lord, what am I that thou shouldst deal so graciously with me: that Thou shouldst pour upon me so abundantly that which Thou has withheld from so many.

That I should still be walking in the light of Thy sun: That my spirit should be rejoicing in the light of Thy word.

That I should not be in the grave with my companions nor sitting in the shadow of death with the heathen; but I am alive to celebrate Thee: I have knowledge to praise Thee.

Therefore I will glorify Thee in thy church: and offer my thanksgiving in the congregation.'[1]

These lines are part of one of thirty-four hymns from 'A Day in the Sanctuary' written by Robert Wilson Evans shortly after he became vicar of Heversham in 1842. Having been a Fellow, classical tutor and chief examiner of Trinity College he was presented to the living by its Master William Whewell, who, incidentally, was an old boy of Heversham Grammar School. For the previous thirteen years Evans had been exercising 'the high office as a priest in the church of God'[2] as Vicar of Tarvin in Cheshire but he had continued his work as a pastoral theologian. His books, rarely if at all read for a hundred years, still convey Evans' deep spirituality which must have been contrasted with the worldly rumbustiousness of his predecessor.'

113

## The Bishopric of Souls

The Good Shepherd was his favourite metaphor and it was also the theme of his most readable work 'The Bishopric of Souls' devoted to the duties of a priest who, he stressed, should see himself as 'an under Shepherd under that Chief Shepherd - and prefer the souls to the bodies of the sheep'.[3] Despite his scholarship he believed that

'a book clergyman is about as efficient as a book farmer, a book merchant or a book statesman or any other man of business who guides himself more by the naked knowledge acquired at second-hand than showing the results of experience'.

Hence a priest should regard visiting as being of

'the utmost importance (so) that the whole flock should have been inspected since the last Lord's Day ... for the shepherd who gathers his sheep together in the fold should also tend them in the pasture'.[5]

At Heversham Evans drew up a timetable of daily visits to each part of his parish including Milnthorpe, Crosthwaite, Crosscrake and Levens (although they had their own pastors) to enable him to visit each family every six weeks.[6] According to his obituary

'his most frequent place was by the bedside of some poor afflicted old man or old woman ... often sought out through the roughest ways and no slight personal inconvenience'.[7]

Death saturated many of his observations such as his description of

'a crowd awaiting the opening of the service..It is still and well drest (sic), and broken into various groups, of which one is gathered round the grave of some dear friend, another is a whole family surrounding and discussing the sundial and apart from the rest you will see the widow at the grave of her husband, the orphan at the grave of his father, the mother at the grave of her child'[8]

Once inside his congregation was not likely to be brightened for he did not approve of 'light' hymns 'for verse even of the simplest kind is more artificial than is necessary'. Thus he composed a massive hymnology on such diverse topics as 'Christian Wrestling', 'Christian Thought while Dressing' and a 'Declaration of the abuse of light'.[9] As a preacher his rule was that a sermon should be simple 'and suitable to the apprehension of the plain mind ... and yet ... come to the high with the same ministrations of freshness and delight as do their green parks and lawns on their return from the artificial and formal scenes of the town'.[10] Always preaching two forty-five minute sermons at Heversham he often went on to preach at a late evening service at Milnthorpe; not surprisingly on one occasion he collapsed from exhaustion in the pulpit.

Convinced that a clergyman's mission should be 'to instruct the children of the Kingdom and the little ones of the household of faith' he called regularly on the church schools at Heversham, Levens, Stainton and Milnthorpe and built Endmoor School in whose class-room is the inscription:

'A.D. 1868. In grateful remembrance that this school was built by the Venerable Robert Wilson Evans vicar of Heversham entirely at his own expense. This tablet was erected by his successor assisted by the teachers and scholars.'

As well as the 'Bishopric of Souls' 1843 and a 'Day in the Sanctuary' 1844 Evans published while at Heversham: 'Parochial Sermons 1842-55', 'Considerations on Church Collections' 1847, the 'Ministry of the Body' 1847, 'Tales of the ancient British Church' 1849, 'Exhortations on the Observance of the Lord's Day' 1850, 'Treatise of Versification Ancient and Modern' 1852, 'Daily Hymns' 1861 and 'England under God'.[11]

## Valehead

However, his most widely read book was the 'Rectory of Valehead' 1830. Ostensibly a work of fiction it is written in a severely rhetorical style lacking conversation and characterisation with descriptive passages similar to those of the gloomier 'Romantic' writers of the late eighteenth century. Accordingly its popularity (it ran to at least 15 editions) in the decades bridging the era of Austen with that of Dickens is difficult to understand. It is based on a dualogue between the rector and a nameless squire entitled 'My friend' with the turgid narrative interspersed with 54 poems including one - 'The Widow' which runs to 468 lines.[12] Some however, have timeless poignancy. 'Good Friday' can still be appreciated:

'Prepare! the holy prophet said
Rise, Son of God, the hour is nigh!
In dust a groaning world is laid,
Hell rears his shameless front on high!
In Mortal Clay
Thy Limbs array.
Uprise, thou Mighty one, to save
Go forth thou Conqueror O'er the grave!

The Son of God went forth, and lo!
Before his steps health's genial heat
Thrilled the wide world of spirits through,
And flesh in vigorous pulses beat.
Hell's hateful door
Was closed once more,
Heaven's wells of bliss o'erflowing ran:
Such gifts the Saviour gave to man.

And man prepar'd the gibe, the jeer,
The scorn, the mockery, hate and spite,
Words, looks, to wring the bitter tear,
The perilous day, the unpillow'd night,
The heart's keen ache,
When friends forsake,
The scourge, the thorn, the errors, the grave,
Such gifts man to his Saviour gave.[13]

Although written before his arrival in Westmorland the imagined description of 'Valehead' could well be Heversham:

'the parish is situated just where a wild and mountainous region meets a fertile champaign country, with which it imperceptibly blends by the gradual opening of its valleys ... with farms prettily scattered with their white fronts and half screening orchards looking over the face of the country'.[14]

Certainly its setting attracted him to Heversham. To quote the 'Manchester Guardian's' 'Obituary' 'One of his first acts was to build a new vicarage house on the shoulder of Heversham Head, a spot from which he ... could command in ordinary weather a glorious panorama of hill and vale and estuary and bay'.[15]

The former vicarage, now called High Leasgill, is Evans' most conspicuous memorial. It replaced the ancient parsonage situated two hundred yards west of the church which having ceased to be a vicarage became a private residence called Elm Lawn until c.1927 when it became the Heversham Hotel now renamed the Blue Bell at Heversham. The decision to build a new vicarage followed a survey (dated 20 May 1843) of the old vicarage made by Miles Thompson of the Kendal architects practice of Thompson and Webster. Thompson found

'the said House and offices are built of stone, slate and thatch and is in a state of great delapidation built at different periods without the slightest regard to architectural Design, the same being placed in a very low and damp situation (very much short of drainage and ventilation) and closely adjoining a large open stagnant sewer or Drain in the adjoining premises ... the floors, plaster work, doors and windows are generally very dilapidated ... and the inferior offices are in ruins'.

Not surprisingly Thompson concluded that 'the present house is quite unfit for the

Residence of the Incumbent of Heversham'.[16] As a result he was commissioned to design the New vicarage on the glebe land on the west of Heversham Head. Apart from the excellent views it was also conveniently close to the parish quarry from which the limestone masonry came.

Although in the 'Bishopric of Souls' Evans had written that the pastor should oversee his flock as a 'shepherd in his cabin' and not care for 'the comfort of your dwelling or the quality and accessibility of your neighbours' he had a fine house built. Costing £2,600 raised[17.] on a mortgage guaranteed jointly by himself and J.Gandy esq. of Heaves Lodge, its accommodation included a palatial drawing-room, dining room, study, kitchens, butler's pantry, housekeeper's room, a cavernous wash house, six principal bedrooms and three servants' rooms (all with fire-places), two staircases, wine and beer cellars, a dairy, stable, coachhouse, shippon, two water closets for the family and an earth closet for the staff. In Evans' day the household comprised his aged father, (until 1849), three maiden sisters, the Misses Jane Amelia, Georgina Elizabeth and Frances Louise, a cook, two maids, a footman and three outdoor menservants. Sadly in its 104 years as a vicarage High Leasgill never had a nursery for Evans was a bachelor and his three married successors were all childless.

Occasionally he used the beauty of his house's setting to illustrate a wider point as in the 'visibility of the church' in 'the Ministry of the Body':

> 'Now I am on the summit, and the valley of my home lies at my feet, betokened
> by the lights which are scattered in a row along its narrow bottom. I dimly descry
> the edge of its further side against the sky, and can trace its course under the deep
> gloom of Whitbarrow, where blazing windows proclaim the presence of man and
> cheer the dreariness of the solitude ... My responsibility immediately rushes upon
> my mind, but brings light rather than gloom. I feel a glow of trust in the chief and
> good Shepherd ... and hope that He will enable me so to teach and labour, that
> some at least of those dwellings, which now shoot forth such bright light into the
> surrounding darkness may be steady beacons... of pure spiritual light to their
> neighbourhood....'

Between 1854-64 Robert Wilson Evans was the first Archdeacon of Westmorland after this part of the Diocese of Chester was grafted onto Carlisle. On his death in 1866 lengthy obituaries appeared in 'The Times' and the 'Guardian' and the local press gave notice of a memorial appeal. Subscriptions were limited to £5 and yet within a few months £200 came in which more than met the cost of £160 for three memorial windows by Clayton and Bell. These were inserted, after the restoration of the church in 1868-71 in the south aisle windows which at the same time had their pannelled tracery renewed. Even when new the brightly coloured glass earned muted praise: the Bishop at the dedication declined to comment on their quality 'as an art product', merely stating that 'their absence of anything like show'[18.] reflected the character of the Archdeacon!

In the centre panel of the middle window appears (perhaps inevitably) the Good Shepherd, a lamb draped round His shoulders touched by the flowing golden locks of an obviously gentile Jesus; on the left the shepherd guards the fold while on the right he rescues a sheep caught by its horns in a thorn bush. The western window depicts the parable of the Sower, the text of the Archdeacon's last sermon, while the eastern window shows the wise and foolish virgins, the former wearing haloes and smug expressions, the latter, dizzily blonde, slumber decoratively on the ground.

That Robert Wilson Evans had trimmed his lamp to meet his shepherd was believed by his flock and the Hon. Mary Howard caused the words 'his wish was granted' to be inscribed on the memorial she set up to him in the sanctuary. This marble tablet has a border of vine leaves, a reference to yet another of Evans' favourite images exemplified in the opening stanzas of his 'Hymn on all Saints' Day':

> 'Array'd in vest of crimson dye
> As one that hath the vinepress trod.

Who art thou, say, that passest by?
Who these that hymn thee on thy road

The world's full vine-vat I have prest
And trampled in my fury there
Blood is the crimson on my vest
They spared not, and I could not spare.'[19]

## THOMAS MORRELL GILBERT

### A Record Span; Late Nineteenth Century Churchmanship; The Disintegration of the Parish

Archdeacon Evans' successor as vicar was a young man of 29, Thomas Morrell Gilbert. Already when he arrived in 1866 he had been Fellow of Trinity 1859-66, Curate of Hurst-pierrepoint 1861-63 and Curate of St.Bartholemew's, Chichester (where his father was the Bishop) 1863-66.[1] Also he had travelled extensively in the Holy Land. A living of £650 p.a. and situated in a beautiful area, inhabited by many agreeably genteel residents was, of course, well worth having. Even so, with his ability and connections the Reverend Gilbert might well have regarded Heversham as being but a step in his career. Perhaps he had an eye on creating a good impression when soon after his induction he flung himself with gusto into the restoration of the church. However, before that long and costly programme was completed he seems to have been caught by the spell cast by the building and the parish with the result that, like all his predecessors since the seventeenth century and his successors (so far!), he stayed until the end of his career. He was made Canon of Carlisle in 1877 and was Rural Dean of Kirkby Lonsdale from 1888-1913. His incumbency lasted 55 years, a span unequalled at Heversham and rarely exceeded in the history of the diocese. Arriving in the midst of the High Victorian era of peace and prosperity he stayed on into the war-weary and impoverished 1920's; one of his last acts being to unveil the war memorial to heroes whose parents he had baptised.[2]

Few vicars can have been so revered or so loved. Yet, unlike Evans, he was not a famous writer; neither was he a great administrator, although he had a passion for composing, in a large, angular hand, innumerable memoranda and rules; nor was he particularly charitable. He did make substantial contributions to the church restoration fund and to St.Mark's Home at Natland but these were in the early days. Later his largesse was restricted to a Christmas dole of a sixpence for each of the school children. They got also a jam turn-over after they had sung 'Land of Hope and Glory' at his front door on Empire Day and Ginger Snaps (three for first, two for second, one for third) as prizes in the summer sports in the vicarage field.[3]

Socially Canon Gilbert mixed almost exclusively with the gentry. In middle age he married

117

a gentleman's daughter, Miss Esther Anne Harrison of Woodhouse. She 'brought him money' and became a great support in his parochial work, even teaching needlework in the village school. Nevertheless Mrs Gilbert expected the girls to curtsey to her as they did the Argles and the Bagots.

Despite an aristocratic manner characterised by his 'ultra church voice',[4] Canon Gilbert was always out and about in his parish. He was a great walker. Hence the sight was familiar to all of the stocky, black-garbed cleric waddling along with his hooked nose and bewhiskered chin jutting purposefully forward from under a tall hat perched on a balding head. Often on encountering a parishioner, whether a burly farmer or embarrassed matron did not matter he would induce him or her to kneel in prayer with him by the roadside. At other times cushioned in his brougham, his wife and nieces, the Misses Whintle in querulous attendance, he would bowl around the lanes on longer journeys.

Of the many and diverse roles of priest he exemplified those of minister of reconciliation and man of prayer. Domestic crises or death brought him instantly into his parishioners' homes where he would give vent to a taste for long and loud extemporary prayer. In 1921 he was said to combine a 'charming sympathetic manner with the humility of a little child'. Not surprisingly the memory of such a paragon lasted for at least half a century and attempts by successive parsons to inaugurate change was confounded often by old parishioners basing their argument on 'in Canon Gilbert's Day ... or ... 'Canon Gilbert always used to say...'[5.]

## Churchmanship

Canon Gilbert continued the tradition of clear protestant worship. Humphrey Hallows in the 'Gazette' in 1880[6.] described the service as being 'about as broad and low as it could be' and tartly commented that the vicar preached an 'undemanding sermon'. The music was damned similarly with faint praise for

> 'the choir is of the old mixed class and with great discretion the service is kept well within its powers. No exalted aim at choral effect is set up, no intoned passages are attempted, everything is done on the simplest possible lines and naturally no conspicuous failure is exhibited'.

As the choir gave little or no lead it was regrettable that there was no clerk to start the responses and 'as a consequence the congregation discharges in an unintelligible mumble and muttering' failing 'to reach the ideal of public worship'[7.] Shortly after 1888, however, spurred on by the Argles and also by Mrs. Gilbert and with a new organ to accompany it, the choir improved considerably. By 1900 its members formed the nucleus of the Eversley Choral Union, performed on 'Messiahs' and won prizes at the Mary Wakefield Festival.

Hallows also 'noticed a common practice observed in Westmorland for parishioners to enter the church after divine service ...' Despite the efforts of Canon Gilbert and his successors and, also, better transport and broadcast time-checks, this weakness characterised the church in subsequent decades.

Canon Gilbert's special interest was education, twice weekly he took the morning assembly at the village school. When it moved to Leasgill, next door to the vicarage, recalcitrant scholars were sent 'to't Canon for punishment'. New pupils were encountered with a pat on the head and the injunction to 'be a good little boy (or girl) and come to school and learn your lesson well', All children were addressed by their full baptismal names. As vicar he was chairman of the managers of the village school for 55 years. He was also manager of the National schools at Milnthorpe for 50 years and a vice-chairman of the Grammar School Governors for 44 years.

Following the passing of the Parish Council Act Canon Gilbert was elected top of the poll to the joint council for Heversham with Milnthorpe. After the division of the civil parish in 1896 he continued to serve on the Heversham Parish Council.

## Break up of the Parish

By the turn of the century Canon Gilbert had presided over the disintegration of the ecclesiastical parish. The process began on the 14th January 1869 when by an Order in Council Crosthwaite and Lythe became a separate parish. On the 3rd March 1873 most of the Preston Richard was transferred to Preston Patrick. The rest of Preston Richard along with Stainton, Sedgewick and Barrows Green became the new parish of Crosscrake on the 11th July 1877. Levens was granted full parochial rights in 1908. Shortly before his retirement Canon Gilbert advised on the final break of the ecclesiastical connection with Milnthorpe formalized in 1923.[8]

For the last twenty years of his ministry Canon Gilbert was aided by a succession of curates including the Reverends Bannerman, Dean, Inglehow, Lowe and Webb. Possibly because his pastoral duties were shared he remained remarkably vigorous in old age, and was known to walk regularly over the Head to Hincaster and then go on to Levens. On one occasion a gang of boys rabitting in the Mabbin Hall woods were chased away by the octogenarian canon wielding a Bible in one hand and a brolly in the other.

## Retirement

When his wife died in 1917 Canon Gilbert's health began to decline. At Easter in 1921 he suffered a slight stroke and in June he wrote to the wardens stating that

'the infirmities of age have increased upon me very much of late and even before the recent attack from which by God's mercy I am now recovered I had to come to the conclusion that the time had arrived when I ought to resign and make way for a younger and more active vicar'.[9]

Naturally, if illogically, the news was greeted with disbelief as well as grief. As in the case of Queen Victoria's death it appeared as if some monstrous reversal of the course of nature had taken place for almost all his parishioners had not known a time when he was not in their midst.

Inevitably there followed an avalanche of presentations. As a 'token of their esteem and mark of appreciation of his earnest work in the school'[10] the teachers and scholars of Leasgill gave him a large photograph of the school. Milnthorpe schools donated four volumes of the history of Russia, the United States of America, Scotland and Europe. The Heversham metal industry class contributed an ornate copper hot water jug and a copper biscuit box. At a tearful ceremony in the Athenaeum the longest serving warden, Mr. T.Inman of Milton Moor, presented on behalf of the congregation 'a deep saddle-backed oak chair with reading stand and hoped that he would be spared to enjoy it'.[11]

Right to the end 'the Canon' took the services and, incidentally, conducted a marriage in the week of his departure. Moreover, he took part in a court case the report of which filled two columns of the 'Gazette'.[12] In the case Canon Gilbert sued Thomas Peet for £3.10s damages caused to his brougham when it had been parked outside Milnthorpe Post Office. The judge agreed with Canon Gilbert that, despite the advent of the motor car, it was reasonable for the brougham to stand in the middle of the road, and that humbler vehicles should wait until it was moved before attempting to pass. The damages were reduced, however, to £2.10s.

Finally on the 27th and 28th October Mr. T.E. Kilshaw offered for sale 515 lots of furniture and effects from the vicarage. Prices were recorded as being 'high' and included £46 for a pianoforte, £10 for a 33 piece Worcester desert service and £1.5s. for 'a brass dinner gong twenty inches in diameter'.[13]

Contrary to his estimate, and perhaps hopes, Canon Gilbert was 'spared' for seven more years. He retired with his library to his niece Miss Wintles's house in Warwick Square, London. Each year he stayed for three summer months at 'Heversham House' Arnside, from where he was taken round his former parish in a taxi. On holiday at the age of 91 he preached his last sermon propped in a chair set under the chancel arch. On his death in London in 1928 at the age of 93 his remains were brought back to Heversham in a lead-lined coffin that took eight men to lift. One of the many press obituaries stated that Thomas

Morrell Gilbert 'combined along with a Christ-like demeanour the urbanity of a thorough going English gentleman'[14] surely a perfect epitaph for an Anglican parson. Sadly, despite a legacy by his neice Miss Wintle of £25 in 1940 for its maintenance Canon Gilbert's gravestone has fallen and is now overgrown. (1982).

### Great Occasions

It was during Canon Gilbert's long incumbency that the church reached its social apogee being the fashionable place of worship for all the great families of the area. Except for the Argles of Eversley, the Swindlehursts of Hincaster House and the Rogers Shaws of Greenside, gentry like the Benson's of Hyning, the Gandy's of Heaves, the Walkers of Brettargh Holt, the Bagot's of Levens and the Keightly's of Old Hall had to by-pass churches nearer their residences on their way to Heversham. In the Middle of the twentieth century older residents recalled how in their Victorian and Edwardian youth the landlords and ostlers of the 'Blue Bell' and the 'Eagle and Child' were kept busy on Sundays unharnessing and watering horses and catering for the coachman and footman. Most of the latter it seemed did not attend divine service. Even had they wished to join the congregation space would have been limited as only three or four pews were reserved for servants. To worship alongside their betters was, of course, unthinkable.

### Weddings

All the village would turn out to see a 'country' wedding when the carriages were drawn by horses 'wearing fancy ear cups with tassels, the lamps filled with flowers', the drivers in tall silk hats with a cockade in the side ... and white gloves holding white reigns'. Two such weddings occurred in April and August 1900 when respectively the Misses Alice Elizabeth and Ada May Walker of Brettargh Holt were married. On the first occasion the 'Westmorland Gazette' gushingly reported that

'special preparations had been made for the event which was one of unusual interest for the villagers of Levens, Heversham and Leasgill who assembled in large numbers ... From the entrance to the churchyard to the church porch an awning had been erected and the pathway lined with baize whilst the interior of the church still embellished with pretty Easter decorations was exceedingly bright. The ceremony was fixed for a quarter to two o'clock but long before that time joyful peals were rung out.'

The service was conducted by Canon Gilbert and by Dr. Bentley, the Bishop of Manchester, 'assisted' by four other clergy. The organist, Miss Germaine, played as well as Mendlesohn's and Wagner's Wedding Marches, the Funereal 'O God our help in ages past' and 'Blessed are they that fear the Lord'. Unfortunately 'the weather was not as bright as the happy occasion demanded and ... fleecy leaden grey clouds scudded across the sky.'

When Miss Sarah was married four months later 'the weather was tropical, there was hardly a cloud in the azure sky and the beautiful country was seen in one of its best aspects'.

The church must have been decorated to an even greater extent than for Miss Alice's wedding for

'the interior of the edifice was very bright and the sun streaming through the windows and lighting up all around. On the communion table there were two lovely bouquets of choice white exotics, whilst the chancel was adorned with beautiful white and purple and blue flowers some nestling and the others springing from beds of lovely evergreens and bouquets of red roses' -

while even - 'the pulpit was entwined with evergreens and the effect was most pretty'.

In the following October when Miss Ada May Holme of Owlett Ash, Milnthorpe, was married the 'Gazette', after describing the church decorations and the lavish musical performance of the valiant Miss Germaine, went into confusing ecstasies over the bride's dress:

'The bride who looked very pretty was attired in a white duchess satin dress trained short trimmed with chiffon a low bodice with transparent (!) chemisette and sleeeves of tucked chiffon trimmed with handsome embroidery of chiffon and orange blossom, and a court train and handsome trouvelle (true lovers knots and flowers) trimmed with orange blossom as was the net veil on which was a wreath of orange blossom'.

The bride also wore the present of the bridegroom, a diamond and emerald pendant. Such an ensemble must have drawn gasps of admiration or envy from the village school girls who invariably were let out of school (fashionable weddings were never on a Saturday) to line the path. Photographs exist of members of the pinafored and curtsying girlish throng holding garlands over the heads of Mr. and Mrs. Henry Melville Gaskell after their wedding in 1905. The bride was the daughter of Captain Josceline Fitzroy Bagot of Levens Hall, the Member of Parliament for South Westmorland.

### A Grand Funeral

It was the funeral in March 1913 of Sir Josceline Bagot, Bart (as he had become the year previously) that drew to Heversham Church the largest gathering in its history. News of the death of the 'beau ideal of a country M.P.' was communicated to the parish via the Mayor of Kendal who had been informed by telegram sent from London by Lady Bagot. Immediately Canon Gilbert organised a special Sunday Service at which Mrs. Nelson (nee Germaine) played selections from Brahm's Requiem and the Canon expressed the loss felt by the whole neighbourhood and also hoped 'that in the elections which must unhappily follow nothing may be said on either side unworthy of those who profess to be followers of the Lord Jesus Christ'.

On the day prior to the funeral the coffin and family party were met at Milnthorpe Station by the vicar of Levens, the Rev.Swann (who later consoled Lady Bagot to the extent of marrying her). The coffin draped with the Union Jack was then put by the eight tenant bearers on a lorry covered with wreaths and drawn through Milnthorpe (where blinds were drawn and the passing bell was tolling) to Heversham. Here the cortège was met by Canon Gilbert and the curate, the Rev. W.A.Inglehow, who together conducted a benediction.

The 'Westmorland Gazette' takes up the account of the funeral day.

'Between nine and 1.30 villagers were allowed to file past the coffin. After the 12.55

*Funeral of Sir Josceline Bagot M.P.*

121

train from the Kendal district arrived began the massing of the thousands who assembled to pay tribute to the memory of Sir Josceline. By the time the two special trains had also discharged their loads at Heversham station hundreds of others had come by road - motoring, driving, cycling or walking so that there were between four and five thousand people gathered about the church. Fortunately the weather remained fine until the ceremony was over, though soon after the crowds had moved away from the graveside the threatening clouds released their burden....

It was not generally known that the seating accommodation of the church had been reserved for public bodies, the representatives of the two political parties and parishioners of Heversham who of course included the tenantry of Levens. Hundreds of the public were around the main entrance long after half past one but only a few score could be admitted.'

Only after the wardens Messrs T.A.Argles, G.Pickthall and J.Inman had packed the church was a message sent to Levens for the cortege to start its journey. On the arrival, the mourners were conducted to the chancel by Canon Gilbert, Rev.S.Swann and Rev. Ronald Symes (who collectively took the service) and five other clergyman including Canon Rawnsley (founder of the National Trust) who with Canon Gilbert signed the register. This time, as well as 'Onward Christian Soldiers', 'O God, our help in ages past' and Brahm's Requiem, Mrs. Nelson extended her repertoire to include 'I know that My Redeemer liveth'.

At the conclusion of the service

'in order to keep space about the grave for the mourners the clergy and choir a cordon was drawn by forty Heversham Grammar School boys in charge of Messrs. Hamilton and A.Adamson (assistant masters) and the first Kendal Scouts (Lady Bagots's Own) in charge of Scout Master Stoker. At no funeral in Westmorland has there been such a wonderful display of wreaths. They came from all parts of the country and all sorts and conditions of people. Around the graveside they spread across the grass in all direction; the rest almost completely carpeted the chancel. When piled on the grave they will form a floral monument that will impress on the visitor to the quiet churchyard the love and esteem in which the dead was held more deeply that by any epitaph cut in marble'.

The 'Gazette' then filled two columns of names of principal mourners and the donors of the 153 wreaths!'

Ironically the village along with the rest of Europe, was soon to have its fill of funerals for 18 months later the Great War broke out. This cataclysm not only claimed many of the village mourners including a score of the Grammar boys, their master Mr.Hamilton but also Sir Alan Desmond Bagot, the principal mourner on this Heversham's grandest solemn occasion.

**EDWARD RADCLYFFE ELLIS**
**Vicar 1921-1939**

When instituted and inducted to the vicarage of Heversham on the 10th November 1921 Edward Radclyffe Ellis had been already a priest for over thirty years. His experience was great. He had been an assistant master and chaplain at Cheam School from 1888 to 1897, curate of St.Stephen Martyr, Portland Town, London 1897-1900, Lecturer (vicar) of Bolton 1900-1910 and Rector of Norris Bank Manchester 1910-1921.[1] Thus when he came to Heversham he was in his middle fifties. In as much as he represented the habits and ideals of the late Victorians he, no doubt, was in tune with the wishes of his new parishioners. Yet, following as he did the inimitable and seemingly interminable Canon Gilbert, his position was not easy. Difficulties of adjustment for him and for the parish were emphasised by the ways in which his character contrasted with that of his predecessor. Whereas 'the Canon' had been ebullient and sociable, Mr. Ellis was cool, reserved and socially aloof. The vicarage was no longer a centre for church activities. The only regular entertainments held there were the choir party and an austere 'evening' for the Bible Class. A reason for the decline in parsonical entertainment could have been that the vicarage indoor staff had been reduced to two and there was only one gardener!

The new vicar's natural reserve was tempered by his wife who 'missed nothing' and 'made the bullets for him to fire' - a constant taunt about vicaresses but in this case it was remembered for 50 years! After a quarter of a century in the parochial ministry it must have been hard for him to hear on all sides the constant reference to the way 'the Canon' had done things and also to be in receipt of frequent letters of advice from the Canon himself. These ranged from the question of the boundary walls to the old school, suggested eulogies for dead parishioners, the glebe, choristers and the Hincaster Mission Room.[2] The latter issue caused some embarrassment. The Mission Room had been opened by the Swindlehurst family of Hincaster House in the 1880's and the Matins, Evensong and a Sunday School were held there weekly. The furniture had been provided by Canon Gilbert. Forty years later in 1923 it seemed that the Canon required payment for the furniture. Eventually Mr. Ellis tactfully induced the Canon to give the furniture to the parish and also won approval by asking him to preach when he came for his summer holidays.

**Parish Business**
Even so in his first few years the records imply that people were prepared to be rubbed up the wrong way. In 1923 the Dallam Agent, Mr. Nanson, informed the vicar and the P.C.C. that

seats were not to be allocated in the Dallam Chapel without the permission of Sir Maurice Bromley Wilson, who also charged 6d a year rent for the altar frontal case kept in the Chapel. All this was especially annoying as Sir Maurice did not worship at Heversham and his parochial tenants sat in the main body of the church. The number of village boys willing to sing in the choir fell off. A fee of 7/6d per quarter 'to be regarded as a prize and not a payment' was introduced and the numbers rose again. Indeed the choir remained at the centre of church life and in 1928 it acted as host for a singing festival in which representatives from eight other parishes took part. In 1926 faint tremors of the General Strike touched the parish when the loyal but stubborn Parish Clerk and Groundsman Robert Squire apparently went on strike after 'another person' had been paid to cut ivy off the wall. Two letters from the P.C.C. failed to get him back to work until he had been thanked formally for all he had done in the past and, presumably, future employment had been guaranteed.[3.]

Yet despite the tea-cup storms the business of the parish was directed efficiently. Much of Mr. Ellis' work was spent in reorganising the finances of the living and the church.[4.] The accounts were put into categories and thanks to the Secretary, Harry Sisson, were beautifully kept. In membership and activities the P.C.C. expanded although the plea by the vicar in 1924 'that members were expected to help spiritually' was ignored. Lay men (not yet women) reading the lesson was still rare. In 1929 the solemn resolution was passed

> 'that the council requests the vicar to use from time to time as he shall think desirable such variations of the services of Morning and Evening Prayer, Litany and Holy Communion as are provided in the Book known as the 'Book of Common Prayer' with additions and deviations proposed in 1928' and have or shall have the sanction of the Bishop of the Diocese.'[5.]

The debates in which Convocation had approved and Parliament refused to sanction the Revised Prayer Book had been followed in the parish with feeling supporting both sides. The resulting compromise at Heversham was that the old form should be used twice monthly at one early celebration and one late with a modified and, incidentally, shortened form of the 1928 book for Matins and Evensong.[6.]

Mr. Ellis encouraged the parish to support a widening range of charities and missions. Occasionally he was over-optimistic. In 1927 a meeting was called for 'grasping the opportunities now possible for working amongst Moslems', and the 'question of what should be done in Heversham was left to a committee'. Owing to the absence of any followers of the Prophet in the parish the committee took the, by that time, already time-honoured decision to hold a coffee morning and send the proceeds to an Indian Mission. Similarly an attempt in 1938 to found a 'Men's Auxiliary for Social and Moral Welfare' in the parish to combat the evils of 'prostitution and degeneracy' came to nothing.

Although from records and memories Edward Ellis' incumbency does not seem to have been particularly productive there was no great decline in church attendance.[7.] Indeed Mr. Ellis was regarded as being a fine preacher. Sometimes, however, he impressed more by the weight of his knowledge than by his eloquence. One gentleman, it is recalled, on hearing Mr. Ellis' first sermon at Heversham said it was the finest piece of preaching he had heard but never attended again.[8.] Another lady paid the vicar the back-handed compliment by stating that she prayed daily for a bishop's mitre for him.[9.] That an effective, if not affectionate relationship did exist between vicar and parish was shown tangibly by the Argles' memorials, the restored organ and the installation of electric light - all achieved during the Ellis years. These and other improvements continued to be provided largely by the richer families with whom, in the tradition of the place, Mr. Ellis kept 'well-in'.

Mr Ellis also played a prominent role in refurbishing the Athenaeum[10.] after it had been given to the parish by the Argles family in 1927. That he was regarded highly by the clergy was demonstrated during his final years at Heversham when he was made Rural Dean of Kirkby Lonsdale.

Finally, at a P.C.C. meeting on the 30th March 1939, 'the vicar spoke of his impending resignation. Mr. Astley and Mr. Kilshaw spoke on behalf of those present, of the great regret they felt at the prospect of his giving up his work at Heversham'. In June a presentation was held in the grounds of Heversham House, the home of Miss Austin and Mrs. Stewart. The Vice-Chairman of the P.C.C. Mrs. Ethel McLeod stated that they 'had had a real friend and leader and all of them had been impressed by his steadfastness and perseverance'.[11] Mrs. Ellis was given a rug and the vicar a photograph of the church, taken by Mr. M.Sisson, and a cheque for £60.[12]

**WILFRED ALEC CLEGHORN**
**Vicar 1939-55**

Wilfred Alec Cleghorn was a native of Darlington. He was ordained in 1921 and before he came to Heversham he had spent his entire ministry in the north-east, having been a curate at St.Cuthbert's, Sheffield, at Rotherham and from 1931, Vicar of Thorpe Hedley. He was descended from an ancient border family and was a Freeman of the Borough of Berwick-on-Tweed.[1]

Instituted by the Bishop of Barrow-in-Furness on the 25th September 1939 his incumbency spanned the Second World War and the first post-war decade. His popularity was great and the memory of him enduring. Even twenty-five years after his death which occured on the 27th December 1955 the vicar[2] could state that in conversation older parishioners implied that 'Cleggy' had only been gone a year or two. Perhaps his appeal could be attributed to the ways in which he resembled a caricature of the stage parson of the period. Of slightly above average height, his lean figure was rendered angular by an outsize and wide low church dog-collar within which his neck would oscilate in a tortoise like motion while chanting the liturgy. He spoke in high-pitched rapid tones but sang sonorously and often off key with gold pinc-nez or horn-rimmed spectacles quivering on the end of his nose.[3]

An assiduous, enthusiastic and often-lengthy visitor, he would either rattle round the parish in a match-box like Austin or plod along the road, avoiding the pavement, staring at the ground, his cassock trailing in the gutter.[4] Once devotional or parish business had been dispensed with, he would embark on a lengthy and gleeful analysis of the news of the day being an accomplished 'fetcher and carrier' himself. Somehow he managed to hold cup, saucer and cigarette in one hand while the other was left free for gesticulation and emphasis[5]

He ministered at a time when church clubs and groups reached a crescendo both in variety and support, before television and secularism won the day. No better master of ceremonies could there have been for the parish kaleidoscope of vicarage parties for the choir, Mothers' Union and 'bible class girls of over 14'[6] for Sunday School trips to Heysham Head or the Christmas Pantomime at Morecambe, or the C. of E. school 'charabanc' summer trips to the Lakes. The latter occasionally included Cartmel Priory where Mr. Cleghorn would encourage budding juvenile historians to show off their knowledge of church history to which he had introduced them on tours of the parish church after the children's services.

In 1946 with the other villages he inaugurated the annual 'Children's Day' fancy dress and sports held in the Princes Way field in June which always started with a short service. At the coronation in 1953 he conducted community singing round the bonfire built by the Church Scouts and Guides on the summit of the Head. Nimbly he managed to duck as the near gale force wind changed and tore the flames horizontally towards the choir.

Perhaps because he and his wife Jessie were childless or because the proportion of old people living in the parish was greatest in his time he delighted in the company of children. While the vicarage was at Leasgill he would pop through the side gate into the school yard at playtime and join the children, especially the girls, in their games. His Wednesday Assemblies and R.E. lessons were a favourite feature of the school week. A regular tale was of his conversation which took place dramatically in the Holy Land in 1917 when, as a private soldier, he had 'marched behind Allenby' into Jerusalem and seen the Union Jack hoisted over the site of Calvary. How he pushed through the refugees and the squalor of war to worship by the silver star set in the floor of the Church of the Nativity at Bethlehem gave an extra thrill to the Christmas story. Memories of this earlier conflict may have been the reason why he invited the German prisoners of war from Bela Camp to sing 'Stille Nachte' at the Carol Services in 1944, 1945 and 1946. This gesture of reconciliation and open friendship was typical of Wilfred Cleghorn. For he was not a stage parson - he was a man of God. The chatter and the public panache were a vehicle for spiritual counselling as often as they were signs of a highly strung nature. His sympathy and advice while ministering to the bereaved, to wives of absent servicemen, evacuees and the sick was practical and often supported by carefully considered reading matter. His preaching had a disjointed style which nevertheless contained telling phrase or topical reference. Occasionally he would ask a pointed question which struck home as to confirmation candidates about 'when' they said their prayers and 'what' was in them.[7]

Apart from memories the records of Wilfred Cleghorn's incumbency are slight, being mainly P.C.C. minutes. They show a few modifications in the forms of worship. In 1940 wafer bread was introduced for Communions, mid-week celebrations were started in 1942, out-door Rogation services in 1945 and Communion servers appointed in 1950. Special events included a St.Andrew's Day of Intercession on 30th November 1942 mid-day prayers and an evening service at the vicarage. In 1944 Heversham parish acted as host for congregations from Beetham, Crosscrake, Milnthorpe and Levens at a cinema service held in the Public Rooms at Milnthorpe. Imperialism was not yet dead for in 1948 an Empire Youth Rally was held at the church at which the preacher was the Rev. E.Shufflebottom.[8] Missionary activity was encouraged and in 1948 the Rev. B.Jayawandena paid a visit to the church and school where he reduced the infants[9] to tears as he was the first real life black man any of them had seen. Immigration had not yet begun!

There were dificulties in maintaining the church's fabric in war time. When wire netting was required for the belfry louvres in 1944 it had to be borrowed from the village tennis clubs courts at Plumtree Hall. Moreover, replacement of the netting could not be obtained until 1949. It also took five years before a hole in the east window was repaired owing to Messrs. Shrigley and Hunt's being involved in repairing bomb-damaged churches. In 1943 the church sent surplus altar linen to the Bishop of Liverpool for use in blitzed churches.

Somehow in the depths of austerity a major repair and redecoration scheme was pushed through. In 1948 Messrs. Hellas of Reading vacuum cleaned the church roof, timbers, walls and tower and treated all the wood for wood worm, leaving behind the stench of cuprinol that pervaded the church's atmosphere for the next thirty years. After the walls had been distempered the bill came to £448. This was met by the sale of securities and by a gigantic Christmas Fayre superintended by Mrs Cleghorn. The staggering figure of £559 was also raised at a Garden Party held with Levens parish at Levens Hall as a contribution to the Bishop of Carlisle's appeal for £550,000 to build more churches. Hyper-inflation and redundant churches were yet to come! One permanent memorial of the Cleghorn years is the Children's Corner. This was placed in the Levens Chapel in 1943 by permission of Mrs. Robin Bagot who, according to the P.C.C. records, has 'to act on behalf of her husband who could not be contacted' as he was a prisoner-of-war of the Germans.

### A Windfall

A more noticeable change was announced dramatically at a P.C.C. meeting on the 29th July 1947 when

> 'the vicar referred to the passing of Mrs Rhoda Thompson and the meeting stood in silence. Before reading an extract from her will the vicar stated that very few clergy had the privilege of imparting such good news as he was to set before the council. Mrs Thompson had been a most generous benefactor to the parish and her intention was that her legacy should be used in anyway that would be for the welfare of the parish as a whole. She had bequeathed her residence, 'The Knoll', for use as a vicarage, the residue of her estate which would be worth at least £4,000 and a reversionary interest after two lives on £10,000. First among the objects for which she wished her money to be used was the maintenance of the fabric of the church'.[10]

Accordingly the High Leasgill vicarage was sold by auction after it had been agreed that none of its grounds would be required by the adjoining school. (Twenty years later part of the ground was in fact obtained when a new drive was made for the school.) £150 was spent on alterations at 'The Knoll' which involved removing the wall between the morning room and the drawing room to create a 30 foot long reception area. This unfortunately meant that the dining room had to double as a study.

The death of Wilfred Alec Cleghorn coming as it did between Christmas and the New Year in 1955 had a profound effect on the parish. The tearful funeral was presided over by the Bishop of Penrith and the church was packed, it was said, as it had not been since the funeral of Sir Josceline Bagot in 1913. Great sympathy was felt for Mrs. Cleghorn whose quieter qualities had strengthened her husband and who 'had also done her best to help the parish in every way. It was unanimously agreed that a gift of money should be given to Mrs Cleghorn to commemorate the life and work of Mr. Cleghorn'. Eventually the, at that time, impressive sum of £500 was sent to Mrs Cleghorn who characteristically presented the handsome silver and crystal communion cruets to the church and donated £100 to the churchyard fund. Yet although she lived for another 23 years Jessie Cleghorn could never be persuaded by her many local friends to visit the parish in which her husband had served so memorably.

*Presentation
Ceremony to
Canon Mrs. Lane 1964*

*L to R:-
J.Latham
N.Chamley
Mrs.Lane
Canon Lane
Churchwardens
J.Sisson
M.Kilshaw
W.Dawson*

## CANON LANE: 1956-64

Stanley Lane was inducted as vicar of Heversham on the 27th May 1956. The next morning at 8 a.m. Communion he dedicated the wine and water cruets, donated to the memory of Wilfred Alec Cleghorn, a gesture reflecting his willingness to tackle sympathetically the job of following a popular predecessor. Neither for the vicar nor for the parish was adjustment to new ways easy. Like the Rev. E.R.Ellis he had been in the ministry for over thirty years before coming to Heversham. He had been curate at Ashton-under-Lyme from 1924 to 1930, vicar of Audenshaw from 1930 to 1942 and Rector of Newchurch in Rossendale from 1942 to 1956. He had become an honorary canon of Manchester Cathedral in 1950.[1]

Both in character and in the exercise of his ministry he differed from the Rev. Cleghorn. As a graduate of Durham he was the first vicar since the seventeenth century not to be a Cambridge man. As the father of two grown up sons, one of whom became a Roman Catholic priest, he was the first vicar for 150 years to be a parent. Always dressed in dark clerical clothes with a rosetted canon's hat on his head, he presented an earnest, if not dour, image to the world which was, however, modified by a willingness to converse on everyday matters as well as those of pastoral importance. As a sick visitor he was most assiduous and several parishioners recalled that, on coming round from an anaesthetic, the first sounds they heard were those of Canon Lane's short, quick steps pattering down the ward.

Always conscious of the distinctive role of the priest and the breadth of the Anglican tradition, he was not a Low Churchman. He did not go in for the spiky extremes of Anglo-Catholic ritual but, he did encourage the congregation, to bow to the altar. Tender consciences were stirred when he obtained, in 1958, an anonymous gift of vestments for use at Holy Communion. The Parish Church Council minute does not record the anguished feelings of some parishioners:

> 'The vicar gave a short address upon clerical vesture according to the Prayer Book Ornaments Rubric of 1549. It was noticeable that church people had appreciated the bringing back into use by the Bishop of their correct vesture for ceremonial occasions. - He explained in detail the meaning and purpose of eucharistic vestments when worn by the clergy. He asked the meeting what the attitude would be if a gift of vestments was presented to the church. No one expressed disapproval. The vicar also mentioned the need for a private communion set for use in the ministration of the sick.'[2]

The vestments were accepted but ceased to be used in the 1970's partly because the then incumbent[3] was considerably taller than the slightly built Canon for whom they had been made. A sick communion set was given to the church by Mr Brownson of 'Colena', Prince's Way, in 1959. Unfortunately this was stolen from the vestry when the church was burgled in 1978.

As a preacher Canon Lane 'made the rafters sing' as they had not rung since the days of Canon Gilbert. At Evensong, which continued to be well supported, he preached often a teaching sermon based on historical as well as scriptural themes. As if to acknowledge his allegiance to the notion of the ministry of the word or to confound those who accused him of popery, Canon Lane wore preaching bands in the manner of non-conformist ministers.

Much of his efforts were devoted to money matters. Even at his first P.C.C. Canon Lane 'spoke about his stipend' and at the next meeting obtained approval 'of the recommendation of the church wardens to pay telephone rent and charges at the vicarage and to give £10 towards the expenses of office'.[4] In 1958 a gift envelope scheme was introduced for missionary appeals and for church offerings which were distributed throughout the parish. Above all the most impressive memorial to Canon Lane was the 'Friends of Heversham' scheme details of which are given in the section on church finances.

In the 1959/60 the church electric lighting was renewed, paid for by Mr Miles Kenyon of Kidside and in 1960 the church clock was overhauled in its centenary year. Another costly scheme quickly and successfully accomplished was the renovation of the Old School, involving the construction of a new kitchen and toilets, making it a much more comfortable meeting room for the Mothers' Union, Sunday School and Confirmation Classes. The latter were one of Canon Lane's special interests and the number of candidates, especially of adults, increased. Moreover, a number of young confirmed men were encouraged by Canon Lane to start their active work for the church by being servers.

### Needlework
Going back to Victorian times the Church had obtained much excellent needlework. Many of the altar frontals had been the work of parishioners like the Misses Austin of Heversham House and Mrs Harry Sisson of 'Birknott'. In Canon Lane's time an ambitious scheme to make embroidered kneelers by Mrs Brownlie of 'Underwood' who, a commemorative book

*Repairs to the roof c.1960.*

*L to R:-*
*J.Sisson*
*W.Dawson*
*R.Sisson*
*James Sisson*
*Ian Sisson*

129

in the vestry records, 'appealed for a group of workers and gave continuous instruction and inspiration in the art of embroidery to those who responded'. In all, between 1960 and 1970 205 kneelers were made by 'lady parishioners'. From the records the most productive ladies were Miss Bessie Handley and Miss Florence Barlow who made 18 kneelers each. Several other ladies completed up to six while the long Communion rail hassock was made by Mary J.Webster, C.Smith, E.M.Brownlie and M.C.M.Fawcett.

Any fear that the Friends of Heversham scheme would put an end to all the social functions in which the parish delighted were removed by Canon Lane and the P.C.C.'s organising Harvest and Rogation suppers, Christmas parties and coffee evenings. More memorably were three 'tableaux vivants' staged in the Athenaeum by Mr George Ashworth from Lancashire who produced a 'Janeite Evening' in 1957, the 'Bronte Story' in 1958 and the 'Dickens Stories' in 1959 - in which members of the congregation of all ages and acting abilities took part, including Canon and Mrs Lane.

That Canon Lane was deeply respected was shown by impressive Easter offerings which each year reached over £100 and by the response to the presentation appeal for him and Mrs Lane on their retirement in 1964. Thus on the 2nd February 1964 despite 'inclement weather' over 100 parishioners were present in the Athenaeum when the vice-chairman of the P.C.C. Mr John E.Latham presented Canon Lane with a cheque for a 'substantial sum of money' and Mrs Tyson for the Mothers' Union gave Mrs Lane a flowering plant and a voucher for rose trees and her new garden. Mr Latham referred to the many qualities by which Canon and Mrs Lane would be remembered by the people of Heversham for their energy and inspiration on launching the Friends of Heversham Church Scheme, to their work in connection with the renovation of the old school and to Mrs Lane's guidance in the Mothers' Union and to the solid foundations on which they had built the church life of the village during the last eight years.[5.]

The parishioners' wishes that Canon and Mrs Lane might have a long and healthy retirement were realised for happily they still lived at Casterton in 1982 to which they had gone on leaving Heversham.

*A Christening by Rev. T.Martin*

**TOM MARTIN**
**Vicar 1964-76**

Tom Martin became vicar of Heversham in June 1964. He had been curate at St.Mary Helliwell, Bolton, from 1937 to 1942 and at Holy Trinity Littleborough from 1942 to 1946 before going to St.Paul's Ramsbottom where he was vicar from 1946 to[1.] 1964. His popularity in his former parish was indicated when several hundred Ramsbottom people attended his induction at Heversham. Although he suffered latterly from poor health which hastened his retirement Tom Martin's incumbency was constructive and successful.

Coming to the village at a time when the population was increasing as a result of new buildings on Dugg Hill, at Hincaster and at Woodhouse, he aimed at harmonising through the church the old and new elements in the community.

Accordingly he and his wife, Dorothy, not only organised with skill and enthusiasm all the usual church activities but also took a full part in the life of the village. In particular, a very real connection was maintained between the church and church school which received during his incumbency new buildings,, staff and curriculum. Falling rolls in the late seventies have meant that nothing resulted from the P.C.C. minute of the 30th June 1975 that 'the field on Dugg Hill has been purchased for a new primary school'.

## Restoration Again

To the surprise of many parishioners it was discovered in 1971 that the condition of the church fabric, which seemed to have received perpetual attention, was in a poor state. In particular the lead roofs were perished and despite temporary repairs could not last long. Inevitably the vicar was the key man in organising the restoration programme and in supervising the fund raising committee. £7,000 was spent on the nave and aisles roofs, and the Dallam Chapel roof cost a further £1,840. When the cost of repairs to wiring, plumbing, the clock, organ, lychgate and furnishings was added to the roof bill almost £20,000 had been spent on the church before the scheme was officially concluded at a Thanksgiving Service held on the 8th September 1973.

Worship and pastoral matters were not neglected. Family communion on the first Sunday in the month was introduced and occasional Young People's Services involving drama were popular. These included a performance of the Creation by the Grammar School in April 1973. When Crosscrake, Holme and Levens parishes decided in 1973 to withdraw from publishing with Milnthorpe and Heversham a joint parish magazine a new parish news letter was introduced. Liturgical changes were envisaged when the vicar and several parishioners attended a meeting at St.John's Windermere to discuss Series III in June 1975. Lay participation was encouraged with increased numbers of sidesmen including the first woman 'sidesman', Miss Ellinor Kirkham,[2] lesson readers and visitors to the sick and housebound elderly. Thus when he retires in 1976 Tom Martin left Heversham Church in every sense in good heart. His testimonial fund was subscribed to by almost every family in the parish including many non-anglicans. His death in 1981 was mourned sincerely by all his former parishioners.

*Decorating Childrens Corner for Harvest c.1965*

## JOHN CLAYTON HANCOCK
### Priest in Charge 1976-77   Vicar from 1977

The impending resignation of the Reverend Tom Martin had presented the church at Heversham with a new but increasingly common situation. For, owing to the 'shortage of clergy and money' the Diocesan Pastoral Committee had informed the P.C.C. of its recommendation to the Bishop of Carlisle that 'the benefice of Heversham be suspended'. Alarm that the church would be deprived of a resident pastor was hardly mitigated by a visit from Archdeacon Ewbank who explained that suspension could be 'up to five years and could then be renewed for another five years'. The P.C.C. had no power of veto of suspension. However, 'a priest in charge' would be appointed, but he would not enjoy a 'parson's freehold' and could be transferred within the Diocese if the need arose.[1]

Supporting their case against the diocesan decision the Church Councillors cited that the church was the mother church of a wide area and that it had recently been restored at a cost of about £20,000 raised by 'public subscription'. Moreover, the vicarage on which some £2,000 was being spent was regarded as an excellent house. They added that the congregation was relatively large for which 'there was no other centre of worship near'. The P.C.C. then put in the ubiquitous request that 'they would like a priest who was a family man of medium persuasion'.[2]

As a graduate of Durham who had received his ministerial training at Cranmer Hall, the Reverend John Clayton Hancock was well suited to the clear protestant tradition of Heversham. Although brought up mainly in the north-east, where his father was a parish priest he was familiar with the north-west having been previously curate at St.Paul's Newbarns, Barrow-in-Furness, from 1960-1965 and vicar of Coniston and Rector of Torver from 1965 to 1976. Despite his full experience John Hancock was, nevertheless, Heversham's youngest incumbent for over a century and as the father of two sons and two daughters his was the first family since the eighteenth century 'to fill the vicarage.'

He was licensed as Priest in Charge on the 3rd July 1976 and exactly a year later tradition was re-affirmed when he was inducted as vicar of Heversham. As in the case of other twentieth century incumbents much of his time has been spent on financial and church fabric affairs, notably the restoration of the organ, the bells and the churchyard.[3] However, from the start of his ministry at Heversham John Hancock has sought to involve all the people of Heversham in the life of the church and to treat its consistently well maintained and revered building as a centre of activities.

### Flexibility

Artistic interests especially music have been cultivated as a form of worship. Even prior to his licensing the P.C.C. had welcomed his plans for a concert by Salisbury Cathedral Choir to be held in the following August. Thereafter a series of concerts by local and visiting musicians including (what has become an annual event) an organ recital by Jonathan Rees-Williams, Organist of Lichfield Cathedral, were put on. To enable greater flexibility the choir stalls were altered in 1979 so that they could be moved to create a central space for drama, mime, orchestras and choirs. At Heversham School Boarders' summer service in 1980 a central altar was set up and for the first time since the Puritan interval in the seventeenth century the celebrant at communion faced the congregation. This was but one of the many adjustments made in response to the liturgical reforms. In 1978 the Rev. Hancock had reported that 'a good cross section of the parish were worshipping together and that with a receptive attitude people are prepared to discuss the need to be outward looking in worship'[4] Already Series III Family Communion had been accepted, 'private baptism' had become a thing of the past but the great tradition of the Older Anglicanism was preserved by the retention of the 1662 Communion at 8 a.m. on Sunday and the use of Authorised Version readings on special occasions like the carol service.

More and more the laity have been encouraged to be active rather than receptive Christians. Traditional forms of service continue to be well supported. The choir still fills most of the choir stalls and since 1977 it has worn robes. The Mothers' Union is one of the stongest in the Kendal Deanery while the St.Peter's Youth Group and the Sunday School (fortuitously staffed by trained teachers) involve the rising generation. In addition to sending representatives to the diocesan and deanery synods a parishioner, Mrs. Ruth Drury, has been a member of the National Synod since 1975. In 1977 John Drury, Malcolm Sisson and Alan Frostick and in 1980 Roger Bingham, Ruth Drury and Ian Entwhistle were appointed to administer communion.

A positive attitude to one of the oldest elements in the church at Heversham, the Grammar School, has been made. Boarders no longer are required to attend every Sunday or to sit segregated in a separate block from other worshippers. Instead special 'boarders' services' are held each term and there are regular celebrations of communion at the school in which the pupils take part.

In the outlying part of the parish the Hincaster Mission Room, used only four times a year in the 1960's, now has a service every three weeks or so. A particularly happy innovation was made in 1979 when Milnthorpe and Heversham congregations agreed to join each other in family communion every fifth Sunday. That links with non-Anglican Christians are friendly was demonstrated informally in 1977 when as the Reverend Hancock was about to remove from his car the beautiful and costly gold-embroidered festival altar frontal, recently completed by the Misses West, the Milnthorpe Roman Catholic priest, Father Benedict Ruscillio, who was passing, stepped forward and helped him carry it into the church.

*The Rev. J.C.Hancock, (Vicar of Heversham from 1976) celebrates communion July 1984 outside The Old Grammar School on Heversham Head prior to the school's merging with Milnthorpe Secondary Modern to form the Dallam School. On the left are John and Ruth Drury, retiring Headmaster and his wife.*

### Celebration

In 1980 the Rev. Hancock master-minded the celebrations to mark the presumed eighth centenary of the oldest surviving part of the church building. The programme of events may be of interest to future historians: In April there was a concert of chamber music; in May a performance of Handel's Messiah by the Levens Village Choir and a special farmyard Rogation Service at Heversham Hall. The key event was, however, a memorable

133

performance of a 'A thousand Years and More' by Martha Bates.' A drama based on an event which happened in Heversham circa 910 A.D. i.e. the attack on the monastery by the Vikings. Also in May were the usual primary school Ascension Day and Grammar School Foundation Day services. In June there was a concert given by the Keldwyth Singers and Choral Evensong by the Church Choir followed by choral and instrumental works by parishioners. The main event was the celebration service at which the preacher was the Bishop of Carlisle, the Right Reverend David Halsey. During the service members of the congregation processed round the church and read extracts of the history of the building concluding with a recital of the names of the clergy who had ministered at Heversham since 1180. On St.Peter's Day the congregation was joined by members of the churches who used to be in the old large Heversham parish.

That Heversham has contributed to the future of the church's ministry was demonstrated in July when Richard Zair a native of the village, was ordained at Bristol Cathedral. At about the same time Roger Bingham, a life-long worshipper at the church, began training for the non-stipendiary ministry.

Celebrations continued in July with an organ recital by Elizabeth Fauntains. On August 31st Johnathan Rees-Williams gave an organ recital. An unorthodox activity was enjoyed by about fifty members of the congregation of all ages in September when they represented on a float in the Kendal Gathering the Viking attack on Heversham. Later in the month the Parish Panorama, a slide history with sound, by the Vicar, John Hancock, drew a large and appreciative audience. Finally in December two large productions of 'Aman and the Night Visitors' and 'Murder in the Cathedral' were performed by the Grammar School pupils in the church.

By involving the young in celebrating the long history of the church its continuity might well be safeguarded. If so, John Hancock's hope will be realised that

'the essential fact in the eighth centenary celebrations is that we are not looking back all the time but today are linking ourselves in a long chain, essentially looking forward and passing on the torch'.[5.]

*Easter Morning c.1970*

## Notes and References to Sources
### Chapter X
### Dr. Lawson

1. The Enclosure Award is kept at CRO(K): A Contemporary copy of plans is in the Vestry safe at Heversham.
2. CRO(K)
3. Enclosure Award CRO(K)
4. Levens Archives; Information Mrs O.R.Bagot F.S.A.
5. See Enclosure Award Map at CRO(K) of H.
6. Levens Archives.
7. *Ibid*
8. *Ibid*
9. CRO(K)
10. Levens Archives.
11. Village tradition.
12. see below
13. see below

### Robert Wilson Evans

1. A Day in the Sanctuary with an Introductory Treatise on Hymnology By Rev. Robert Wilson Evans B.D. London Rivington Printer 1843. From Evening Hymn XIX. A Thanksgiving for the privilege p.200.
2. 'The Bishopric of Souls' Robert Wilson Evans;Gilbert Rivington 1843. Intro. Chap.I 1-2.
3. *Ibid* p.3
4. *Ibid* p.40
5. *Ibid* p.30
6. *Ibid* p.30
7. Westmorland Gazettee 17 March 1866.
8. Bishopric of Souls p.101.
9. A Day in the Sanctuary p.86, p.74, p.140.
10. Bishopric of Souls p.125
11. All printed London by Smith, Elder & Co.
12. Rectory of Valehead p.231-248.
13. *Ibid* p.61
14. *Ibid* p.1-2
15. Westmorland Gazette March 1866.
16. CRO(K) WPR/8
17. *Ibid*
18. Westmorland Gazette 1872.
19. Valehead p.60.

### Canon Gilbert 1866-1921

1. Crockfords
2. see above
3. Reminiscences Mrs L.Lister: Mrs. J.Wilson: Mrs. Frear, Mrs Birch; Mr M.Kilshaw; Mrs E.Dix.
4. *Ibid*
5. Author's memories.
6. Westmorland Gazette 12 June 1880.
7. *Ibid*
8. CRO(K) WPR/8
9. P.C.C. Minutes.

10. Westmorland Gazettee 17 September 1921.
11. *Ibid*
12. Westmorland Gazette 27 August 1921.
13. Westmorland Gazette 5 November 1921.
14. Westmorland Gazette 12 December 1921

### Edward Radclyffe Ellis 1921-1939

1. Crockfords
2. CRO(K) WPR/8
3. P.C.C. Minutes (H)
4. see above
5. P.C.C. Minutes
6. *Ibid*
7. Service Registers.
8. Reminiscenses of Mr Harold East.
9. Reminiscences Mr Malcolm Sisson.
10. The possibly 'unique' name for Heversham's Village Hall (at Leasgill) opened in 1872 and still (1982) extant. See Curwen Heversham with Milnthorpe p.32.
11. P.C.C. Minutes.
12. Westmorland Gazette June 1939.

### Wilfred Alec Cleghorn 1939-55

1. Crockford's
2. Reverend J.C.Hancock.
3. Author's memory.
4. Memories Mr J.Sowerby.
5. Memories Mrs R.W.Hall.
6. P.C.C. Minutes.
7. Question to author, within a month of W.A.C's death.
8. P.C.C. Minutes.
9. Including the author aged 6.
10. P.C.C. Minutes.

### Canon Lane 1956-64

1. Crockfords.
2. P.C.C. Minutes.
3. Reverend J.C.Hancock.
4. P.C.C. Minutes.
5. Westmorland Gazette 6 February 1964.

### Reverend Tom Martin 1964-76

1. Crockfords
2. P.C.C. Minutes.

### Reverend J.C.Hancock 1976-

1. P.C.C. Minutes.

**RULES**

FOR THE

## SUNDAY & WEEK-DAY SCHOOLS,

IN CONNECTION WITH

### THE PARISH CHURCH OF HEVERSHAM,

OPENED JULY, 1842.

CHAPTER XI

# Heversham Church of England School

One of the more enduring legacies of the nineteenth century church at Heversham is the village school. In the provision of Elementary Education the parish was neither unique nor early. Between 1820 and 1870 the Anglican National Schools Society and the Non-conformist British and Foreign Schools Society set up schools in over half the parishes of England. In the neighbourhood the school at Beetham, allegedly dating from c.1500,[1] catered for girls as well a boys by 1800; while a National school was started at Burton[2] in 1817. Within the parish a National school was founded at Milnthorpe[3] in 1819; at Levens the Hon. Mary Howard built a school to accommodate 100[4] pupils in 1828 and the ancient schools at Crosthwaite and Crosscrake were also functioning. In the 1830's Heversham Grammar School was making one of its periodic attempts to become an exclusive public school by expanding the boarding side and charging fees to day boys[5] Some of the children from Heversham village, Leasgill and Hincaster did not attend either Levens or Milnthorpe schools but the majority of girls and infants received no education. As the numbers unable to sign the marriage registers show many remained totally illiterate.

At Heversham no recourse was made to the National Schools Society. In 1839 James Gandy of Heaves offered to build a school at his sole cost. Possibly his offer was prompted by a wish not to be out-done as a philanthropist by Mrs Howard of Levens who was currently embarking on building a church and school at Holme. Certainly Mr Gandy's offer was accepted immediately by Mrs Howard's enemy, the vicar Dr. George Lawson. Building work began in the north-west corner of the churchyard. Unfortunately Dr. Lawson had not consulted the churchwardens who called a special meeting on the 29th May 1839 to decide if 'the building for the purpose of a female school and residence for the person taking charge thereof shall be sanctioned for the purpose intended'.[6] The main problem was the feeling that a house should not be built on consecrated ground. A committee under the chairmanship of Major Swain, a veteran of the Peninsular War who lived at Old Hall, Endmoor, was appointed to consider the matter. Eventually the vicar of Kendal Rev. John Hudson was called in to adjudicate. He decided that the school could be built but not the house. James Gandy accordingly paid for the completion of the school and his initials with the date 1839 appear on the south gable. Even so no scholars were enrolled for two more years, the rather lame reason being that without a house a mistress could not be appointed. Incidentally no house was provided for the teachers at Milnthorpe or Beetham. Mr Gandy, no doubt believing that the church wardens had looked a gift horse in the mouth, refused to pay for the house. To the rescue came his neighbouring landlord, George Wilson of Dallam Tower who donated land adjoining the smithy as a site. Virtually in a death bed reconciliation with Dr.Lawson, who only had a matter of months to live, Mrs.Howard paid for the house. Thus her initials and the date 1841 are carved on the gable end of the delightful cottage ornée that so prettily overlooks the churchyard.

### The School Opens

Finally a broadsheet was issued announcing the opening on the 12th July 1842 of 'Sunday and Weekly Schools in connection with the Parish Church of Heversham'. Below an engraving of the new buildings is a list of twelve rules:

1. No child will be admitted under the age of five years.
2. Every child who attends the day School will be expected to attend the Sunday School.
3. The School will begin with prayer, at nine o'clock in the morning, at which time all the children are expected to be assembled.
4. The charge for each child is two-pence per week, to be paid every Monday morning.
5. Any child neglecting to pay the School fee for a fortnight will not be allowed to continue in the School until the same be paid.
6. The children are expected to come with their hands and faces clean, their clothes neat, and their hair short and well brushed.
7. Any complaint must be made to the Visitor and not to the School Mistress.
8. The holidays will be a fortnight at Midsummer a fortnight at Christmas, a week at Easter, and every Sunday.
9. The days of admission will be the first Monday in each month.
10. If any child make her appearance at School, later than the time of calling over the names, she will be kept the same number of minutes after the School closes, unless a satisfactory reason be given.
11. The School hours will be from nine to twelve in the morning, and from one to four in the afternoon; and on Sundays to commence at nine in the morning, and a quarter before two in the afternoon.
12. The children are to go from School to Church together, and in an orderly and quiet manner; they are to remain in their seats after service until the congregation have dispersed.[7]

It seems that, despite the original intention, boys as well as girls were admitted. Older boys went on to 'the Masters Schools'[8] at Levens or Milnthorpe. Soon after the opening of the School the following 'distressing incident', related by Curwen, occurred in February 1845.' A poor woman in a state of great destitution tramping from Manchester to Kendal, sleeping out in the wet and mostly without food, left Milnthorpe with an infant three months old. On arriving at the School she asked if she might warm herself and her baby at the fire. She then uncovered the child and found that it was dead ... Mrs White of the 'Blue Bell' took her in and administered to the disconsolate mother every comfort in her power'.[9]

The first Mistress was Mrs Ann Robinson[10.] who remained until 1869 when Miss Parker took over. No records survive of the curriculum but probably it was based on the rigid drilling on the four 'R's:

1. Reading - learned by recitation,
2. Writing - on slates and occasionally in copy books,
3. Arithmetic - with an abacus as a teaching aid, and
4. (Above all) Religion, involving a thorough knowledge of the Catechism.

Some instruction was given in sewing, often by ladies of the parish.

W.E.Forster's great Education Act of 1870, generally held to have inaugurated state education, did not have much effect on denominational schools like Heversham's. To begin with, it did not make education compulsory because there were not sufficient school places for all the nation's children; nor did it make education free (although grants were available from the school boards for 'necessitous children') and 'school pence' were levied at Heversham until 1891.[11] Aid, towards salaries and books, was forthcoming from the Privy Council Committee for Education but this was on the strict basis of 'payment by result'. Henceforward the School was subject to almost annual inspection. Moreover, for the benefit of central bureaucracy, the headteacher had to keep a log book. Heversham's school log is kept in four volumes beginning respectively in January 1872, March 1897, June 1924 and October 1951. As in the church's main story no dramatic change is revealed. Even so it is possible to discern shifts, adjustments and innovation which, despite periods of apparent stagnation, have contributed step by step to an educational revolution. Moreover, at Heversham the association with Anglican-based Religious Education has continued.

## Attendance

In the early decades attendance was a major problem. Thus on the 28th February 1872 the Headmistress, Miss Helen Elizabeth Ord Watts, recorded:

'Heversham was visited by a rather severe snowstorm. Although the snow had almost gone by Thursday still the children did not come out, probably the reason being that parents did not wish to pay for two days so the registers have not been called at all this week'.[12.]

In 1874 the school roll numbered 42; the average attendance was 31. Often the children were absent for reasons other than illness as in August 1880 when nearly all the boys were helping with the harvest or in 1889 when Miss. Wood recorded 'four girls in the upper school have been absent for a fortnight being wanted at home to assist in spring cleaning' The first mention of a school attendance officer was in 1884. However, he could not stop, for example, six boys 'following the hunters' in 1893 or almost all the children being late as they were 'helping with some somewhat unruly cows'.[13.] In every generation children's succumbing to the happy temptation to dawdle on the Head or play in the old quarry adjacent to the school rather than come into lessons is recorded.

## Supervision

Victorian and Edwardian teachers received considerable assistance and also close supervision from non teachers. Canon Gilbert regularly took morning assembly. His twice weekly lessons in scripture and arithmetic were on the official timetable for over fifty years. The curates also helped out with poetry, drawing and, in the case of the Rev. Law, gardening. Mrs Gilbert and her sister, Miss Harrison, taught needlework. Even so at any moment in the day managers like Mrs Argles of Eversley, Mrs Curwen of Horncop, Lady Bagot of Levens and Misses Woods of Elm Lawn were liable to descend on the school and try their hand at teaching. Canon Gilbert, as the official Visitor, was required to check the register and every month the comment 'I have this morning tested the attendance register and found them quite correct' was entered in the log book. He also made unheralded checks on the education of the pupil teachers when he would record 'I visited the school between eight and nine o'clock whilst the mistress was instructing the P.T.'s and found all going on correctly'. In serious cases 'punished in the presence of the vicar' appears by the names of miscreants.

The pupil teachers stayed for about three years during which period they attended on Fridays and Saturday mornings the training centre in Kendal. There were also monitresses and an adult assistant who was in charge of the infants. With the exception of Miss Wharton B.A. (1940-46) the latter were all uncertified until 1964. Incidentally the log books show that the list of mistresses given by Curwen in the 'History of Heversham and Milnthorpe' is neither complete nor correct. Miss Helen Watt left in June 1874 and was followed by Miss Isabella Ritchie who stayed until May 1979 when Miss Isabella Robinson became the Mistress. She lasted only until December 1880 when Miss Jane Brocklebank took over. At Christmas 1885 the log book records that Miss Brocklebank 'had left in a hurry'.

## Difficulties

The 1870's and 1880's were harrowing for pupils and teachers. With the power to grant or withhold aid of £10 for basic subjects and £6 for sewing and drawing the visits of Her Majesty's Inspectors were dreaded by all. In the weeks preceding a forewarned visit the Mistress spent hours attempting to extract blood out of stones by drilling basics into the pupils while 'the Canon' assisted in rounding up truants. Even so, every report was critical. The 1874 report was fairly mild stating that

'the order is good and the children have passed upon the whole a fair examination. The spelling and arithmetic certainly admit of improvement. Mending and darning should be more systematically taught.'

In 1875 arithmetic was 'still very weak. The smallness of the school makes the failure in this subject more emphatic ...' Moreover,

'the boys offices should be kept in a more cleanly state. One tenth of the grant has been deducted. The issue of Miss Ritchie's Certificate (she had hoped to be promoted to the second class) is deferred until a more satisfactory report on arithmetic of her school is received.'

The next year the elementary subjects were 'creditable' though spelling was inferior and sewing was 'not very good'. Maps of Scotland, Ireland and the County of Westmorland 'are wanted'. Miss Ritchie obtained her certificate. Under the brief rule of Miss Robinson geography and grammar were introduced but 'were very little known' but Arithmetic was 'especially creditable'. This improvement did not continue under Miss Brocklebank for in 1880 'out of 60 sums set out only 23 were worked absolutely correctly. The writing was ill-formed and much too small'. However, the classes were 'kindly taught' and it was noted that 'one boy John Handley having hurt his wrist was allowed to learn other lessons instead of writing'. The school's performance continued to deteriorate. Punctuation was 'moderate', arithmetic 'defective' while in 1883 'needlework specimens worked at inspection were not satisfactory'.

Poor Miss Robinson also had discipline problems. The punishment register lengthened. As in any badly-ordered school the same names appear over and over again; in this case they were E. and J.Kilshaw, J. and W.Handley, J.Smith, G.Shane, J.Varley and J.Birkett who were caned collectively and individually several times each week. In 1884 it was reported that 'the schools attainments were decidely weaker'.

## Improved Teaching

When in January 1886 Miss Annie Wood 'late student of Warrington Training College' arrived an improved and ambitious curriculum was introduced. Parsing, Compound and Personal Pronouns, Comprehension of the Predicate and enlargement of the object, and decimal fractions were recorded. Geography was diversified with lessons on 'the chief watering places of England, the chief towns in Westmorland and a study (detailed?) of Patagonia and Tierra del Fuego.' Examining the infants, Miss Wood found, apparently to her surprise, that 'the five year olds did not give satisfactory results in writing'. So she set about 'rousing the listless ones' by introducing 'object lessons' on such topics as 'the bee, the whale, the knife, the fork, the shovel'. Needlework now included 'cutting out a chemise'. Discipline also improved and in two years only one boy was caned. Social welfare was attempted, though not for long, for in November 1887 'cheap dinners chiefly for children who live a distance from school' were provided. That the improvements were not merely window dressing was shown in 1889 when inspectors reported 'more diligent application among the pupils'.

## Songs

The Victorian curriculum emphasised singing. Many of the song titles are recorded. They range from Nursery Rhymes and infants' songs like 'Little Toddlekins' through patriotic airs like 'Hurrah for England', and morale-boosting 'Try, Try Again' and 'Shall School Acquaintance be forgot' to the sentimental 'Little Sister's gone to sleep', 'The vacant chair', 'Kiss me Mother, kiss your darling' and 'O call my brother back to me'. The weather was serenaded in 'To the sun' and, perhaps, more usefully, 'Lo, the Heavens are breaking'. Seasonal songs were apparently taught without reference to the calendar as 'Beautiful bird, Spring has come' was taught in October 1876. 'The Last Rose of Summer' in April 1877 and 'Spring' in July 1887.

## Leasgill School

In 1891 the school moved from the Churchyard buildings to Leasgill. There were several reasons for the move. Firstly numbers had increased from about 40 in 1880 to 56 in 1890 and attendance averaged 80% compared to about 60% previously. The addition of a gallery for infants in the corner now occupied by the small kitchen did not help much. Proper recreation, let alone 'musical drill', started in 1886, was impossible in the minute yard. Nevertheless hygiene was probably the reason for the move. The school had been closed in 1889 during a diphtheria epidemic. Typhoid broke out especially 'amongst the infants'[14.] periodically. In 1890 the inspectors reported that 'arrangements for securing personal cleanliness' were unsatisfactory. This opinion was not exaggerated for the school's privy was built on top of the wall below which, on the lower road level, was St.Mary's Well, the school's only water supply. Perhaps poor sanitation was the reason why Miss. Wood did not occupy the mistress's house.

The obvious site for a new school was in the field where the Crow Wood Council houses were built in the 1950's. Unfortunately the tenant, Sergeant Rhudham of the 'Blue Bell', refused to move. As an alternative the Dallam estate offered the field to the north of Plumtree Hall. A Victorian spirit level found there in 1964 might indeed have been dropped when this site was surveyed. This idea was abandoned when Mrs Susannah Argles of Eversley offered Bank Field at Leasgill which, though steeply sloping, commanded marvellous views down the bay to Humphrey Head and up the Lythe Valley to the Langdales. Moreover, it was next door to the vicarage. The price was a nominal ten shillings.

The building designed by the County Surveyor, Mr C.Bintley, was constructed of stone hewn from the adjacent parish quarry. It consisted of one large classroom, a cloakroom, a hallway entered through a tall tudor door emblazoned with prison-like iron work, approached by 'the slope from the playground. The new school still had earth privies emptied weekly by the vicarage menservants, Ambrose Fox and Proctor Birkett. The privies were, however, tucked behind the bushes on the north side.

## The Cost

Work began after the land was vacated at Lady Day and the school was completed by August 31st 1891. The total cost was £471.16s4½d. The largest bills were £206.6s.2d. from the mason William Scot; £104.14s.6d from H.Sisson, the carpenter and £14.9s.9 from the glazier and decorator, G.Semple. Shrubs were obtained at £1.18s2½. from 'Mr Webb of Kendal' and G.Squire was paid 3d for planting them.

Funds were raised very quickly. Canon Gilbert, the vicar, gave £50 initially and, by stages, a further £40. Captain Bagot of Levens Hall gave £25 but the largest subscription was £200 from William Tattersall whose father had been on the committee which established the old School in 1842. A staggering sum of £140 was brought in by the first recorded bazaar in the church's history.[15.]

The money was well spent. In May 1892 the inspectors found that 'the school had made a good beginning in its new and much improved premises' while the next year the pupils showed 'respectable intelligence'.[16.]

Miss. Wood left in August 1893 and was replaced as headmistress of 'Heversham mixed school' by Mary Halstead. She found the children 'very restless and backward in elementary subjects'. Confirming this poor impression the inspectors only 'reluctantly' made a grant for English. They found that the good scholars had been drilled in 'finding synonyms for particular words rather than being led to perceive the general meaning'. In 1899 'a tendency to noise and confusion' was noted as being responsible for causing the 'inaudibility and want of expression which undoubtedly prevailed'. Nevertheless Miss Halstead had introduced 'patriotic history', 'marches and hoop drill' and a metric chart for use in mathematics. Also the school entered the 'Wakefield Music Festival at Kendal'! On the 19th March 1897 the first photograph of the school was taken. On leaving in August 1900 Miss. Halstead was presented with a testimonial by the pupils.

**Extension**
After a year under Miss Emma Bullock Miss Isabella Slinger began a reign of 23 years. Miss Slinger was the last teacher to occupy the old mistress's house.

Her first problem was shortage of pupil space. In 1902 the school inspector, one Herbert Grime, stated that 76 was an 'excessive number'[17] for a one-roomed school. On the 5th May 1903 he threatened that the grant from the newly founded Board of Education would be endangered if the school was not enlarged. The managers acted instantly. On the 8th June building work began and on the 27th June the Mistress recorded

'owing to the necessary removal of the south wall of the school during alterations school will be held in the Athenaeum by kind permission of Mr and Mrs F.A.Argles'.[17.]

At £457.13s.8d the extension also designed by Bintley cost almost as much as the 1981 building. Once more the bulk of the cost was met by private subscription plus a bazaar which made £139.6s.6d., only just short of the 1890 record.[18.]

The 1902 Education Act meant that London-based bureaucracy pushed its nose into the building programme. A protracted correspondence was conducted by Canon Gilbert with the formidable Permanent Secretary to the Board, Sir Robert Morant, who insisted that 'an open fire is essential in the room intended for the babies although there may be one or more radiators under the window'.[19] The managers successfully resisted the demand that a dormer window be installed to light the gallery in the new infants' room. The gallery was, in fact, removed in 1908.[20] Similarly the request that hot water be installed in the washroom was ignored, despite periodic reminders, until 1966! Ironically as soon as the extra room was opened numbers began to fall, dropping to 49 in 1913.

Miss Slinger was deemed to be an 'energetic and industrious' teacher. However, she barely altered the Victorian curriculum and formal methods. As late as 1920 recitation by the whole class was the method of teaching poetry while the inspectors noted that no essay had been set for three months. In 1909 the older girls began to attend cookery classes at Milnthorpe in the former Agricultural Hall which later became the 'Bull's Head' dining room.

Until the 1918 Education Act pupils could leave or become 'half-timers' at the age of 12 if they reached Standard IV. During the Great War total exemptions were given to eleven year old boys so that they could work on farms. Most children left at 13 or 14 but one deaf girl was allowed to stay on until she was 16.[21]

In 1918 the minimum leaving age was fixed at 14, boys over 11 were transferred to Levens or Milnthorpe schools and up to three 'scholarship places' were awarded to Heversham Grammar or Kendal Girls' High School. Also in 1918 the start of the school year was transferred from April to August.

### Developments

Miss Slinger resigned on the 30th June 1924. Her successor Mrs Anderton lasted only a year when Miss Elizabeth Gibson took over. She developed music and drama. The school won the Mary Wakefield Festival's 'Schools banner', staged Christmas Pantomimes and older pupils took part in 'Village Players' performances provided by Miss Gibson. On the 9th February 1926 the children 'paid a visit to Kendal Kinema to see Ben Hur'[22] With almost unique benevolence the inspector reported in 1928 that the 'school is now working on correct modern lines and the children give a pleasing account of themselves'. In 1928 Miss. Ann Newby Smith became headmistress. Under Local Education Authority rules she was summarily dismissed when she married in August 1931. As, however, there was no rule to prevent the managers from appointing a woman who was already married, she was reinstated in September as Mrs Mackay and only lost a month's pay. She was remembered for many years as an enthusiastic if 'over bossy' and not particularly popular teacher who, however, arranged a wide programme of visits including one to see her husband spinning and weaving in his Kendal arts and crafts studio.

The H.M.I. report for 1935 was mixed. Special praise was given to the infant teacher, Miss Mona Marjorie Dunn, who was 'able to obtain genuine effort from the children'. However, in the tradition of the school, mathematics was criticised:

> 'the children seem to lack patience and perseverance and most of them are very helpless when required to deal with problems in arithmetic involving careful thought and application'.

It was no doubt with some asperity that the mistress appended to the report the comment that 'a thunderstorm occurred during the arithmetic test' and many of the older girls were 'at cookery' during the inspection.

### Miss Wright

On the 1st September 1937 Miss Nancy Wright began her headship which lasted for an unprecedented 30 years. During this time the numbers on the school roll helter-skeltered from a mere 24 in 1938, rose to 64 with the first influx of the evacuees in 1939, dropped to 22 in 1943, zoomed up to 51 with the doodle-bug evacuees in the autumn of 1944 before trickling down to 29 by V.E. Day in 1945. The post-war bulge and the raising of the school leaving age in 1948 to 15 brought numbers up to 51 in 1950. When Milnthorpe Modern School opened in 1951 the older girls left and the school became a two class primary school with 43 children in 1952. New housing and the attraction of about a quarter of its pupils from outside the parish raised the number to 60 in 1963 when a third class was started. Until the 1960's only a few improvements in the fabric were made. Water lavatories - one for mistresses, one for girls and one plus a drain for boys had been installed in 1935. Following a successful garden fete given at Eversley (then the residence of Mrs E.S.Drew) electricity was installed. The vicar and managers attended on the 7th November 1938 to witness the switching on of the five lights and a power point. Soon a Philips radio was obtained and in January 1939 the school began 'to listen in to the B.B.C. wireless lessons'.[23]

Throughout the 1940's and well into the 1950's war time shortages and financial stringency imposed appalling difficulty on school work. Often only the fair copy was entered into exercise books, rough work being done on scrap paper including envelopes, and pupils with tiny hand writing were especially praised. Fortunately Miss Wright possessed, except in matters of discipline, a gentle temperament and also had the instinct of a Westmorland farmer's daughter for 'make do and mend'. These qualities were invaluable in coping with the administrative and educational nightmare imposed on this hitherto small, quiet school by the surge of urban evacuees who came with different academic standards and full range of social problems.

### Evacuees

The records barely hint at the impact of the Second World War. On the 30th August 1939 the headmistress recorded that 'the piano had been tuned', five Newcastle evacuees had arrived, the children had a gas mask inspection' and 'an air raid practice' (contemporaries recall that this involved trooping outside, answering the register and then hiding in the bushes) and that 'at 3.30 the school was closed during the present emergency'.[24.] When the school re-opened on the 15th September 44 children from Wingrove School, South Shields, currently billeted at the Hincaster House hostel, were waiting to be entered on the roll. At first the local authority demanded that as the evacuees were chargeable to the Newcastle rates they should be taught separately. Five Tyneside teachers came and went in quick succession en route for the Forces or increased responsibility at home and in January 1940 Mrs Latham née Miss Dunn was brought in to help out until a permanent assistant, Miss Wharton, was appointed. Three classes were organised in 1940. In the school there was the top class of 15 Heversham and 12 Wingrove children and the infant class of 14 Heversham children and 7 Wingrove children. The middle class of 5 Heversham and 25 Wingrove children were taught in the Athenaeum. A further complication was that the evacuees brought their own furniture and equipment with them. No sooner had the last lot of Tyneside or Barrow desks arrived, than the evacuees began to drift home with the result that the equipment drifted back, too.

The source of evacuees did not remain constant. By August 1941 only 14 Wingrove children were left but 19 Todds Nook children from Tyneside had arrived. By the end of the autumn term there were only 26 Newcastle children but, with the bombing of the Barrow docks, 16 children came from Walney Island. Possibly because their parents could pay occasional visits to Heversham the Barrow children stayed longer - the last only left in 1943.

During the peak of the emergency welfare and education were kept separate. There were no school meals - Horlicks which had been provided at break time since 1933 was unobtainable after April 1940. When in 1943 there was a lull in the evacuee invasion and school numbers had dropped to 22 it was decided to start a canteen; the food would be brought in 'containers' from the Levens school kitchen. War time red tape insisted that all equipment described as 'emergency allocation' had to come from the Ministry of Supply depot at Manchester. Thus it was nine months before the canteen opened on the 7th November 1944. By that time 31 'south country evacuees' had arrived. Most of these children stayed until 21st March 1945.

### The 11 + and all that

The 1944 Education Act had considerable effect on the curriculum for all the 11 + selection - called the 'scholarship' at Heversham until the 1960's - shaped the education of the juniors. By 1948 'Schonell tests A and B', 'Verbal reasoning', 'Speed and accuracy' and 'Intelligence testing' had arrived in force. Though never popular the 11 + saved the school. For, the reputation of Miss. Wright and her assistant from 1946-64 Miss Alice Mary Davidson for thorough instruction combined with formal discipline attracted many, mainly middle-class, children from other parishes who augmented the Heversham village children to bring the numbers up to a 'viable' level. In the 1920's and 1930's such children would probably have attended the private schools in Arnside and Kendal. These had, however, either closed because of the war-time problems or had been condemned as 'inefficent' under the terms of the 1944 Act. The school certainly realised the hopes of most parents and also of the school managers as over the 20 years the so called 'pass rate' in the 11 + was over twice the local average and often exceeded 70% of the entry.

The means of such success did not earn the approval of the inspectors. The 1951 report commented on the excessive formality of the lay out of the class room and of the teaching, and denounced the over-concentration on the 3 'R's which had led to a weakness in 'creative work' and had failed to develop in those children 'naturally endowed with lively minds' their potential in creative writing. Moreover, as far as any child at the school could remember, there was no effect on the curriculum in the 1940's and 1950's following the 5th March 1945 'when school was closed all day and the teachers attended a lecture on Sex Education at Kendal High School'.[25.]

### The School Expands

In 1959 the H.M.I's report stresses the inadequacy of the accommodation. The junior room was far too small and 'would be a deterrent were the school inclined to liberalise its practice.' However, the 'intellectual vitality' of the children and the fact that the teachers were 'assiduous for their welfare'[26.] as well as growing numbers meant that after twenty years of uncertainty there was no question of closing the school. Since 1949 the Athenaeum had been used afresh for school dinners, P.E. and Country Dancing lessons. In 1963 a class of 7 to 9 year olds was accommodated there.

Building work on a new extension began in January 1966 when the Leasgill buildings were closed. Children up to 9 were taught in two classes in the Athenaeum. Juniors, after a gap of 76 years, re-occupied the Old School in the churchyard. Eventually on the 30th August 1966 the headmistress recorded

'School re-opened. All three classes are being taught in Heversham Church of England school which has been extended and altered. A new entrance and drive have been made and a new front door, entrance hall and corridor have been created. The following have been added: a third classroom with quiet bay, a practical bay, a book store, a cloakroom, toilets, a staffroom with book store, a canteen kitchen with dinner hatch, a P.T. store, a store for bicycles and indoor toilets for the infants. In the old rooms the walls have been replastered, shelves fixed on the sloping window sills (still too high for

*Heversham School. Group II 1910.*

144

anyone under 5ft. 6ins. to be able to see out), expanded polystyrene fitted in the beams in the ceiling and an oil fired central heating system fitted.'[27.]

Miss. Wright ended her successful career on the 21st December 1967 and was followed by the school's first headmaster, Mr. Harry Barnes, who stayed until April 1976. He expanded the musical tradition of the school and virtually from scratch introduced modern P.E. which before long led to the school's taking part in, and frequently winning, local sporting competitions. In 1975 he could record 'today was the primary school's swimming gala in Kendal - won by Heversham Primary School yet again'. The academic traditions were maintained and, as Heversham was in one of the last areas in the country to retain Grammar Schools its success continued to be measured by the 11 + results. In 1973, for example, 4 boys 'passed' to Heversham Grammar School, 6 girls passed' to Kendal High School while 5 'went' to Milnthorpe Secondary Modern School.

After a summer term under a temporary head, Mr John Watson, Mr Croft became head in September 1976. Also in 1976 Mrs Elizabeth Henneberry who had been on the staff since 1964 became the school's first official deputy head. In Spetember 1979 Mr Charles Bethel became head of the school which in September 1980 had 63 children on the roll.

**Not Just Work**

The school records provide evidence of more than building changes, staff and the basic curriculum. They tell of school treats, special events, health and even the weather. There are many references to the climate and its effect on the attendance in log books. Heavy rain in the second week in September and snow in the second week in March are, for example, mentioned frequently. On the 11th September 1914 only 15 children came to school[28] while on the 12th March 1891 snow 'precluded any child from attending'.[29.] Until 1938 when electric light was installed the curriculum and school times were changed during the darker months. Hence in December 1897 Miss Halstead stated that school would open at 1 p.m., instead of 1.15, and close at 3.45 p.m. instead of 4 p.m. until the end of February. She had also 'changed the copy book lessons as the days are so short the children cannot see to write in them during the latter part of the afternoon'.[30] The school continued to function in conditions which would produce howls of indignation from parents and the unions in the 1980's. Although snow was covering the playground on the 28th November 1912 'the Drill inspector, Miss Dodd, considered it warm enough to drill outside'. In 1914 Miss Slinger recorded that there were but

'three pieces of coal in the classroom fire and six in the big room, the rest is composed of cinders and if it were not for the pipes the room would be unbearably cold'.[31.]

The thermometer read 45 degrees! During the 1947-48 fuel crisis the school was closed for three weeks but when it reopened Miss Wright noted classroom temperatures of '38 degrees in the infants' room and 40 in the junior room. Desks were brought as close as possible to the coke and wood fires and as it was too cold to write there were dancing, singing and recitation lessons.'[32.]

**Health**

The effect of disease was more acute in the nineteenth century than in modern times. 'Hooping cough' closed the school in 1872 an 1876, diphtheria in 1901, 1911, and typhoid in 1890[33.] and 1899. The end of the Great War is not recorded in the log for the school was closed by 'German or Spanish flu'' from the 26th October to the 18th November and again from the 29th November to the 7th January 1919. Cases of infestation are rarely mentioned though two children were sent home because of 'sore heads' in 1905 and there were ring worm outbreaks in 1886 and, with scabies, in 1940.

The most persistent disease was scarlet fever with severe outbreaks in 1879, 1905, 1914 and 1918. In 1914 the epidemic spread because of the neglect of the parents. Miss Slinger recorded on the 11th November:

'On reassembling the headmistress caused children to 'show hands' thereby discovering two of them on whose hands the skin was peeling. They and their sisters were sent home. This morning only 23 children arrived. On showing hands again two other children were seen to have the skin on the hands peeling. Evidently the 'cold' epidemic has been something more. Canon Gilbert was of the opinion that it would be best to close the school. (It did not reopen until the 5th January)... The mistress burnt the boxes, books, sewing and knitting used by the 'peeling ones' and by James Lancaster as a preventative measure.'[34]

In recent times there were severe epidemics of chicken pox in 1942, 1948 and 1951, measles in 1949, 1957 and 1963. The first medical inspection was held on the 21st January 1909 when 'Dr.Henderson examined 12 children and gave a short practical talk about Health before he left'. The second inspection was almost a public occasion for as well as parents, the district nurse and the doctor, Canon and Mrs Gilbert, Mrs Curwen ('Lady Manager') and the Rev. A.D.Brown also attended.[35] Even so 49 children were examined and thereafter the children were weighed, measured and had head inspection three times a year. Dental inspection began in 1916, eye tests in circa 1920 and hearing tests in 1960.

**Special Events**
Enlivening the story of the school are many references to special occasions and local and national events. Some like Milnthorpe Fair held in May and October, Milnthorpe Show and Gala in August, Arnside Regatta in September, Milnthorpe Agricultural Show in October and the Spring hiring fair In Kendal invariably cut attendance by half. Visiting menageries and circuses as in 1872, 1877 and 1891 also caused truancy.

Similarly, before 1914 holidays for local weddings occurred almost annually and the whole school attended Mr Argles' funeral in 1885 and Sir Josceline Bogot's in 1913. In 1880 children were presented with 'buns and book by Mr and Mrs Argles in remembrance of their son's coming of age'[36] and in 1885 they were let out early in order to see Mrs Bagot arrive as a bride at Levens Hall. Annual treats were given by the Misses Wood of Elm Lawn at Christmas, the Argles in January and Canon and Mrs Gilbert either in June or August. Both the Argles and the Misses Wood gave the children a Christmas tree in January - after they had finished with it. In 1886 the Misses Wood's tree did not get to the school until the 23rd January! Noblesse oblige![37]

Royal occasions guaranteed a holiday as on the 24th-25th June 1887 and the 22nd June 1897 for Queen Victoria's Jubilees, and in June 1893 for the wedding of the Duke of York and Princess May of Teck. In 1902 the children did well getting two days in June 'in accordance with the King's wish that festivities decided for the Coronation should proceed although the ceremony itself is postponed by reason of the serious illness of the king', two days when he was crowned in August and a half day when peace was proclaimed in South Africa, also in August. On August 27th 1903 the mistress noted 'Owing to Princess Louise, the Duchess of Argyle passing through Heversham this morning and the children having got very wet with watching, it is thought advisable to close school early this morning'.[38] On the 25th October 1907 'the children and teachers went to bottom of the lane to cheer Princess Louise of Schleswig-Holstein'. In 1911 there was a holiday on the 16th June for the Coronation of King George V and Queen Mary. The school also won as an attendance prize large framed photographs of these monarchs which dominated the infants' room until c.1960. As a four year old pupil the author can remember a five year old pupil saying they were God and Jesus!

An unusual act of regicide occured in 1912 when seven boys collected 330 Queen Wasps for which they were paid 4d a dozen. Despite the war one feature of the traditional social pattern was observed in February 1917 when the children trooped up to Levens Hall to congratulate Sir Alan Bagot on his coming of age and were afterwards 'entertained to tea at Levens Welcome.' The Peace of Versailles was celebrated with two days' holiday in June

1919; single day's holidays were given for the wedding of Princess Mary on the 27th February 1922, the Duke of York on the 23rd April 1923, the Duke of Kent on the 29th November 1934 and the Duke of Gloucester on the 6th November 1935. On the 28th January

'being the day of the burial of our beloved king George V the registers were not marked and the children marched to Heversham church where a service was held. The children then returned home to spend the day as a day of Remembrance'.

In May 1937 the children were given Coronation mugs and also one shilling each from a school manager, Councillor John Handley. Later in the year on the 22nd September the school closed at 3.15 p.m. in order that the children could see Queen Mary as she passed through the village.[39.]

Two days were given for the V.E. Day holiday on 1945, and one day for the wedding of Princess Elizabeth and Lieutenant Mountbatten on 23rd November 1947, for the silver wedding of King George VI and Queen Elizabeth in April 1948 and two days for the Coronation in June 1953. On the latter occasions one of the school's oldest pupils who was also the youngest member of the Church Scout troop[40.] had the honour of lighting the beacon on the Head. More memorably for most, the headmistress recorded on the 25th June

'this morning the children who were early to school went to the Princess Way to see Queen Salote, Queen of Tonga, as she passed along the road.'[41.]

She was clad in an outsize fur coat on what for Heversham was a hot day. One day's holiday was given for Princess Margaret's wedding on the 6th May 1960, the Queen and Prince Philip's Silver wedding in November 1972, Princess Anne's wedding in November 1973 and two days for the Silver Jubilee of Queen Elizabeth II in June 1977.[42.]

## Empire Day
The most ostentatiously observed event was Empire Day which was celebrated from 1909 to about 1960. The first Empire Day set the pattern for future years. The headmistress recorded on the 25th May 1909:

'Yesterday was Empire Day. Mrs Argles kindly presented a flag and staff to the school. At 11.45. a.m. visitors, teachers and scholars assembled in the play ground and pro-

*Empire Day c.1914*

ceedings commenced with the singing of 'Hurrah for England', followed by a little play by the older scholars, 'Brittannia's Birthday'. The vicar next gave a stirring and appropriate address. Then the flag was hoisted by Harriet Townley and Percy Shane, the two senior scholars. After saluting the flag the children recited 'The Union Jack' and after a hearty vote of thanks to Mrs Argles and the singing of 'God Save the King' followed by cheers, the company dispersed. A half-holiday was given in honour of the day.'[43.]

In 1924 on the 20th May

'Queen Mary's birthday ... partly as a preparation for the forthcoming visit to Wembley Empire Exhibition each child took the part of one or more British possessions ... and the opportunity was taken to speak a few words on what it is meant by being a good citizen and a true member of the British Empire'.

The day of the visit was the 24th June - the Prince of Wales' birthday. Spurred on by an adulation later reserved for pop singers, the five girls who went to Wembley learnt to sing 'God Bless the Prince of Wales'[44.] as they hoped to see him. Their hopes were not rewarded.

## Religious Education - the fourth 'R'

Appropriately the most extensive information in the school records concerns Religious Education. This has always included an understanding of the Anglican liturgy, the Church's seasons, the Apostles Creed and, until the 1950's, the Catechism. No vicar has taught twice weekly at the school since Canon Gilbert's time but all his successors have scrupulously attended assembly once a week and taken a short lesson afterwards. In order to qualify for a grant after the 1870 Act the school was bound to take non-Anglicans. Because of this scripture lessons had to be taken either at the beginning or at the end of each session so that non-Anglicans could be withdrawn. However, except for six members of one Roman Catholic family who attended the school from 1945 to 1963,[45.] the withdrawal of children from Religious Education is not recorded.

Until the 1920's denominational teaching governed the syllabus. Even so there were complaints in 1875, 1877, 1880 and 1910 that children were not conversant with the theology behind the tenets of the catechism which they had memorised parrot fashion. As a result of Canon Gilbert's tuition their knowledge of the Bible, especially the Old Testament, was generally good. The 1901 Diocesan inspector was so carried away by the children's having caught the 'meaning and spirit' of Christianity that he enthused 'I wish that I could find a stronger term than excellent to do justice to this exceptionally good report'.[46.] Twice in the early years of the twentieth century the school obtained the highest marks in the Diocesan Scripture examination, while under Miss Gibson in the 1920's the 'keen and enthusiastic work in dramatising' Bible stories earned special praise.

In modern times the R.E. report for 1960 stated that 'the children were very recollected throughout the morning service, their own part was spoken in voices both natural and reverent, a dual quality sadly rare in assemblies of young children in school'.[47.] Ten years later the assembly was said to be taken 'reverently and enthusiastically' and the R.E. syllabus sucessfully 'linked Biblical knowledge to life'.

## The Continuing Purpose

When in 1891 Mrs Argles provided the site for the new building she expressed the hope that the school should continue 'as long as possible' as a Church of England School.[48.]

The qualification 'as long as possible' hints at a fear that the church might in the foreseeable future not have been able to continue the task. She need not have worried. Ninety years later Christianity is still of key importance to the school and R.E. is regarded as being more than just another school subject. The school's 'aided status' safeguards a measure of freedom for the governors whose chairman is the vicar. The children attend and take part in services at Christmas, Ash Wednesday, Ascension Day, St.Peter's tide, Harvest and St.Andrew's Day. In song, drama, reading and through the school's orchestra's accompanying the congregational singing the latest generation of Heversham Christians demonstrate not only their training in the church school but also contribute to the preservation and advance of the Church at Heversham.

*C of E School 1951*

*Top Row:    Ann East, Bobby Handley, Colin Townshend, Dorothy Nelson, David Chin, Patricia Byrne, Michael Newhouse, Goeffrey Brown, Hazel Garnet.*

*Middle Row:   Janet Dawson, Raymond East, Pamela Bingham, Roger Bingham, Jane Ireland, Janet Miles, Herbert Wilson, Susan Byrne, David Brownlie, Irene Nelson, Basil Cornthwaite.*

*Bottom Row:    Valerie Jackson, Lesley Fell, Allan Richardson, Sandra Dickinson.*

**Notes and References to Sources    Chapter XI**

1. History and Topography of Cumberland and Westmorland 1860   Whelan p.818
2. *Ibid*
3. History of Heversham and Milnthorpe Curwen p . 3 8
4. Whelan p.835
5. R.D.Humber p.34-37
6. Vestry Book (H)
7. Original Document in the possession of Mrs N.Tyson.
8. Term used in log book.
9. History of Heversham with Milnthorpe Curwen p.25-26
10. *Ibid* p.25-26
11. Log Book I (Log I) Heversham C. of E. School, kept at the school at Leasgill.
12. Log I.
13. *Ibid*
14. *Ibid*
15. School Records CRO(K)
16. Log I.
17. *Ibid*
18. CRO(K)
19. Log 2.
20. *Ibid*
21. *Ibid*
22. Log 3.
23. *Ibid*
24. Log 3.
25. *Ibid*
26. Log 4.
27. *Ibid*
28. Log 2.
29. *Ibid*
30. *Ibid*
31. *Ibid*
32. *Ibid*
33. *Log 1.*
33. log 1.
34. Log 2.
35. *Ibid*
36. Log 1.
37. *Ibid*
38. Log 2.
39. Log 3.
40. The present author!
41. Log 4.
42. *Ibid*
43. Log 2.
44. *Ibid*
45. Michael, Patricia, Susan, Eileen, Jane and Kevin Byrne
46. Log 2.
47. Log 3.
48. Vestry Book, also School Records CRO(K)

# INDEX

151

*Printed by Carnmor Print & Design*
*95/97 London Road, Preston.*

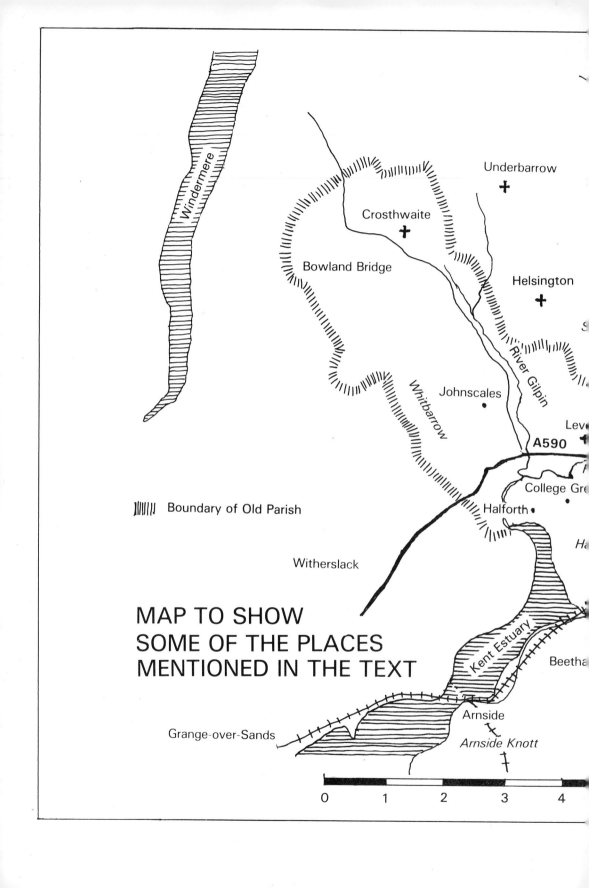

MAP TO SHOW
SOME OF THE PLACES
MENTIONED IN THE TEXT